Argentina, the United States,
and the Anti-Communist Crusade
in Central America,
1977–1984

This series of publications on Africa, Latin America, and Southeast Asia is designed to present significant research, translation, and opinion to area specialists and to a wide community of persons interested in world affairs. The editor seeks manuscripts of quality on any subject and can generally make a decision regarding publication within three months of receipt of the original work. Production methods generally permit a work to appear within one year of acceptance. The editor works closely with authors to produce a high quality book. The series appears in a paperback format and is distributed worldwide. For more information, contact the executive editor at Ohio University Press, Scott Quadrangle, University Terrace, Athens, Ohio 45701.

Executive editor: Gillian Berchowitz
AREA CONSULTANTS
Africa: Diane Ciekawy
Latin America: Thomas Walker
Southeast Asia: James L. Cobban

The Monographs in International Studies series is published for the Center for International Studies by the Ohio University Press. The views expressed in individual monographs are those of the authors and should not be considered to represent the policies or beliefs of the Center for International Studies, the Ohio University Press, or Ohio University.

Argentina, the United States, and the Anti-Communist Crusade in Central America, 1977–1984

Ariel C. Armony

With a foreword by Thomas W. Walker

Ohio University Center for International Studies
Monographs in International Studies
Latin American Series, Number 26
Athens • 1997

05 04 03 02 01 00 5 4 3 2

Library of Congress Cataloging-in-Publication Data

Armony, Ariel C.
   Argentina, the United States, and the anti-communist crusade in
Central America, 1977–1984 / Ariel C. Armony.
      p.   cm. — (Monographs in international studies. Latin
American series ; no. 26)
      Includes bibliographical references (p.   ) and index.
      ISBN 0-89680-196-9
      1. Argentina—Foreign relations—1955–1983.   2. Military
government—Argentina—History—20th century.   3. Argentina—
Military relations—Central America.   4. Central America—
Military relations—Argentina.   5. Counterinsurgency—Central
America—History—20th century.   6. Argentina—Relations—
United States.   7. United States—Relations—Argentina.
I. Title.   II. Series: Monographs in international studies. Latin
America series ; no. 26.
F2849.2.A86   1996   96-8612
327.82—DC20   CIP

Typeset by Professional Book Compositors
Cover design by Chiquita Babb
Cover painting: *El titiritero de la muerte* (*Death's Puppeteer*) by Leoncio
   Sáenz of Managua, Nicaragua.

To Mirna, Ian, and Alan

Contents

Maps

Figures

Foreword

The politics of individual Latin American countries cannot be understood fully if one examines only the internal workings of political systems. Especially during the cold war, many governments rose or fell primarily, or in part, because of external intervention or manipulation. The main external actor in the Americas was the United States. Among many electoral victories influenced by U.S. funding were those of Eduardo Frei Montalva in Chile in 1964, José Napoleón Duarte in El Salvador in 1984, and Violeta Barrios de Chamorro in Nicaragua in 1990.[1] Three of the most prominent U.S.-sponsored interventions or machinations against chosen enemies include the CIA-orchestrated overthrow of the democratically elected, mildly revolutionary government of Guatemala in 1954; the U.S. military intervention to block the return to power of the democratically elected but deposed President Juan Bosch in the Dominican Republic in 1965; and CIA involvement in the destabilization leading to the overthrow of democratically elected President Salvador Allende in Chile.[2] All of this was done in the name of fighting "Soviet-backed Communists" as very loosely defined by Washington and the conservative elite of Latin America.

Yet, while the United States was the primary external actor in the internal affairs of Latin American countries, it was by no means the only one. In the 1980s, for instance, Israel—the biggest recipient of U.S. aid and loans in the world—became a surrogate arms supplier to countries such as Guatemala[3] or forces such as the Contras[4] when it became difficult for U.S. administrations—for domestic political reasons—to supply that support directly. There is also evidence that international drug operatives may have cooperated with the CIA in its project in Nicaragua.[5]

What is particularly interesting and, until now, not really well-studied, is the role played by other Latin American countries in the anti-Communist crusade in Central America. That—or more specifically, the role played by Argentina—is the focus of Ariel Armony in this book.

From the late 1970s onward there were rumors and bits and scraps of information that seemed to indicate that Argentina had become involved in the turmoil in Central America. Nevertheless, until Ariel Armony undertook this study, no one had done a systematic examination of this matter. Because of this gap in the literature, most of the scholarly community—myself included—labored for a long time under a number of false assumptions. First, most of us assumed that the United States had created the first units of Contra army which would fight against the "leftist"[6] Sandinistas in the 1980s. For example, even in the second edition of our *Understanding Central America* (1993), John Booth and I still state, "In 1981, Reagan gave the CIA $19.8 million to organize and train in Honduras an exile army of anti-Sandinista counterrevolutionary elements."[7] No mention of Argentina. Second, most specialists assumed that whatever involvement the Argentines had with the Contra cause represented nothing more than a failed ploy by Buenos Aires to win U.S. support or neutrality in the Malvinas/Falkland Islands War of 1982. This, in turn, was part of a broader third assumption that, in its involvement in various counterrevolutionary activities throughout Central America from the late 1970s onward, the Argentine military, like Israel, was simply acting as a U.S. surrogate.

The scholarly community should be very grateful to Ariel Armony for this study since it fine-tunes our knowledge of the Central American drama of the late 1970s and early 1980s by deftly demolishing all three of the assumptions mentioned above. Armony shows that the Argentines first became involved in Central America in 1977 when they became alarmed that Jimmy Carter, with his emphasis on human rights, had betrayed the anti-Communist cause. Thus, they felt compelled to fight on the "ideological frontier," in this case in Central America where "Communism" appeared on the verge of victory. Soon, they were also motivated by the fact that many "Communist" refugees from their "dirty war" in Argentina had begun to show up in Central America, especially Nicaragua. Thus, the Argentine military's decision to become involved in Central America was entirely its own. Though U.S. training of the Argentine military in cold war ideology and tactics may have influenced the decision and while certain elements within the U.S. military and CIA may have heartily approved, the move itself ran counter to the foreign policy posture of the United States as it was being articulated at the highest levels.

Further, Armony also shows how the Argentine military's association with, and support for, Anastasio Somoza's Nicaraguan National Guard flowed naturally into its decision in 1979 and 1980 to gather together the exiled remnants of that sultanistic army and mold them into the first 1,000-person force of counterrevolutionaries (Contras) to fight the Sandinistas. In addition to disproving the assumption that the Contras were originally created by the CIA, this information destroys the argument that Argentine involvement with that irregular counterrevolutionary force was designed primarily to influence U.S. behavior in regard to the Malvinas/Falklands matter. True, the Contra army would eventually become a wholly U.S.-owned and -operated venture, but it was originally set up by the Argentines to promote *their* foreign policy interests.

The information in this book is also important in that it should demolish the myth—if anyone still believes in it—that the Contras were essentially "freedom fighters" and, as President Reagan liked to put it, the "moral equal" of the U.S. Founding Fathers. Instead, Armony shows not only that the first Contras were remnants of Somoza's brutal National Guard—which had killed around 50,000 people, most of them civilians, in 1978 and 1979—but also that their original international handlers were agents of the Argentine Army Intelligence Battalion 601—precisely the group that was then playing a central role in that country's infamous dirty war. For both the Argentines and the Nicaraguans, the old French/U.S. tactic of "counterterror"[8]—the use of torture, murder, and disappearance as a device to politically demobilize target civilian populations—was second nature and would be a hallmark of Contra behavior throughout the war.

This book, however, is much more than just a study of Argentine involvement in Nicaragua. Armony examines Argentine activities in El Salvador, Guatemala, and Honduras where Battalion 601 advisors taught local security forces the fine points of the "Argentine method" of counterterror. He also looks into the history and nature of the Argentine base of operations in the United States and the Argentine international links with anti-Communist actors.

The research that went into this study was exhaustive. It involved not only a thorough examination of primary and secondary documentation available in the United States, but travel to and interviews in both Nicaragua and Argentina. This is a very important book that fills a significant gap in the literature and, in so doing, corrects a number of false assumptions. Thank you, Ariel Armony, for this exceptional work.

Thomas W. Walker, Ohio University

Preface

The principle of accountability is essential to securing a democracy based on the rule of law. This is especially important for democracies that have recently emerged from authoritarianism. In these cases, accountability begins with truth-telling. Truth can be a powerful impetus for a society to redress past human rights violations. The task of telling the truth is a long and difficult one. However, this effort is necessary if society wants to undertake a genuine healing process and build a democratic system that will prevent these atrocities from happening again.

Latin American societies are still trying to come to terms with their recent past. The tragic events experienced throughout the hemisphere in the 1970s and 1980s have had a major impact on democracy and human rights. In spite of important efforts to restore truth and justice, there remains a sense of impunity that impedes genuine pardon and reconciliation. In spite of the efforts of some elected leaders to impose forgetfulness, not a few believe that strengthening collective memory is crucial for building democratic governance.

This book seeks to understand a little-known aspect of Latin America's recent authoritarian past: the extraterritorial role played by national security forces responsible for unprecedented programs of state terror in their countries. A crucial case of these activities beyond borders was the anti-Communist crusade led by the Argentine military in Central America in the late 1970s and early 1980s. This book shows in detail how the perpetrators of the infamous "dirty war" in Argentina transferred their model of mass repression to Central America and how the United States supported this effort, endorsing the barbaric methods applied by the Argentine military in Central America.

In this study, I focus on a complex, dark chapter in U.S., Argentine, and Central American history. I aim at understanding the process of cooperation between state and nonstate actors in the counterrevolutionary campaign in Central America and to establish their responsibility for many of the atrocities committed in the name of anti-Communism. The confluence of Argentine dirty warriors, Central American death squad leaders, and U.S. intelligence operatives in the fight against indigenous forces seeking to change their societies illustrates how counterinsurgency policy can be a catalysis of mass murder and terror. The moral responsibility of all actors involved in this effort has yet to be faced by both governments and individuals.

When I arrived in Argentina in 1993 to conduct fieldwork, I did not imagine that this topic was still very sensitive. Soon I found out that it was not only in Argentina where relevant actors were reluctant to talk about the Argentine involvement in Central America, but the same was also true for Nicaragua and the United States. In Nicaragua, most of the files concerning this issue had been destroyed under the administration of Violeta Chamorro. In the United States, many of the documents related to the U.S.-Argentine collaboration in Central America were classified. As I write this preface (in the fall of 1996), the new Human Rights Ombudsman of Honduras, Leo Valladares, is waiting for the U.S. and Argentine governments to release documents on their counterrevolutionary operations that can help Honduras to prosecute armed forces personnel linked to death squad activity in that country during the 1980s.

This book is based on a variety of primary data. I conducted in-depth interviews with military officers, government officials, former Contra leaders and rank and file, diplomats, journalists, and other relevant actors. I made initial contact with strategic informants and gathered additional names using the technique of snowball sampling. In most of the cases, respondents authorized me to record the interviews. Some interviewees requested anonymity or that certain statements not be credited to them by name. Interviews were conducted in Argentina, Nicaragua, and the United States. All translations from Spanish are mine.

Key sections of this study are based on original documents. I collected them from a number of sources including government agencies, human rights organizations, research institutions, and journalists who had worked on related aspects of this topic. Several individuals opened their personal archives to me and shared valuable data.

In completing this project, I received the cooperation and support of many people in Latin America and the United States. They contributed to this book in many ways, always with generosity and enthusiasm. They facilitated my research, helped me to understand concepts and issues, and guided me in the painful task of polishing my thoughts and ideas.

From the very beginning of this project, I benefited from the advice of Thomas Walker. His academic and intellectual integrity served as a model for which to strive in my own work. Thelma Wais and Jorge and Natalio Kolbowski played an essential role in the making of this study. They greatly facilitated my research in Argentina and provided encouragement and wisdom along the way. To them, my deepest thanks.

While in Argentina, various individuals and institutions provided generous support and access to data sources. I am especially thankful to Jorge Listosella, Juan José Salinas, Rogelio García Lupo, Horacio Verbitsky, Gerardo Noto, and the Center for Legal and Social Studies (Centro de Estudios Legales y Sociales, CELS). I would like to stress my gratitude to my friends Leonardo Bechini and Marcelo Sosa, who bore with me and my research in Buenos Aires.

While in Nicaragua, several people collaborated with this project by offering me access to key interviews and documents. I am particularly indebted to Ricardo and Milagros Chavarría, Isa Zúñiga, and several anonymous Nicaraguans who generously volunteered their time and effort to this research.

In the United States, various scholars and researchers contributed to this study with resources, suggestions, and criticisms. Peter Kornbluh, from the National Security Archive in Washington, D.C., facilitated access to important documents. Robert White, Wayne Smith, Robert Chisholm, Mitchell Seligson, Harold Molineu, and Michael Grow read drafts of various chapters and offered very useful insights. Margaret Crahan shared her expertise on the topic, provided guidance and close readings, and encouraged the conceptual development of this project.

Ohio University and the Center for Latin American Studies at the University of Pittsburgh provided generous financial support for different phases of the research. I am thankful to Ohio University Press and its Monographs in International Studies for the support given to this project. My editor, Gillian Berchowitz, demonstrated that patience and understanding still exist in this troubled world. Dennis Marshall's superb job as copy editor contributed to improving the manuscript in innumerable ways. As already noted, a great many people helped me at various stages of this project. If I have inadvertently overlooked someone, my apologies and my thanks.

I wrote this book because of my wife Mirna. With love, dignity, and intelligence, she taught me the most valuable lessons I have learned in my life. This book is for her and for my children, Ian and Alan. When I felt overwhelmed by the tragic events I describe in this book or disheartened about the future of Argentina and Latin America, their eyes, laughs, and silences helped me to understand that it is worth trying once more.

Introduction

State terror convulsed Argentina in the 1970s, particularly toward the end of the decade. As a result of a state-sanctioned program of massive repression, tens of thousands of people were kidnapped, tortured, and murdered. During the authoritarian regime that ruled the country from 1976 to 1983, the military sought to restructure state, economy, and society.

In their efforts to impose a highly exclusionist, sociopolitical model—indeed, to annihilate all perceived opposition to the regime—the armed forces adopted a clandestine, repressive strategy. This became the trademark of the Argentine national security state. A key component of that strategy was the implementation of a systematic program of "disappearances." The intelligence apparatus, which emerged as an autonomous core within the authoritarian state, played a central role in the deployment of state terror during what became known as the "dirty war."

Meanwhile—and particularly during the later part of the Argentine repression—Central America was experiencing an upsurge of rebellious activity. A number of guerrilla organizations, with varying degrees of popular support, challenged the institutional order of their nations and sought to seize power in the name of a disenfranchised majority. Faced with such a threat, the region's armed forces responded with massive programs of state-sponsored violence. Consequently, tens of thousands of civilians got caught between "two fires," suffering murder, exile, and gross violations of human rights in the hands of military and paramilitary forces. Continuing into the 1980s, increased state violence was responsible for an unprecedented level of human devastation in Central America.

In Nicaragua, following the revolutionary triumph of July 1979, that country entered the worst civil conflict of its history: the so-called Contra war. A counterrevolutionary armed movement made up of exiled national guardsmen and disgruntled peasants fought against the Sandinistas—erstwhile revolutionaries and now in power as the government—in an apparent effort to overthrow the regime. Initially organized by Argentina and later backed by the U.S. government, in the mid-1980s the Contra army evolved into a major military force. A decade of intense struggle left a total of more than 30,000 deaths (combatants and noncombatants) on both sides. The protracted Contra war devastated Nicaragua's economy.

Foreign and indigenous actors, engaged in armed reaction against the Sandinista government, wanted to impede revolutionary change in Nicaragua. The adhesive that had brought together the variety of actors that made up the anti-Somoza coalition was their common opposition to the ruthless, corrupt rule of Anastasio Somoza Debayle rather than an interest in the pursuit of social revolution. Therefore, the counterrevolutionary movement that became known as the Contras did not want to restore the Somoza regime; it strove to halt structural transformation of society as promoted by the Sandinistas.

These events constitute the historical core of this book. The following chapters analyze the Argentine military involvement in Central America and its collaborative venture with the United States in the region. In the late 1970s and early 1980s, the Argentine military regime sought to internationalize its repressive apparatus throughout Latin America. The Argentines wanted to transfer their expertise in counterinsurgency to countries fighting Communism. A final phase of that extraterritorial venture was their participation in the Central American conflict.

The Argentines initiated their involvement in Central America during the civil war in Nicaragua (1977–1979) and immediately afterward provided counterinsurgency training and military assistance to El Salvador, Guatemala, and Honduras. The Argentine military program, conducted by veterans of the dirty war, reached its peak with the organization of the Nicaraguan Contras. Following this independent venture against the Sandinistas, Argentina became a U.S. surrogate. The administration of Ronald Reagan bought into Argentina's covert program in 1981.

This book examines the role of Argentina and the United States in the wave of Central American counterrevolutionary activity. It attempts to understand Argentina's extraterritorial activities in the light of the armed forces' military, ideological, and geopolitical doctrines, the growth of the country's intelligence apparatus during the dirty war, the motivations of the military leadership and factions within the armed forces, and the process of generation and transfer of expertise in internal security. It discusses U.S. foreign policy motivations and actions toward Central America, the role of the CIA in the counterrevolutionary effort in the region, and the dynamics of U.S.-Argentine relations under the Carter and Reagan administrations. It also provides a profile of the Argentine military missions in Central America, their technical capacity, and their coordination with local security forces.

The book highlights the transnational process that involved state and nonstate organizations in the mobilization of resources, both economic and coercive, for counterrevolution in Central America. It thus brings attention to the transnational coalitions that resulted from complex linkages between ideological actors. The book is largely focused on the international connections and dynamics of surrogacy on the anti-Communist side of the cold war.

The chapters trace the origins, development, and termination of the Argentine military involvement in Central America and its cooperative venture there with the United States. Chapters 1 and 2 establish the context for the study and introduce key conceptual elements. Chapter 1 discusses state terrorism in Argentina—the security doctrines, the military intelligence apparatus, and the co-ordination of antidissident forces in Latin America. Chapter 2 lays out the main features of U.S. foreign policy toward Central America and Nicaragua under the Carter and the early Reagan administrations and discusses U.S.-Argentine relations during that period.

Subsequent chapters provide a detailed account of Argentina's involvement in Central America and its links with the United States and other ideological actors. Chapter 3 traces the Argentine military role in Nicaragua under Somoza and in El Salvador, Guatemala, and Honduras. Chapter 4 assesses the relationship between Argentina and the Nicaraguan Contras (1979–1984) and the three-sided arrangement of Argentina, the United States, and Honduras. Chapter 5 traces the main transnational networks that participated in the counterrevolutionary effort in Central America and discusses their ultimate impact on the Argentine state.

Argentina, the United States,
and the Anti-Communist Crusade
in Central America,
1977–1984

Latin America

Chapter 1

Argentina: State Terror and Counterinsurgency Warfare

AN INQUIRY INTO the *extraterritorial* enterprise of the Argentine military in the late 1970s and early 1980s requires that we note four major features of the 1975–1981 dirty war, which served as a prototype for the military venture beyond the country's borders. But first, briefly, I want to give a sense of the backdrop to the events in Argentina. For a powerful core of hard-liners within the Argentine military, the dirty war initiated in 1975 was, as a former senior adviser to an Argentine president observed, "an endless enterprise."[1] Launched against "subversion"—a concept defined by its very unpredictability and measurelessness—the dirty war was waged against an enemy that was perceived to range from locally armed guerrillas to international human rights organizations that denounced the military's abuses.

The Argentine armed forces adapted and refined a comprehensive counterinsurgency methodology from French and U.S. sources. The resulting National Security Doctrine was a native product shaped by institutionalized features of Argentina's political life, by long-standing intramilitary conflicts centered on technical and ideological questions, and by the changing military perceptions of the "Communist-revolutionary" threat. In the mid-1970s "anti-Communism" became the dominant paradigm within the armed forces. It became an "enunciation of the truth" and served as a measure of a person's allegiance or resistance to the military regime's policies.[2]

The first of the four major features of the dirty war to be noted is that the "antisubversive" war was a result of the combination between National Security principles adopted by the leadership of the armed forces and the swell of a secret repressive machinery (the intelligence apparatus) that emerged as an autonomous core within the authoritarian state. This network of intelligence services, in which younger military officers and civilian agents played a major role, acquired immense power. This was a consequence of the generals' clandestine strategy to annihilate political dissent.

The second feature of note is that, although the decentralized and autonomous intelligence services had a significant impact on Argentina's political and civil societies, as Alfred Stepan has pointed out, they were not integrated into a national intelligence system, such as that of Brazil. Stepan indicated three reasons for this: (1) the questionable professional capacity of the intelligence community in the eyes of the military; (2) the 1976 separation of power between the junta and the president, with formal distribution of one-third of government posts for each of the three branches of the armed forces; and (3) the intense competition between the army and the navy for political power. In addition, there was a long-standing trend of rifts within the intelligence community.[3]

This brings us to the third relevant feature of the dirty war: the existence of a network of largely autonomous intelligence services deepened the country's pattern of corruption and gross abuse of human rights and eroded institutional mechanisms of control. Interestingly, the potential damaging effect of a clandestine antisubversive strategy on the military institution had been stressed in the 1950s by an influential Argentine officer educated in France (see later in this chapter).[4] Indeed, the experience of the French army in the Algerian war had shown that Western-Christian values were not enough to guarantee the army's integrity, discipline, and morality.[5] I argue that the corruptive character of the intelligence services and their informal operational power and autonomy were key elements impacting the Argentine extraterritorial operations.

Finally—the fourth feature—state terror blurred the boundaries between action and sanction.[6] Individuals could find no rules by which they might guarantee their personal safety. However, in spite of the randomness and unpredictability built into the repressive system, state terror was not exclusively the outgrowth of perverted or sadistic military officers. Although this does not condone the moral reprehensibility of the military's repressive campaign, gross human rights abuses were, to a large extent, a function of the logistics associated with annihilation of the subversive enemy, as perceived. This is important: it exposes the way in which *expertise* was a key dimension in the unconventional campaign waged by the Argentine security forces. In my opinion, a central aspect of the Argentine extraterritorial venture was the transfer of antisubversive know-how. Military and paramilitary forces engaged in counterrevolutionary wars elsewhere were given tools.

This chapter discusses the nature of state terrorism in Argentina in the 1970s. Attention is given to the questions of technical knowledge, ideological-military significance of the National Security Doctrine, foreign influences on the Argentine military's unconventional, antisubversive methodology, and the role of the intelligence services in the dirty war. The National Security Doctrine expressed a conception of war, the state, and the role of the military in society with an emphasis on internal security. The Argentine doctrine reformulated French and U.S. national security concepts according to the country's political culture, the institutional history of its armed forces, and the nature of civil-military relations.[7]

The chapter also focuses on the doctrine of ideological frontiers as a rationale for extraterritorial operations and on the coordination of antidissident forces in the hemisphere. The chapter concludes with a view on the Argentine involvement in the 1980 Bolivian coup d'état—a determinant stage in the process of military expansion to Central America.

State Terror

On March 24, 1976, a military junta comprised of the commanders in chief of the army, navy, and air force seized control of the government in Argentina. Removing President Isabel Perón from power was the armed forces' response to a situation of increasing political violence. The country was in the throes of right- and left-wing terrorism, guerrilla activity, economic disarray, and a vacuum of political power. This combined with a marked erosion within the ranks of the official Peronist party. The March 1976 coup inaugurated a new political period that would be marked by the implementation of a vast program of state-sponsored repression aimed at the annihilation of "subversion" in Argentina. The combination of political violence and institutional chaos accounted for "the initiation of the 'machine for killing' that continued its antiterrorist activities even after the guerrillas had been militarily annihilated."[8]

For the armed forces, their political role went beyond the task of destroying the enemy. The new military authorities announced that their prime objective was to strengthen and integrate the nation so as to enable Argentina to attain its political and economic potential. This long-term goal, which entailed a broad effort to restructure the state, the economy, and society (along the lines of a free-market, highly exclusionist model), required the armed forces staying in power indefinitely.[9] The disruption of democracy in Argentina represented, as the head of the military junta, General

4

Jorge Rafael Videla, stated, "the final closing of a historic cycle and the opening of a new one whose fundamental characteristic will be manifested by the reorganization of the nation."[10]

Assuming that the confrontation with the Marxist enemy was a boundless war, the military maintained that the response to internal subversion had to involve a comprehensive political, economic, psychosocial, and military strategy.[11] "Subversion is not a problem that requires only military intervention," said Videla in April 1976. "It is a global phenomenon demanding a global strategy covering all areas: politics, economics, culture, and the military."[12] In fact, mass repression was the central component of the security forces' "reactive logic" to popular mobilization.[13]

The military sought to solve the political problem of order by implementing a program of fear that fused "fear of the known" with "fear of the unknown."

> Fear of the known was instilled through actual physical repression, threats, control of the society, propaganda, and the omnipresent power of the state. Fear of the unknown was instilled primarily through omission: disinformation, the absence of the defined rules of the "war," and the absence of spaces where people could meet and acknowledge the presence of one another.[14]

State-sponsored terror disabled the individual's capacity to predict the relation between action and sanction.[15] As Tulio Halperin Donghi strikingly put it, the quality permeating the social fabric was "the overwhelming monotony of living with fear."[16] Furthermore, the cycle of terror was made complete: obedience to authority was reinforced by mutual surveillance.[17]

The military claimed to act on behalf of "the highest interests of the nation" and to be preventing "the dissolution of Argentine society . . . [and] the disappearance of [the] Fatherland as a state."[18] Their "process of restoration," heavily influenced by their "conspiratorial vision of history," tolerated no opposition. To the military regime, all dissent to the new national project was a betrayal of indigenous beliefs and threatened the physical and spiritual survival of the nation.[19] Subversion was construed as "any concealed or open, insidious or violent action that attempts to change or destroy a people's moral criteria and way of life, for the purpose of seizing power or imposing from a position of power a new way of life based on a different ordering of human values."[20]

The Military's Repressive Methodology

The military had a rationale for the adoption of its clandestine repressive strategy. First was the assumption that this strategy (compared with a conventional approach contingent upon judicial and public accountability) would render faster and more effective results in the confrontation against the internal enemy. The secret deployment of state violence would protect the security forces from legal restraints and domestic and foreign pressures. In addition, its clandestine nature guaranteed the security forces the freedom of action necessary for the annihilation of subversion.[21]

A methodology of this type would inhibit the insurgents' ability to mobilize mass support by creating fear among the population. The implementation of a systematic program of "disappearances" after the coup was a key component of this strategy. Under torture, disappeared prisoners relinquished information that was believed to be vital for counterintelligence activities. The tactic of disappearance caused uncertainty within the ranks of the rebel organizations and terror among society as a whole. To be kidnapped by the security forces literally meant to be "sucked-up" (*chupado*), i.e., to be placed "out of society."[22] As an Argentine human rights organization stated,

> The detention-disappearance has a double objective: to facilitate the
> speed and efficacy of investigations and operations, and to permit the

6

location of the detained person on the . . . [secret] level of repression. From this moment, the prisoner may be tortured, forced to collaborate, held indefinitely or killed, without anyone knowing anything more about him. Uncertainty over his fate is also created, which may paralyze the activity of family and friends on his behalf.[23]

Another aspect of the military's methodology further guaranteed protection for the security community.[24] "It was viewed as particularly important that personnel from the three branches of the armed forces participated [in the operations], because in that way we would all be contaminated," said a retired navy officer. "It was a contribution that had to be given by all members of the armed forces. All must face the same political and military risks, whether in urban or rural areas."[25] In this way the armed forces sought to take responsibility for the antisubversive campaign as an institution, guaranteeing individual officers protection from future accountability to society.

The methodology followed a pattern: a presumed subversive was abducted, confined in a clandestine detention center, tortured and made to confess, and then summarily executed. Usually, torture was a regulated procedure; it involved technique—state-of-the-art methods and special equipment. The torturer was frequently escorted by a medical doctor, who was responsible for determining the ability of the prisoner to tolerate torture without cardiac arrest. Personnel underwent specialized training in torture techniques.[26] Methods and instruments routinely used to torment prisoners traveled across national boundaries (for example, electric prods—a basic gadget in torture sessions that was adopted by most Latin American security forces).[27]

To the security forces the elimination of enemies was a logistics problem. As already noted, state terror—"a premeditated, patterned, and instrumental form of government violence"[28]—was not the product of perverted military officers but a response of "terribly and terrifyingly normal" men (to use words written by

Hannah Arendt about earlier atrocities).[29] The authoritarian regime sanctioned the standard tactic of disappearances to deal with suspected enemies because it worked: it was effective. "Moral and long term political costs appear less important than security considerations" to the Argentine government, said a cable from the U.S. embassy in Buenos Aires.[30]

The Argentine armed forces, particularly the security community, mastered a logic of repression and extermination. This expertise ranged from sophisticated torture techniques to the so-called "naval solution"—the practice of throwing drugged or already dead captives from aircraft over the Atlantic Ocean.[31] This method, the so-called death flights, was a trademark of the Argentine armed forces. The army and navy employed this method to kill hundreds of political detainees during the late 1970s. As disclosed by military officers, tortured detainees were drugged into unconsciousness before they were stripped and tossed into the sea. "When there were too many [prisoners at the clandestine torture center] we had to 'evacuate' them," an Argentine sergeant said.[32] Referring to his participation in the death flights, Navy Capt. Adolfo Scilingo asserted, "I had no doubts at all that we were employing absolutely legal means, as required by the situation. . . . I did not hesitate to follow my superiors' orders." Scilingo said that part of the Roman Catholic Church hierarchy condoned the military regime's method of disposing of political opponents by ordering them thrown out over the ocean, considering it to be a Christian and clement form of death for those who represented a danger to society.[33] This Argentine practice was a doubly terrible punishment: not only did it kill the victims, it deprived them of the right to know they had been condemned summarily to death.[34]

The prestige achieved by the Argentine security forces within key military circles in the hemisphere was a function of the effectiveness of their unconventional counterinsurgency methodology. The Argentine case demonstrated that, in the 1970s, state terrorism worked. The U.S. embassy in Buenos Aires acknowledged, "It will remain difficult for us to argue against Argentine 'success' in its undeclared war against terrorism and para-military guerrilla activities."[35] It was precisely this kind of expertise that the Argentine security forces were transferring to Central America.

Foreign Influences

The major ideology behind the Argentine state terror was the National Security Doctrine (NSD). This doctrine resulted from the military's own interpretation of a set of concepts about national security, cold war politics, and counterinsurgency warfare. The NSD placed "national security above personal security, the needs of the state before individual rights, and the judgement of a governing elite over the rule of law."[36] In Argentina, the NSD was the result of a complex, extended process that combined a variety of sources, including German geopolitical thought, Roman Catholic Church canon, and, principally, French counterrevolutionary doctrine and U.S. cold war security policies.[37] The French current of thought developed in the wars of Indochina (1945–1954) and Algeria (1954–1962) emphasized an ideological, global approach to the phenomenon of insurgency. In turn, U.S. influence served as a rationale for military involvement in internal security and development (these concepts were viewed as dependent upon one another) and stressed the need for a collective defense of the Western Hemisphere against Communist expansionism. The Argentine interpretation of the NSD gave preeminence to the dimension of security over that of development, claiming that Argentina was a main theater of operations in an international confrontation, in which opposing blocs were divided along ideological frontiers.[38]

French National-Catholicism exerted a strong influence on the Argentine military.[39] The Catholic version of the *doctrine de guerre révolutionnaire* stated that all civil authority must be subsidiary "to the natural order and to natural law." This current of thought emphasized that "subversion and revolution must not be allowed to undermine the natural moral order of society because they are undermining the order of Creation."[40] Nationalism was viewed as the only tool for emancipation, because both Marxism and liberalism were perceived as doctrines that violated "the organic-statist ideal of the harmonious community."[41] Subordinate parts had to play their proper role in the organic whole; the state's mission was to advance the common good.[42]

In the 1950s, the French counterrevolutionary doctrine became an important subject of study in Argentina's official war school. Gen. Carlos Jorge Rosas, who graduated from the French military academy in the mid-1950s, played a major role in the dissemination of the *doctrine de guerre révolutionnaire* to key Argentine army circles. That influence rapidly increased with the arrival of a French military mission to Buenos Aires and the publication of several articles by French authors in Argentine military journals. Anti-communism and psychological warfare were two themes that had a strong impact on the military's conception of antisubversive war. By the end of the 1950s, the army organized the first courses and military exercises in counterrevolutionary warfare. Even though the role of the French doctrine in military training faded a few years later, its principles and ideas continued to influence the upcoming army cohort. The French model also had a strong impression on military antisubversive rules and regulations in Argentina.[43]

The messianic undertones of the French counterrevolutionary doctrine, in conjunction with nineteenth- and early-twentieth-century Spanish Catholic thought, contributed to strengthening the belief among Argentine officers that the armed forces had a preeminent role to play in society because of their commitment to the common good. Understood as "the final cause of the state, its intimate end," only the common good endowed political power with "its moral authority and legitimacy."[44] This notion of the common good was intimately related to the organic theory of the state, which conceived of the state as an autonomous organic force subject to a life cycle. Such theory originated in Iberian Catholic thought and German eighteenth- and nineteenth-century philosophy. This biological conception of the state is a central notion in geopolitical thought.[45] The influence of German geopolitical theory (*Geopolitik*) on South American military thought was pivotal in shaping the rationale of national security, particularly the central notion of national power, a major topic in the NSD.[46]

In sum, French National-Catholicism, communitarian Catholic Church doctrine, and European (mainly German) geopolitical thought found a receptive audience in Argentina's nationalist, anti-communist and antiliberal military milieus.[47] Disorder in society, a consequence of subversion and revolution, was perceived as a major source of weakness for the national state. Only God and Fatherland, construed as homologous entities, could serve as sound founding principles for a truly moral social order. As stated by an Argentine officer who gained preeminence in the 1980s as a paradigm of the Christian civic soldier, "without God and Fatherland, it is emptiness, nothingness . . . oblivion, death."[48] According to this belief system, it was the mission of the armed forces to maintain and guard national sovereignty against the threat of dissolution.[49]

The French ideological-military doctrine of unconventional warfare, combined with the U.S. counterinsurgency techniques used in the Vietnam War[50] and Argentina's own sources of expertise in the repression of political dissidents, shaped "the new professionalism of internal security" of the Argentine armed forces. Their central mission was transformed from external defense to internal protection against communist infiltration.[51] Counterrevolutionary doctrines and cold war principles also influenced the manner in which such a mission was carried out. Accordingly, the armed forces' new professionalism emphasized the need for direct military involvement in politics and domestic intelligence, the use of unconventional methods to increase effectiveness in the anti-subversive war, and the adoption of a new hypothesis of conflict based on the concept of ideological frontiers.[52]

National Security and the Transition to Globalism

The doctrine of national security emphasized the international dimension of the revolutionary war. Local conflicts were interpreted as an effect of Soviet strategic actions in the framework of an East-West confrontation. This defense doctrine reduced Communism "to the condition of internal aggression at the service of a foreign power" and directed the armed forces to create a new societal model that would eliminate any interference with the agenda defined by the armed forces (the so-called "national objectives").[53]

The concept of global balance of power played a significant role in the Argentine military's world view. In the domain of global strategy, every achievement of the Soviet Union was seen as a triumph for Communism, and every progress of Marxism in the world political arena was perceived as another step toward the final victory of the Kremlin. According to this world view, the intensity of the East-West conflict forced developing countries to avoid a neutral, or "third," position in order to preserve their national independence in face of Soviet-sponsored expansionism.[54]

The Argentine military claimed that the defense of the Western system could not be restricted by geographical borders. Under the aggression of the Marxist-Communist International, the concept of national frontiers was subordinate to an ideological dimension. The Communist revolutionary war determined a new type of confrontation in which there was no geographical partition circumscribing military operations into separated conflicts. If the Marxist foe applied a global strategy that disregarded the notion of conventional borders, the Western bloc's reply could not be launched from independent national positions.[55]

An outgrowth of national security principles, the concept of ideological frontiers gave support to the idea that Argentina could "occupy the empty spaces in the hemispheric struggle against Communism" generated by the Carter administration's policy of human rights[56] (for a discussion of the Carter administration's foreign policy see chapter 2). The Argentine military high command believed that the failure of the Carter administration to face Communist imperialism in Latin America posed "an overarching need for an alternative source of military and political assistance within the region."[57] In light of U.S. abdication of responsibility in hemispheric security, the armed forces launched an ambitious program of continental expansionism aspiring to place Argentina in the international context.

The concept of ideological frontiers was first proclaimed by Gen. Juan Carlos Onganía in a speech at West Point in 1964. Onganía stated that the Argentine armed forces welcomed U.S. hemispheric leadership and were committed to "the common cause of the Americas"; i.e., the defense of the "Western and Christian" way of life against Communist totalitarianism.[58] The Argentine army defined the main threat to national security as an "indirect maneuver" of international Communism. In the cold war theater of operations, the enemy's strategy was to promote insurgent movements in the Third World with the objective of winning over the minds of the population. The problem of internal security became a central concern for the state, which was compelled to fight insurgency in all areas, particularly in the ideological realm.[59] In turn, the principle of ideological frontiers defined a new kind of security cooperation throughout the hemisphere. Conventional multilateral assistance against external aggression—as established by the Inter-American Treaty of Reciprocal Assistance (Tratado Interamericano de Asistencia Recíproca, TIAR)—was viewed as insufficient to counteract the new type of conflict. Accordingly, hemispheric security cooperation evolved into a coordinated counterinsurgency program based upon a model of unconventional, clandestine military operations.[60]

At the Thirteenth Conference of American Armies, held in Bogotá, Colombia, in 1979, the then army commander in chief, Gen. Roberto Viola, said that the Argentine armed forces had both the responsibility and the right to intervene in other Latin American countries in defense of regimes threatened by "internal aggression."[61] The global conflict in the 1970s, Viola stated, was a new kind of confrontation: "Unlike classic wars, this war has neither a definite beginning in time nor a final battle crowning its victory. Neither does it have large concentrations of men, arms, and other materials of war, nor clearly defined battle lines."[62] According to this view, the hemisphere was a single battlefield in the war against international Communism. Therefore, it was imperative to guarantee the victory over internal subversion by destroying the enemy's ideological attack from abroad.[63]

The military assumed a state of permanent war against Marxist aggression. Accordingly, after defeating the local forces of the Left, the military turned its attention to the external "conspiracy" threatening the Western world.

The Argentine military sought to unite Southern Cone countries into a security pact, with the objective of crushing the Marxist forces as well as opposing Carter's "alienated" foreign policy toward Latin America. Argentina attempted to persuade Brazil to take an active stand in the hemispheric anti-Communist effort. However, the Brazilian military government, embarked in the process of *abertura*, had moved from the doctrine of ideological frontiers to a more pragmatic attitude in the international arena. As the *Latin America Weekly Report* commented in September 1980, "President Jorge Videla's recent trip to Brazil was a failure, as far as inducing the Brazilians to underwrite Argentina's grand strategy was concerned."[64] Brazil's attitude of nonintervention in the collective effort against Communism may have helped trigger Argentina's decision to project itself as a continental power.

The doctrine of ideological frontiers, for which national boundaries were irrelevant in the confrontation against Communism, served the Argentine military as a rationale for meddling in regional conflicts in Latin America.[65] The Argentine armed forces became responsible for a series of military actions in the hemisphere: the intervention in the July 1980 "cocaine coup" in Bolivia; counterinsurgency training and military assistance to El Salvador, Guatemala, and Honduras; and the organization of exiled Nicaraguan national guardsmen into an anti-Sandinista force. Argentina's authoritarian regime undertook an ambitious military expansionist design after crushing its own local guerrilla movements, launching an unprecedented program of state-sponsored terror at home. Consistent with an old pattern of nationalism that viewed Argentina as a potential power with predominant foreign interests,[66] the Argentine military sought a series of extraterritorial operations that would contain the perceived Communist threat while extending Argentina's influence abroad.

If Argentina had been only a battleground in a global confrontation against Communism, escalating turmoil in Central America could be seen as the continuation of the same conflict. As had been the case of Argentina in the early 1970s, Nicaragua, El Salvador, and Guatemala were perceived as targets of an indirect Soviet attack. The principle of ideological frontiers gave a rationale to a powerful sector of the armed forces that saw the venture of transferring Argentine counterinsurgency expertise to Central America as a potential source for immense economic and political benefits.[67]

In addition, a group of high-ranking officers perceived the existence of a small guerrilla nuclei abroad as a strategic threat that had to be eradicated. Notwithstanding the military victory over the Montoneros and the People's Revolutionary Army (Ejército Revolucionario del Pueblo, ERP) in 1977, those officers continually focused upon the fact that exiled guerrillas, including the Montonero leadership, had found a safe haven in Nicaragua. The Montoneros identified themselves as Peronist. The Montonero leadership was drawn largely from right-wing Catholic Church activists. The ERP was the armed offshoot of the Revolutionary Workers' Party (Partido Revolucionario de los Trabajadores, PRT). Initially a Trotskyist group, the ERP followed the model of the Cuban revolution and the example of guerrilla leader Ernesto "Che" Guevara.

From the point of view of some Argentine generals, the Sandinista-led revolutionary triumph proved that the forces of the Left had not been defeated. As an army officer recalled, the Argentine uneasiness with respect to Nicaragua emerged when Somoza was deposed and "all the democratic sector that had participated in the anti-Somoza revolution was entirely displaced, jailed or forced into exile." At that point, according to that officer, it became clear to the Argentine authorities that there would be no chance of reaching an understanding with a Sandinista Nicaragua.[68] Even though the Argentine military intelligence ruled out the possibility of a renewed guerrilla offensive against the Argentine regime out of Nicaragua (based on a certitude that the insurgent organizations had no capacity to resume military action), some analysts argued that a Sandinista Nicaragua could serve the exiled Argentine guerrillas as a platform for intelligence operations in South America. Accordingly, the recourse to military actions beyond national borders was viewed within some influential army circles as a final, essential phase of the internal war against subversion.[69]

The Intelligence Services: Key Actors in State Terror

The commanders in chief agreed early on that it was necessary to establish a de facto legal order to fight "subversion" in Argentina. But they also decided that the adoption of a *clandestine strategy* was the only course to guarantee the annihilation of the political opposition.[70] This strategy gave the intelligence community a central role in the repressive campaign. As an army officer stressed, "since the war against subversion was ideological, power was transferred to the intelligence sector of the armed forces.[71] Intelligence personnel attained a high degree of organizational autonomy. The so-called task forces enjoyed inordinate power and independence to wage "their" dirty war. The intelligence community was responsible for gross abuses of human rights and widespread corruption associated with the antisubversive campaign. Even though the repressive strategy adopted by the military regime profoundly shaped the role of the intelligence services in the deployment of state terror, their traits and power were, to some extent, a result of historical developments in Argentina's system of state coercion.

Intelligence specialists began collecting information on political dissidents in the 1930s. A vast apparatus of coercion was created following the military coup d'état of 1930. The new coercive state agencies were rapidly bureaucratized during the regime of Agustín P. Justo (1932–1938). Specifically aimed at political policing, the state surveillance apparatus was based on a military and police intelligence network characterized by fragmentation and internal conflict.[72] In the 1940s, the administration of Juan Domingo Perón (1946–1955) organized the controversial State Intelligence Agency (Secretaría de Inteligencia de Estado, SIDE), which served to spy on the political opposition to the regime.[73]

A decade later, the military intelligence services began a gradual process of professionalization. In the 1960s, the emphasis on counterinsurgency warfare and the emergence of the first guerrilla attempts in Argentina gave domestic intelligence a strategic role within the military structure.[74] In the next decade, the intelligence apparatus evolved into a clandestine facet of the state, developing its own autonomous logic and rules of rationality.[75]

During the dirty war of the 1970s, the military command established two parallel structures, one official and one secret, that conducted repressive operations throughout the nation. Argentina was divided into zones in order to facilitate the implementation of counterinsurgency actions. The secret state was run by "the intelligence services of all the branches of the armed forces, under the authority of the commanders in chief, the commanders of zone and subzone, and the chiefs of the different areas."[76] Actually, the clandestine apparatus of repression was under the operational command of the army with direct support from the navy and the air force (see figure 1.1).[77] The core of the repressive apparatus included also the Superintendency of Federal Security, a division of the Federal Police, and the State Intelligence Agency (SIDE), under the authority of the president's office.

The security community was responsible for major human rights abuses during the dirty war. In the period 1975–1979, Argentina ranked the highest in terms of the percentage of "disappearances" compared with the other bureaucratic-authoritarian regimes of South America.[78] The significance of the *desaparecidos* issue was so relevant for the Argentine public that Raúl Alfonsín won the 1983 presidential elections campaigning on a human rights platform.

Figure 1.1. The structure of the army intelligence community—the leader in clandestine operations.

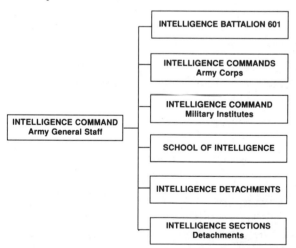

Sources: Interviews with army officers in Buenos Aires, July–August 1993; Federico Mittelbach, *Informe sobre desaparecedores* (Buenos Aires: La Urraca, 1986), p.19; *Página 12*, various issues.

Unlike Brazil, Argentina did not have a nationally integrated system of intelligence. None of the Argentine intelligence agencies paralleled Brazil's prime national intelligence organization, the National Information Service (Serviço Nacional de Informações, SNI).[79] In Argentina, most military and paramilitary intelligence organizations operated with a high degree of autonomy, often in competition with each other and responding to parallel chains of command. Their covert actions tended to bypass the regime's own institutional regulations. The emergence of this dual state contributed to the erosion of the hierarchy within the armed forces and to escalation of intramilitary tensions.[80] As the U.S. embassy in Buenos Aires noted in 1980, U.S. sanctions designed to compel "the security forces to abandon the tactic [of disappearances] would involve confrontation between the political level of the government and very powerful elements in the security forces. The potential costs of such a confrontation make it a very unattractive alternative to a government which must count on a military institution that is more or less unified."[81]

The Argentine security community was made up of various intelligence agencies with operational autonomy.[82] The intelligence apparatus emerged as an omniscient center of power within the national security state with its own procedures and responsible to no one but itself. The officers and civilians associated with the area of intelligence had considerably more power than officers assigned to regular combat units. Not only did intelligence units have exclusive jurisdiction to carry out operations; they also had control over the most profitable dimension of the counterinsurgency venture: the looting of the property of victims of state repression and the extortion-kidnapping of wealthy businessmen under the pretense of the "war against economic subversion." The unusual degree of power enjoyed by the intelligence community during the dirty war was a source of intense conflicts and resentment within the armed forces. Several years after the human rights trials of the Alfonsín administration, some officers claimed that the failure to prosecute intelligence personnel, particularly civilian agents who worked within military intelligence structures, was testimony to the partisan political nature of the trials.[83]

The network of intelligence agencies operated with great autonomy from military and police rules and command structures, and maintained secret budgets, staff, and procedures. By the time the intensity of the antisubversive war in Argentina decreased, the intelligence apparatus had become a full-scale autonomous force of professional agents with capacity to engage in extraterritorial operations.[84] Army Intelligence Battalion 601 was a central actor in this process. A key counterintelligence unit,[85] this battalion played a vital role in the dirty war and later led the Argentine counterrevolutionary operations in Central America.

Intelligence Battalion 601

Intelligence Battalion 601 had a central position in the repressive apparatus and intelligence gathering. It possessed unparalleled power capabilities, both formal and, especially, informal, to centralize and carry out secret intelligence operations. During the dirty war, all military intelligence units were directed to maintain a permanent exchange of information with this army battalion and to route to it all unidentified military equipment and documentation captured from the guerrillas by the security forces.[86] Battalion 601 was under the umbrella of the Army Intelligence Service (Servicio de Inteligencia de Ejército, SIE) and under direct command of the Army Intelligence Chief (Jefatura II Inteligencia, Estado Mayor General del Ejército, EMGE).

Though formally under the sole command of the Jefatura II, Intelligence Battalion 601 had a parallel chain of command to the First Army Corps (Buenos Aires) via its chief, Gen. Carlos Guillermo Suárez Mason. Presumably, it was Suárez Mason, from his post as commander of that army corps, who promoted and first led the Argentine military involvement in Central America. His interest in a war against Marxism beyond national borders—an enterprise subsequently embraced by the president and commander in chief of the armed forces—was closely linked to his illegal transnational operations (see chapter 5).[87]

The Military Intelligence View of Subversion

It is worthwhile to study how the military, and specifically the army intelligence command (Jefatura II), construed the subversive threat in the period 1975–1981. Army intelligence documents exposed a map of the "Marxist subversive war" from the viewpoint of the military. From their beginning in the early 1960s (with the first attempt to start a guerrilla *foco* in northern Argentina), the "subversive-terrorist" groups were perceived as having evolved into complex clandestine organizations "comprising a *political apparatus* of leadership, propaganda and indoctrination, and an *armed apparatus* responsible for specific terrorist action including the formation of an 'irregular army'."[88] The creation of the Organization for Latin American Solidarity (OLAS) and the guerrilla warfare led by Ernesto Guevara in Bolivia were viewed as the key events in the rise of revolutionary movements in Latin America.[89]

A 1975 army intelligence report stated that the Marxists' first objective was to win over the psyche of the population and, subsequently, to take control of the nation's resources. It was stressed that the local revolutionary organizations, the Montoneros and the ERP, had launched a total war against Argentine society. The armed forces (particularly the army) of course constituted the main obstacle to the potential success of the insurgent venture; hence, it was argued, the revolutionary organizations would seek to "erode, demoralize, and annihilate" the military forces.[90]

A 1977 army intelligence report stressed that, given the erosion of the insurgents' military structure and their inability to gather support from the population, the strategy of the Montonero organization had shifted toward a priority of political action over armed struggle. The ERP was perceived as centered almost exclusively on psychological action following the annihilation of its leadership and the devastation of its personnel and military infrastructure.[91] This report warned of the threat of new domestic terrorist acts against selected government and military targets, but it also underscored that a crucial confrontation against the guerrilla organizations was being waged in the international arena, where the Marxist enemy, it said, sought the political isolation of the military regime.[92] In spite of the high international political cost of the antisubversive campaign for the Argentine government, the powerful security community dictated the need to continue the campaign in the domestic realm[93]—to be supplemented by extraterritorial operations in conjunction with neighboring forces—with the objective of cleaning up the remnants of the subversive threat.[94]

Military intelligence gave particular attention to transnational links among insurgent organizations. Reports stressed the importance of the Revolutionary Coordinating Junta (Junta Coordinadora Revolucionaria, JCR), an umbrella organization created "to continue the Marxist subversive awakening of the 1960s, instilling new stimulus and goals in it."[95] The core of the JCR consisted of guerrilla organizations from Argentina, Chile, Uruguay, and Bolivia. One report said that, following its initial strategic objective of creating a unified Latin American revolutionary vanguard, the JCR established contacts with insurgent organizations from Brazil, Paraguay, Peru, Venezuela, Colombia, Mexico, Guatemala, Nicaragua, El Salvador, and the Dominican Republic.[96] In the late 1970s, military intelligence sources maintained that leftist guerrilla organizations in Central and South America were integrated into a unified structure commanded by the Soviet Union, Cuba, and the Sandinista government in Nicaragua.[97]

The increasing emphasis on extraterritorial intelligence operations may have been a response to the military's perception of a threat, particularly the Jefatura II's assessment of the subversive strategy (see figure 1.2). Growing concern with an internationally coordinated attack against Argentina was possibly associated with the regime's expansion of security operations abroad. As later revealed, an army intelligence document showed that the main focus of concern for the armed forces in the period between 1979 and late 1981 was the allegedly subversive propaganda campaign against the military regime being carried out by human rights organizations, both Argentinean and international, and by the Montonero movement.[98]

The First Attack in Central America

In the face of the military's perception of an ideological offensive against Argentina, army intelligence chief Gen. Alberto A. Valín (who ran Argentina's anti-Sandinista program) directed his staff to improve and intensify counterintelligence activity. The military's claims of a subversive ideological offensive against Argentina were not sustained by any concrete evidence of a terrorist or guerrilla campaign. However, the military intelligence command stressed the importance of the Marxist ideological aggression. "One of the main attacks against the PRN (*Proceso de Reorganización Nacional*)," said a secret document subscribed to by Valín, "comes from support organizations (*organizaciones de solidaridad*) and from radio stations established abroad that interfere openly with the country's internal affairs."[99] Indeed, extraterritorial intelligence operations were initially focused on targets perceived as sources of anti-Argentine propaganda. The first operation conducted by Argentine-trained exiled Nicaraguan guardsmen was an attack on the shortwave radio station Radio Noticias del Continente on the outskirts of San José, Costa Rica, in December 1980. Allegedly run by the Montoneros, the radio station denounced human rights abuses in Argentina. The Nicaraguan exiles agreed to conduct the operation in exchange for Argentine continuing support for the Contra venture.[100]

23

Figure 1.2. Subversion in Argentina according to army intelligence command, 1979–1981.

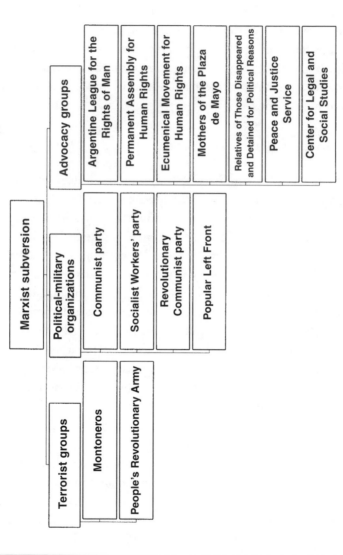

Source: Comando General del Ejército, Jefatura II Inteligencia, Annex 1 (Intelligence) to the secret directive of the Army General Commander no. 604/79, Buenos Aires, December 24, 1981.

According to a former Intelligence Battalion 601 operative—who testified before the U.S. Senate in 1987—the CIA provided the Argentines with intelligence and logistical assistance for the attack on the radio.[101] The U.S. agency was thus involved in an unauthorized operation during the Carter administration. Even though the attack failed, it was a first attempt to coordinate U.S. intelligence expertise with Argentine military training for a covert operation carried out by former Nicaraguan guardsmen against a target in Central America.

The Coordination of Repression in South America

The threat allegedly posed by revolutionary movements served as an ideological foundation for the coordination of antidissident forces throughout Latin America in the 1970s. The military intelligence services of Southern Cone countries organized a clandestine infrastructure for the persecution of political enemies. Neighboring paramilitary groups operated collectively. Foreigners were kidnapped and "transferred" to the security forces of their respective countries. Sometimes intelligence agencies worked in conjunction to carry out political assassinations. By establishing common provisions for their countersubversive activities in the region, the South American military regimes created a multinational repressive apparatus based on the exchange of intelligence on political opponents.

In the 1960s, the Southern Cone security forces had established links to cooperate in counterinsurgency operations. The professionalization of the intelligence services, the exchange of military missions, and the growing number of officers trained in neighboring countries abetted this process of cooperation. In 1974, Southern Cone police forces and intelligence services formally agreed to collaborate in the illegal detention and exchange of exiled political dissidents. On behalf of national security concerns, the region's security forces established shared rules and patterns of cooperation to fight an unconventional war without borders.[102]

Operation Condor

In the 1970s, Chile's National Information Directorate (Dirección de Información Nacional, DINA), in conjunction with the intelligence services of Argentina, Brazil, Uruguay, and Bolivia, organized Operation Condor. This transnational network aimed at coordinating efforts to hunt down exiled political dissidents and exchange intelligence information. The collective venture was based on the rationale that there was a common enemy—international Communism; therefore, a country had "the right, in fact the duty, to silence not only the opposition to one's own regime but also the opposition to any neighboring regime."[103] Dissidents were kidnapped by local security forces and transferred to secret detention centers in their original homeland. Some of them were refugees but legal residents; some were under the custody of the U.N. High Commission for Refugees (UNHCR).[104] This transnational repressive network was responsible for numerous operations (that included kidnapping, torture, and assassination) against political dissidents not only in Latin America but in the United States and Europe.[105]

In Argentina, the first wave of transnational repression began in 1974 with the murder in Buenos Aires of Gen. Carlos Prats González, former commander in chief of the Chilean army and minister of the interior during the Socialist administration of Salvador Allende. Allegedly, the Argentine paramilitary organization Triple A (Alianza Anticomunista Argentina, AAA) rejected the Chilean request to assassinate Prats, obliging the DINA to carry out the operation.

In addition to this killing of Prats (September 1974), the DINA also carried out, under the auspices of Operation Condor, the assassination of Orlando Letelier, former foreign minister of the Al-

26

lende administration, in Washington, D.C. (September 1976), and the terrorist attack against a former Chilean vice president, Bernardo Leighton, in Rome (October 1975). In a second wave of transnational state-sponsored repression, several South American political exiles were killed in Argentina, among them, Gen. Juan José Torres (former president of Bolivia), Zelmar Michelini (former Uruguayan senator), and Héctor Gutiérrez Ruiz (former president of the Uruguayan House of Representatives).[106]

It may be presumed that the Argentine intelligence operative who served as link to the DINA agents in Argentina, the United States, and Italy was Juan Martín Ciga Correa. A SIDE agent and former member of ultrarightist Argentine groups, Ciga Correa was allegedly involved in the logistics of the Prats operation. Under the command of Army Intelligence Battalion 601, this Argentine operative became involved in the counterrevolutionary program in Central America in the early 1980s. (Battalion 601 agent Héctor Francés, who served as intelligence adviser in Costa Rica with the mission of organizing a support network for the anti-Sandinista operation, identified Ciga Correa as one of the paymasters to the Argentine advisers in Honduras.[107] See chapter 4.)

The DINA network in South America—whose key operative in Buenos Aires was Enrique L. Arancibia Clavel—included Italian neofascist terrorists Stefano delle Chiaie and Pier Luigi Pagliai, who played a major role in the repressive apparatus of Gen. Luis García Meza in Bolivia. Other important actors linked to this network were Battalion 601 Col. José Osvaldo Ribeiro, who would serve as head of the Honduras-based Argentine general staff in charge of the anti-Sandinista program, and Colonel (at that time Captain) Mohamed Alí Seineldín, who operated as link between the army and the Triple A and would become an influential ultranationalist leader of military rebellions in Argentina.[108]

Miami-based Cuban exiles worked as contract agents for Operation Condor. Anti-Castro terrorists Orlando Bosch, Gaspar Jiménez, and Luis Posada were involved in the killing of Cuban diplomats in Argentina in 1976. Cuban-exile terrorist organization Omega 7 provided support for the DINA-led assassination of Letelier. The Cuban-exile network, in particular Omega 7 and Alpha 66, would cooperate with Intelligence Battalion 601 in the training and organization of anti-Sandinista forces in the early 1980s.[109]

Having achieved hemispheric prestige as a result of its success in the dirty war, Argentina sponsored counterinsurgency courses for Latin American officers in the late 1970s. Argentine experts provided instruction on their antisubversive methodology, with particular attention given to the use of torture to extract information from prisoners. Some of the courses took place at the Navy Mechanics School (Escuela de Mecánica de la Armada, ESMA), one of the most nefarious clandestine detention centers in Argentina. A former prisoner at the ESMA stated before the Argentine National Commission on the Disappeared (CONADEP) that in early 1979 the ESMA Task Force—Grupo de Tareas (GT) 3.3.2—organized a course on countersubversive techniques to which Latin American officers from Nicaragua, Bolivia, Uruguay, and Paraguay (and possibly Brazil and Guatemala) were invited. The Argentine GT 3.3.2 prepared several reports:

> One dealt with the history of the guerrilla movement in Argentina, another with the organization and creation of the task forces. Another report covered the most effective methods of torture and its different phases, physical torture . . . psychological torture, isolation, etc. They also prepared a dossier with photographs, description and background information on the people they were looking for, which was distributed to the participants.[110]

From 1977 on, Argentine paramilitary groups stalked, kidnapped, and assassinated Argentine political refugees throughout Latin America and Europe. Hit teams were sent from Argentina to track down exiled dissidents in Brazil, Uruguay, Paraguay, Bolivia,

Peru, Venezuela, Mexico, Spain, Italy, Switzerland, and Belgium.[111] By the late 1970s, Intelligence Battalion 601 had set up bases of operations in several Latin American countries, as well as the United States (see chapter 5).[112]

A Major Operation: Coup in Bolivia, 1980

In July 1980, the Argentine military became involved in a major, and violent, extraterritorial operation: the coup d'état in Bolivia led by army commander General García Meza. García Meza requested military assistance to oust Lidia Gueiler, the civilian president designated by the Bolivian Legislative Assembly, and the Argentine army and navy actively participated. The coup was characterized by precise planning and brutal execution.[113]

This involvement was a key step in the process of Argentine military expansion throughout the subcontinent. According to General Videla, the Argentine armed forces helped overthrow interim President Gueiler—in spite of the Carter administration's decided opposition to the interruption of the democratic process in Bolivia—to prevent the emergence of "a Cuba in South America."[114] Argentina was the first country to recognize the new Bolivian regime. "It was part of the cold war game," said a high-ranking navy officer. "We had to do the dirty job in Bolivia."[115] In addition to East-West considerations, traditional tensions in the Southern Cone region—particularly, Argentina's rivalry with Brazil—and the importance of buffer states such as Bolivia for the regional balance of power played a significant role in the decision to support García Meza's coup. However, geopolitical logic was not the only reason for the cooperation with the Bolivian military. Powerful groups within the Argentine armed forces were closely linked to transnational illegal networks, mainly drug trafficking, and their participation in the coup—known as the cocaine coup—yielded huge economic benefits.

García Meza's regime, according to Human Rights Watch/ Americas (formerly Americas Watch), "attracted international condemnation due to its widely reputed involvement in cocaine trafficking as well as gross abuses of human rights."[116] García Meza's partner was drug baron Roberto Suárez Levy, considered one of the world's prime cocaine traffickers in the 1980s (the regime was accused of protecting two other important cocaine rings, one led by Alfredo Gutiérrez and another by José Gasser). Money supplied by Suárez Levy helped pay for Argentina's involvement in the coup. In turn, those funds supported Argentine military activities in El Salvador. Army General Suárez Mason, a partner of major cocaine traffickers—including García Meza and his minister of the interior, Col. Luis Arce Gómez—led a powerful network within the Argentine military and paramilitary apparatus that successfully combined anti-Communist operations with drug trafficking and other illegal transactions.[117]

Under the regime of García Meza, Bolivia became a sanctuary for Nazi war criminals and Italian neofascist terrorists. Klaus Altmann—better known as Klaus Barbie, the Butcher of Lyon—received the honorary rank of lieutenant colonel in the Bolivian army from Arce Gómez. Altmann advised the Bolivian security forces on interrogation and torture techniques.[118] Pier Luigi Pagliai and Stefano delle Chiaie operated within the Bolivian military intelligence service. Pagliai "used to go in and torture prisoners, and he also extorted narcotraffickers."[119] Delle Chiaie, an associate of Suárez Mason and protégé of the Italian secret lodge Propaganda Due (P-2), worked in the Bolivian army operations section (G-3), commanding paramilitary groups. One author has suggested that he had been an adviser to the Triple A and the Argentine army intelligence service.[120]

Veterans of Argentina's antisubversive war played a key role in García Meza's military takeover and the ensuing campaign of state terrorism. Argentina had at least two military intelligence units operating in Bolivia. Some Argentine officers were "almost an integral part of the Bolivian army. They were working in the high command headquarters . . . directly assigned to help the Bolivians." The Argentine military intelligence service actively collaborated with García Meza and Arce Gómez in the planning and execution of the July 1980 coup. The military communiqués broadcasted by the new Bolivian authorities had been produced in Argentina and with the assistance of Argentine intelligence experts.[121]

One of the irregular paramilitary units most heavily involved in the ruthless repression that followed the July coup in Bolivia was the Special Security Service (SES), a branch of the National Directorate of Investigation (DIN). Headed by Col. Freddy Quiroga and directly responsible to Arce Gómez, "the SES was reportedly established under the supervision of Argentine advisers, including former officers from the notorious Navy Mechanics School [ESMA]."[122] The SES carried out what was considered the most serious human rights crime committed under the García Meza regime: the assassination of eight members of the Leftist Revolutionary Movement (Movimiento de Izquierda Revolucionaria, MIR) in January 1981. Paramilitary agents working under SES auspices were also responsible for the killings of Socialist leader Marcelo Quiroga Santa Cruz, congressman Juan Carlos Flores Bedregal, and trade unionist Gualberto Vega. Following a SES-commanded raid on the headquarters of the Bolivian Trade Union federation (Central Obrera Boliviana, COB), Quiroga and Flores were seriously wounded and dragged off to army facilities. They died there after being brutally tortured. Allegedly, Argentine navy advisers used Quiroga to teach the Bolivians how to keep a prisoner alive while inflicting maximum pain. Argentine advisers were possibly involved in torturing other survivors of the raid on COB.[123]

The Bolivian "cocaine coup" contributed to the financing of an Argentine-led transnational anti-Communist network known as the Andean Brigade or Group Andes: "a sort of secret foreign legion whose job was rooting out Communists wherever they happened to be, especially the Montoneros guerrillas and those assisting them."[124] This paramilitary network worked in conjunction with Intelligence Battalion 601. The key Argentine links to Andes were General Suárez Mason and Raúl Guglielminetti, a civilian intelligence operative who headed Argentina's Extraterritorial Task Force (see chapter 5). The brigade allegedly collaborated with U.S. military personnel assigned to Central America.[125]

The Qualified Surrogate

As a result of its undisputed success over the subversive enemy, the Argentine military perceived itself as having developed a sophisticated counterinsurgency methodology. This perception was shared, to a large extent, by several other armed forces throughout the hemisphere. Coupled with the generalized view that the Carter administration's human rights policy was responsible for a surge in "Communist expansionism," this contributed to the Argentine decision to transfer its expertise on internal security to Central America and to apply it to the organization of an anti-Sandinista armed movement. Underlying that decision was the assumption that contemporary technological progress made a direct superpower confrontation improbable, which gave primacy to indirect struggle through peripheral, unconventional conflicts.[126]

Once the guerrilla movements had been defeated in Argentina, state-sponsored terrorism was deployed as a mechanism of social control of the population.[127] From the viewpoint of the armed forces, the military victory over "subversion" required an analogous triumph in the political realm.[128] Indeed, some officers would argue in the 1980s, i.e., in the aftermath of the resumption of civilian government, that the political battle against subversion had been lost.[129]

Argentine extraterritorial operations were conducted by the

core of the security community that had fought the dirty war in Argentina, primarily, Army Intelligence Battalion 601.[130] As this chapter has shown, the intelligence network that played a central role in the clandestine repressive campaign attained an unusual degree of operational autonomy. It became responsible for gross violations of human rights and numerous crimes committed either out of desire for personal vengeance or for economic motives. This clandestine face of the authoritarian state would be the dominant force in the Argentine counterrevolutionary venture abroad.

Argentina's decision to fill in for the United States during the Carter administration in the hemispheric struggle against Communism indicated the determination of the armed forces to project their influence throughout Latin America. The Argentine intervention against "international Marxism" in the hemisphere was consistent with the generals' claim that their country had suffered "a Soviet invasion through the Cuban surrogate."[131] As one of Argentina's most notorious ideologues of state terrorism argued, Argentina was the battleground of an international confrontation that continued in Central America.[132] Accordingly, anti-communism served as an effective rationale for a complex operation that combined military and ideological training of counterrevolutionary forces with a broad network of illicit transactions that continued the pattern that emerged during the dirty war.

In the early 1980s, Argentina, which first operated as an independent actor in Central America, emerged as a qualified surrogate for the Reagan administration's design in foreign policy for that region. The U.S.-Argentine cooperation in Central America was not an incidental concurrence on security issues, but the corollary of a coinciding paradigm. This paradigm viewed popular unrest as a result of a Communist scheme aimed at deepening indigenous sources of discontent. In addition, the Argentine involvement in hemispheric counterrevolutionary initiatives in the late 1970s and early 1980s was not an isolated case of extemporaneous interventionism; rather, it conformed to the military's long-standing view of Argentina as a natural leader in Latin America.[133]

A concise discussion of U.S. foreign policy toward Latin America under the administrations of Presidents Carter and Reagan is necessary to understand the cooperation between the United States and Argentina in Central America. It is also important to analyze some key features of the troubled relations between the United States and Argentina in that period. Attention should be given to evidence that exposes a little-known face of such relations. To those tasks I turn in the next chapter.

Chapter 2

The U.S. Lurches into Cooperation with the Argentine Military

CENTRAL AND SOUTH AMERICANS WERE key actors in the counterrevolutionary efforts that took place in Central America in the 1970s and 1980s. In other words, the military and political struggle, especially the anti-Sandinista venture, was not the exclusive result of a sophisticated strategy formulated and implemented by the United States. True, the administration of Ronald Reagan and many U.S.-based groups and individuals—some of them strongly supported by U.S. congressmen—played a crucial role in encouraging military and paramilitary demobilization efforts, but the war in Central America was driven by a combination of indigenous forces and international players that responded to specific threat perceptions.[1] The origins of a devastating conflict such as the Contra war were largely shaped by international coalitions that resulted from complex linkages between ideological actors. This book is focused mainly on the dynamics of the rightist side of that ideological confrontation (see, in particular, chapter 5).

Argentina, traditionally an aggressive actor in foreign policy, perceived empty spaces left by the Carter administration in the hemispheric anti-Communist conflict and took the opportunity to assume a position of leadership in that struggle. In response to what it perceived to be a pool of Communism in Central America, the Argentine military sought to expand its extraterritorial antisubversive campaign to that region. Initially an autonomous actor in the Central American counterrevolutionary effort, Argentina took over a surrogate role on behalf of the United States when the Reagan administration "bought into" the Argentine covert military program in early 1981. That cooperative period ended with the Malvinas/Falklands conflict, beginning in spring 1982.[2]

This chapter delineates the most significant features of U.S. foreign policy toward Central America and Nicaragua under the Carter and early Reagan administrations. It also outlines the key elements that shaped the relations between the United States and Argentina during that period. Attention is given to the role of the U.S. Central Intelligence Agency (CIA) in supporting Argentine covert paramilitary efforts in Central America, and the role and impact of the United States in the origins of the regional anti-Communist venture is clarified. In addition, the chapter shows how Reagan's policymakers sought to unsettle what they perceived to be a totalitarian regime in Nicaragua—an effort in which they were aided by the intelligence apparatus of the ruthless Argentinean regime.

Carter's New Approach: Human Rights and Stability

"It is a new world that calls for a new American policy," stated President Jimmy Carter on May 22, 1977. A world that had changed dramatically in less than a generation required the United States to abandon the principles that had guided its policy since the end of World War II. The perception that the Soviet threat had become less intense created a situation viewed by the Carter administration as an opportunity for the United States to free itself from "that inordinate fear of Communism which once led us to embrace any dictator who joined us in that fear."[3] Accordingly, the United States had to find a new approach for its foreign policy, oriented to create a more flexible framework of international cooperation based on the principles of human rights, democracy, reductions in strategic armaments, and détente with the Soviet Union.

The new foreign policy approach was aimed in part at restoring faith in government after the moral crisis spawned by the Vietnam War, Watergate, and the revelations of widespread abuses by the U.S. intelligence community, extending from plots to overthrow foreign governments to illegal surveillance of U.S. citizens. The Carter administration stressed its commitment to abandon what was perceived as a tradition of U.S. "policy by manipulation" toward the Third World, seeking to assume instead an open attitude of cooperation with Latin America, Africa, and Asia.

The new policy assigned a distinctive role to Latin America. This region was chosen to serve as a laboratory to implement the administration's pledge to implement a sincere North-South dialogue. The focus was on negotiations toward a Panama Canal treaty, commitment to human rights and democratization, and the intention to improve relations with Cuba. Latin America, as a gray area on the international geopolitical map, could serve as a suitable and secure place for the administration to implement its innovative agenda.[4]

Carter's new approach, even though presumably sincere, did not last long. It gave way to a more traditional agenda aimed at managing a series of regional security crises that emerged in the context of an increasingly hostile domestic and international environment. Cuban military activities in Africa, the fundamentalist revolution in Iran, and the July 1979 oil shock affected the administration's strategic world view and unleashed a wave of conservative pressure at home. A number of events in the Caribbean Basin (namely, the Grenadan and Nicaraguan revolutions, the

Non-Aligned Movement summit in Havana, and the "discovery" of a Soviet brigade in Cuba) alerted Washington to the increasing threat of Soviet-Cuban expansionism.[5] With the capture of the U.S. embassy in Teheran, the Soviet invasion of Afghanistan, and aggravation of the war in El Salvador, the administration's favored agenda of "constructive global involvement" was definitely replaced by a "determination to give a measured and effective response to Soviet competition and to Cuban military activities around the world."[6]

The same day the Panama Canal treaties came into force (October 1, 1979) President Carter delivered a national address focused on the relevance to U.S. national security of the Soviet brigade spotted in Cuba. While the treaties aspired to symbolize a new era in inter-American relations, Carter stated that cold war times were not over.[7] The United States was still concerned with ensuring "the ability of troubled peoples to resist turmoil and possible communist domination."[8] That October day exemplified the impossibility for the Carter administration to articulate its new approach with U.S. traditional security interests. The "fresh start" announced in 1977 ended in early 1980 with a country that "felt bullied by OPEC, humiliated by the Ayatollah Khomeini, tricked by Castro, out-traded by Japan, and out-gunned by the Russians."[9] The efforts to protect U.S. economic and security interests worldwide, particularly vis-à-vis the increasing turmoil in the Third World, led the Carter administration to abandon its emphasis on human rights in favor of a policy centered on the defense of order and stability.

Carter Initiates Covert Activity

Fearing a wave of revolutionary change throughout Central America triggered by growing instability in Nicaragua, the Carter administration sought to prevent the emergence of "Cuban-style" regimes in the region. By 1978, Nicaragua had entered a cycle of extreme state-sponsored repression and massive popular insurrections that accelerated the country's political crisis.

Washington's strategy regarding turmoil in Nicaragua was largely formulated in light of the experience of the Vietnam War. Vietnam had shown that the United States should not support a regime that lacked popular legitimacy, and initially the Carter administration designed its policy toward Nicaragua in accord with such a principle. The dictatorial regime of Anastasio Somoza had no chance to achieve even a minimum social consensus. It could not rule without brutal repression. However, as turmoil escalated in the whole of Central America—particularly in El Salvador— the United States increasingly viewed the Nicaraguan crisis as a U.S. national security issue. It became clear to the Carter administration that unrest in Nicaragua demanded a more effective U.S. policy—one designed to "avoid a radical outcome" in the insurrectional process.[10]

The U.S. mediation strategy in Nicaragua was driven by an effort to prevent a Sandinista-led military victory. After a number of failed attempts to control the outcome of the revolution, a U.S. "damage-limitation policy"[11] focused on "preserving some kind of effective but reconstituted [National] Guard presence so as to avoid leaving the FSLN [Sandinista National Liberation Front] as the only organized military force" in Nicaragua.[12] According to U.S. officials, it was critical to show concrete evidence that a reconstituted national guard could be sustained, and thus attract "moderates" to play a leading role in a post-Somoza transition period. Such a plan was largely dependent upon the selection of a new national guard commander with "the capacity to bring the GN [Guardia Nacional] together and deal in a transitional environment." (One such candidate, favored by the U.S. government, was Col. Enrique Bermúdez, later military leader of the Contra forces.) U.S. guidance and assistance were perceived as critical for the success of this strategy.[13]

In spite of U.S. damage-limitation efforts, the Sandinista forces assumed a prime role in the successful Nicaraguan revolution. In response to this outcome, the Carter administration shifted its strategy toward a policy of containment: the aim was to restrict the prospects for radical change. The disintegration of the GN and the Marxist-Leninist background of the Sandinista leadership appeared to represent a severe blow to the U.S. quest for stability in Central America. Thus the Carter administration moved promptly to find a modus vivendi with the triumphant Sandinista-led coalition to prevent the risk of having "another Cuba" in the hemisphere.[14] A key decision was to request Congress to provide economic assistance to the Sandinista government with the objective of preventing the radicalization of the new regime. This line of action was accompanied by the administration's decision to provide military aid to the Salvadoran government to bolster its counterinsurgency campaign.[15]

The Carter economic aid program intended to prevent Nicaragua from leaning toward Cuba and the Soviet Union. The key U.S. assumption was that economic assistance oriented to strengthen the private sector could maintain "the monetary/economic system viable and enmeshed in the international economy." If moderate components within the anti-Somoza coalition could survive and gain strength, there was, in the view of the Carter administration, "a good chance that the internal process [could] evolve toward a Mexican rather than a Cuban model."[16]

In early November 1979, the Carter administration requested congressional authorization for $75 million in assistance funds—largely targeted to strengthen the non-Sandinista private sector. The debate in Congress focused on the matter of "whether Nicaragua was salvageable or had already been lost to Communism."[17] Following consideration of the magnitude of Soviet and Cuban influence on the new Sandinista regime, Congress agreed to provide Nicaragua with the requested economic aid. However, the release of the funds was conditioned on a presidential certification that the "Government of Nicaragua has not cooperated with or harbors any international terrorist organization, or is aiding, abetting, or supporting acts of violence or terrorism in other countries."[18] The core of U.S. concern in Central America was the Marxist threat in El Salvador; Congress, therefore, wanted Carter's certification that the Sandinistas were not supplying weapons to the Salvadoran guerrillas. Once Carter finally certified, in September 1980, that there was no evidence of Nicaraguan government involvement with the Salvadoran rebels, the aid funds for Nicaragua were made available; however, as an analyst noted, by that time the monies' "symbolic importance as a gesture of U.S. friendship had faded."[19]

As the Carter administration perceived that it could not prevent the Nicaraguan revolutionary government from approaching the Communist bloc, it authorized a CIA covert action program to funnel approximately one million dollars to a number of anti-Sandinista labor, press, and political groups in Nicaragua.[20] Even though Adm. Stansfield Turner, then director of the CIA, indicated that "the Carter administration had no program of covert action that would have permitted any paramilitary support to the contras,"[21] the fall 1980 presidential finding that approved covert operations in Nicaragua opened a track substantially different from the candid foreign policy proclaimed by Carter three years earlier.[22] Undoubtedly, the Carter administration did not intend to set up the context for a paramilitary effort to overthrow the Sandinista regime. However, as one commentator pointed out, "the fact that Carter had initiated covert activity of any kind made the next step—Reagan's paramilitary operation—more palatable to congressional Democrats."[23]

Before leaving office, the Carter administration renewed military assistance to El Salvador, which had been cut off on a human rights basis, and halted economic aid to Nicaragua because of the alleged Sandinista role in furnishing arms to the Salvadoran rebels. In January 1981, Carter said that restrictions on the press and political activity in Nicaragua, as well as an excessive Cuban presence in that country, were a source of significant concern to the U.S. government. Carter pledged the incoming Reagan administration not to "abandon Nicaragua to the Cubans."[24]

The Friction between Carter and Argentina

The friction between the United States and the Argentine military regime was intense during the Carter administration, with the tension converging on human rights issues, Argentina's nuclear policy, its refusal to adhere to the U.S.–Western European embargo on grain sales to the USSR, and the military regime's involvement in the 1980 coup d'état in Bolivia.

The Carter administration's human rights policy was perceived by Argentina as an expression of U.S. "moral imperialism" and was strongly contested on the basis of nationalism, prestige, and rejection of any interference in its domestic affairs.[25] While Argentina upheld its adherence to the anti-Communist coalition in the Western Hemisphere, it stressed a position of "non-automatic" alignment with respect to the United States and the Western bloc.[26] Argentina's ambitions for regional preeminence were heightened during the Carter administration, as the Argentine and other Latin American military regimes perceived Carter's human rights policy as a U.S. failure to fulfill its hemispheric security responsibilities.[27]

The Carter administration chose Argentina as one of the countries in which to implement its foreign policy oriented toward human rights. The horror of the dirty war prompted the U.S. government to apply sanctions to the Argentine military regime to drive it to improve its human rights record. As part of this policy, the United States placed an embargo on military aid and training to Argentina, opposed Argentine loan requests at the World Bank and the Inter-American Development Bank (IDB), denied Argentina credits from the Export-Import Bank (EXIMBANK), and periodically condemned the military junta at international forums.[28]

With the support of Congress and U.S. public opinion, the Carter administration advanced a policy based on one of the key congressional initiatives of the 1970s: the importance of contemplating the human rights record of countries receiving U.S. assistance.[29] The relative absence of vital strategic or economic U.S. interests in Argentina facilitated the pursuit of a policy that intensified a long-standing pattern of distrust and mutual antagonism between the two countries. Moreover, the Carter administration's efforts to isolate the Argentine military regime because of its human rights abuses alienated a postwar ally in the U.S. policy of anti-Communism.[30]

The Argentine military government viewed the tension with the United States as a clash between Carter's lack of political realism (a result of his moral approach to foreign policy) and Argentina's need to fight and annihilate an insurrectionary armed movement sponsored by Cuba and the Soviet Union. The military claimed that such a movement had contributed to placing the country on the verge of national disintegration. "It was assessed that there were 20,000 activists [in Argentina]; that is, 20,000 potential combatants," said an Argentine army general. "They launched a war . . . which, perhaps, the United States failed to understand."[31]

Even though U.S.-Argentine relations under the Carter administration were largely distinguished by open hostility, there were isolated instances in which both governments tried to find ground for mutual understanding. It has been argued that these minimal exchanges were effectively used by the Carter administration to obtain concrete results in its human rights policy toward Argentina. As one analyst observed, in September 1978 the U.S. vice president, Walter Mondale, and the Argentine president, Jorge Rafael Videla, agreed on a quid pro quo that linked domestic human rights practices with economic aid.[32] As a result of that meeting, Videla invited the Inter-American Commission on Human Rights (IACHR) to conduct an on-site inquiry on the human rights situation in Argentina. In exchange, the Carter administration agreed to unblock an EXIMBANK loan to Argentina. Presumably, this temporary accord contributed to improve the human rights situation in Argentina. "Especially noteworthy was the decline in the practice of involuntary disappearance for which the Argentine regime had gained international notoriety."[33]

Various sources suggested that the military faction led by Videla and Viola sought to improve relations with the United States and the international community as a way to strengthen its position vis-à-vis the hard-liners within the military regime.[34] The Videla-Viola faction was interested in promoting a gradual process of political liberalization under military tutelage. Navy commander in chief Adm. Emilio Eduardo Massera promoted a political plan with populist coloring. The hard-liners, Suárez Mason and Luciano Benjamín Menéndez, advocated a strong military government and a resolute decision to annihilate all vestiges of political opposition to the regime. Presumably, the EXIMBANK/IACHR quid pro quo with the Carter administration was used by Videla to obtain a basic consensus within the military to advance a policy of limited negotiation on the human rights issue.

As recalled by a close aide to President Videla, a retired general, Miguel Angel Mallea Gil, the 1978 meeting between the Argentine president and Mondale in Rome led to some improvements in U.S.-Argentine relations:

> President Videla told [Mondale], "How do you intend that I improve human rights in Argentina if every time I open the newspaper I find a strong condemnation from the State Department or Democrat congressmen, which—deserved or undeserved—has a major domestic impact, particularly upon the army, which is the one that is fighting and whose men are being killed?"[35]

According to the same source, Mondale guaranteed Videla that the level of U.S. criticism against the Argentine military regime would decrease, with special attention to public statements issued by the State Department. Mondale's commitment "was implemented, it lasted for a while, and then we started again with the same problem." It became clear to the military authorities that the interests of Argentina and the United States were "basically irreconcilable." Videla exemplified the officers that were "in favor of respecting human rights," said Mallea Gil. "But there was a war to be won and we chose that path instead of the politically erroneous, in our opinion, moral logic advanced by President Carter."[36]

By 1980, national security concerns and domestic political pressures forced the Carter administration to adopt a stronger position vis-à-vis perceived Soviet gains in the international arena.[37] Consistent with this refurbished foreign policy agenda, the United States gradually changed its attitude toward Argentina. The decision to improve relations with the authoritarian regime quickened following the Soviet invasion of Afghanistan. Compelled to make his reactive policy work, Carter sent a mission to Buenos Aires to solicit the military junta's adherence to the grain embargo against the Soviet Union. However, the generals maintained their decision to replace in part the U.S. grain sales to the USSR, and Argentina's determination contributed to the eventual failure of the U.S. sanctions. A further source of conflict with the United States was Argentina's contribution to the breakdown of the democratic process in Bolivia. It was in July 1980 that the Argentine security forces actively participated in the so-called cocaine coup (see chapter 1).

In spite of the tensions, the Carter administration initiated a policy shift toward Argentina. In early 1980, the assistant secretary of state for human rights, Patricia Derian, had announced her resignation to the press, denouncing "a move to normalize our relations and to end our official criticism of the [Argentine military] regime."[38] Derian had learned earlier that the U.S. military and intelligence agencies commended the Argentine armed forces for their successful counterinsurgency campaign. "Through these agencies," Derian stated, "the United States government is sending a dangerous and double message. If this continues, it will subvert our entire human rights policy."[39] Derian's account concurred with Argentine sources that suggested a double message was indeed being sent by the United States with respect to the military's clandestine strategy of repression in the dirty war. While the U.S. government condemned Argentina for its abominable human rights record, U.S. military and intelligence officials secretly praised the Argentine leaders for their triumph over the Marxist enemy.[40]

The CIA Support for Counterrevolution

Testimony in Congress in 1987 indicated that the CIA, under the Carter administration, collaborated with extraterritorial operations conducted by the Argentine intelligence services.[41] Ostensibly without the approval of the White House or Congress, CIA operatives facilitated Argentine intelligence activities in the United States and Central America. Those operations sought to organize an anti-Sandinista force and to support the Salvadoran counterguerrilla warfare.

Carter's decision to make the CIA a "highly moral" organization, regulated to operate on the basis of a moderate Soviet threat, was perceived by many of its veterans as a policy of "purging" the agency.[42] Old CIA hands believed that Carter's approach to the "Communist tide," particularly in Central America, was soft and ineffective. But reports of secret U.S. Congress hearings declassified in the early 1990s suggest that in fact the role of the CIA under Carter went beyond the covert assistance program to anti-Sandinista moderates in Nicaragua.

Leandro Sánchez Reisse, who worked for Intelligence Battalion 601 from 1976 to 1981, disclosed to a U.S. Senate subcommittee that the Argentine government, in cooperation with the CIA, established a covert business in Florida, which served as an operations center for Argentine military activities in Central and South America from 1978 to 1981. Sánchez Reisse asserted in his 1987 deposition that the CIA collaborated with his intelligence unit in Florida and that the Argentines conducted operations on behalf of the U.S. intelligence agency (see chapter 5).[43]

Sánchez Reisse declared that he had dealt with CIA agents firsthand when he was running intelligence operations in Fort Lauderdale. According to his testimony, the U.S. agency provided the Argentines with support for military operations in the areas of intelligence and logistics (see chapter 1). Asked about the real purpose of the Argentine base in Florida, Sánchez Reisse stated: "We had to be in Fort Lauderdale to make easier the shipments of weapons and money to support the activities in Central America of Argentine troops, Argentine advisers, and people working from [the] United States in that area."[44]

The Argentine military placed intelligence operatives in the United States to coordinate the transfer of funds and arms to Central America. This special intelligence unit, the Extraterritorial Task Force (Grupo de Tareas Exterior, GTE), had been created as an extension of Army Intelligence Battalion 601.[45] Allegedly, the nature and extent of the GTE activities in the United States—arms trafficking, illegal financial transactions, and money laundering—were made possible because of the connivance of the CIA. The Argentine intelligence unit handled covert funds in several countries, including the United States and Switzerland. The funds were usually transferred to Central America through Panama (see chapter 5, "The Argentinean Front Companies").[46]

Other sources such as Edgar Chamorro and Sam Dillon stated that CIA operatives were engaged in secret contacts with early Contra organizers under the Carter administration. It appears that, in spite of Carter's efforts to curtail the power and leverage of the CIA, the agency supported a hemispheric network of right-wing government officials and independent players united under a mandate of anti-Communism. Two of the most prominent actors of that network were Nicaraguan exile Francisco Aguirre and a former CIA deputy director, Lt. Gen. (retired) Vernon Walters. In 1980, Aguirre and Walters traveled to Argentina to discuss with high-ranking officers the details for a plan to organize a counter-revolutionary army in Central America. These early efforts were critical for the rapid implementation of a U.S.-sponsored anti-Sandinista program under Argentine supervision.[47]

Reagan Advocates Containment and U.S. Leadership

Ronald Reagan became president with a clear agenda based on a foreign policy philosophy of "cold war internationalism."[48] An anti-Communist crusader, Reagan was committed to recovering U.S. global military preeminence and to counterbalancing Soviet strategic expansionism in the Third World. Whereas, to him, the United States was suffering the devastating consequences of its self-imposed human rights mission, the Soviet Union perceived itself as a dynamic power "interested in the ultimate goal of its philosophical fathers, the global triumph of its political system."[49] Under Reagan, the U.S. response to the Soviet expansionist goal was to be translated into a foreign policy devoid of human rights concerns and heavily grounded on the assumption that regional conflicts were largely a function of external factors.[50] The Republican president's intelligence doctrine, which equated anti-Americanism with Communism, would drive his administration to view all threats to U.S. interests as Communist-inspired.[51]

The Reagan administration's view of the Third World responded to a cold war geopolitical approach according to which regional conflicts were part of an East-West confrontation. Such conflicts demanded decisive U.S. action to fight a perceived expansion of Soviet hegemony. Accordingly, the Reagan administration saw Central America and the Caribbean as a key place to show the world U.S. commitment to reassert its role as a superpower.

The rhetoric against Nicaragua, "the new Soviet beachhead" in the hemisphere, had escalated before the Republican administration came into office. In early 1980, Gordon Sumner, a retired lieutenant general and one of the authors of the so-called Santa Fe Document,[52] asserted that "the Sandinistas are blood brothers of the Marxist militants—red terrorists, who are holding this nation hostage today in Teheran."[53] The 1980 Republican platform condemned "the Marxist takeover of Nicaragua and Marxist attempts to destabilize El Salvador and Guatemala" and committed the party to "support the efforts of the Nicaraguan people to establish a free and independent government."[54] Following the elections, Reagan's future national security adviser, Richard Allen, stated that "the Reagan administration will move rapidly to reverse a feeling of utter helplessness with respect to Fidel Castro's Soviet-directed, armed and financed marauders in Central America, specifically Nicaragua, El Salvador, and Guatemala."[55]

The Santa Fe Document, produced in the summer of 1980, was a blueprint for Reagan's hemispheric strategy. All the document's authors—with the exception of L. Francis Bouchey—occupied positions in the area of Latin American affairs during the Reagan administration. David Jordan and Lewis Tambs were appointed ambassadors to Latin America; Gordon Sumner became special adviser to the assistant secretary of state for inter-American affairs; Roger Fontaine joined the National Security Council as an expert in Latin America.[56]

The document argued that the United States should strengthen hemispheric security against the Communist threat on the basis of acknowledging an "integral linkage between internal subversion and external aggression." U.S. foreign policy, according to the Santa Fe Document, had to revitalize the core postulate of the Monroe Doctrine: "No hostile foreign power will be allowed bases or military and political allies in the region." Accordingly, the United States could no longer tolerate "the status of Cuba as a Soviet vassal state" nor a permanent Marxist Sandinista regime in

Nicaragua. The document recommended the pursuit of effective hemispheric integration by the promotion of regional security agreements and reactivation of traditional links with Latin American armed forces. Assuming that the very survival of the United States was in danger, the report encouraged the United States to reestablish continental leadership in order to "protect the independent nations of Latin America from Communist conquest and help preserve Hispanic-American culture from sterilization by international Marxist materialism."[57]

At confirmation hearings in January 1981, Secretary of State-Designate Alexander M. Haig depicted a turbulent global environment in which major nuclei of instability in the Third World represented a threat for U.S. national security.[58] Such a hostile international environment compelled the United States to restore its leadership in the Western world and to deter Soviet adventurism in regions sensitive to U.S. national security. Communist interventionism, according to Haig's view, focused on strategic areas with routes and resources critical to the economic and political independence of the West: "When the Soviet Union exploits local conditions for its own strategic aims, the problem is no longer local but a strategic threat to our own survival."[59] Haig rejected the notion of a world "divided into distinct strategic zones in which wars can be discretely fought and contained"; instead, he favored the principle of an extended conflict in which a regional U.S.-Soviet confrontation might spread and at once become global.[60]

Jeane Kirkpatrick, Reagan's ambassador to the United Nations, in an article entitled "U.S. Security and Latin America," described national security as "the strategic perspective which had shaped U.S. policy from the Monroe doctrine down to the eve of the Carter administration, at the center of which was a conception of the national interest and a belief in the moral legitimacy of its defense."[61] Drawing a distinction between traditional autocracies (authoritarian regimes), which had the capacity to evolve into democracies, and totalitarian regimes, in which there were no prospects for a political change in that direction, Kirkpatrick helped to promote the need for U.S. pragmatic support for right-wing dictatorships in Latin America.[62]

Reagan Era Rhetoric: "The Moscow-Havana-Managua Axis"

The Reagan administration's strategic agenda in Latin America was defined in terms of the principle of global balance of power. U.S. efforts in the Western Hemisphere were aimed at correcting the perceived "tilt" in favor of the Soviet Union. Latin America, a key battleground in the East-West conflict, proved vulnerable to Soviet aggression. If the region were to fall into communism, the Reagan administration claimed, the United States would lose access to critical raw materials and vital sea lines of communications in the Caribbean, the Gulf of Mexico, and the South Atlantic.[63] But, most importantly, the administration's design to protect U.S. economic and security interests in Latin America was viewed as a means to correct the global balance of power and to restore U.S. will and credibility. From the point of view of U.S. foreign policy, the region became a place where the United States and the Soviet Union were to "play out the drama of international politics."[64]

The Reagan administration placed Central America at the core of U.S. foreign policy concerns. The region became a symbol of U.S. ability to preserve the Western alliance. As Reagan pointed out, if Central America were to fall into Communist control, "our credibility would collapse, our alliances would crumble, and the safety of our homeland would be put in jeopardy."[65] The need to maintain the Caribbean Basin on the U.S. side of the balance of power responded to both political and military imperatives. In the political domain, a triumph of anti-Communism in Central America was viewed as decisive to U.S. credibility. At the military level, the guiding "economy of force" principle demanded concrete measures to prevent the region from turning Communist; the United States must not be required to divert resources to the Caribbean Basin to the detriment of other critical areas.[66] In his testimony before the congressional committees investigating the Iran-Contra affair, former national security adviser Robert McFarlane outlined the reasons for thwarting the creation of a "hostile axis" on the U.S. southern border. "The danger is not Nicaraguan soldiers taking on the United States," McFarlane explained,

> it is that country serving as a platform from which the Soviet Union or other surrogates like Cuba can subvert neighboring regimes and ultimately require the United States to defend itself against a Soviet threat, whether by spending more dollars on defense that we didn't need to, to worry about our southern border, whether we need to worry more about the Panama Canal now that Russians are here, whether we need to be concerned about the half of our oil imports that come from refineries in the Caribbean within MIG range of Nicaragua.[67]

Three major tasks were delineated for U.S. foreign policy in the Western Hemisphere. First, to improve relations with Mexico; second, to make the Caribbean Basin a safe area for U.S. national security; and third, to restore U.S. friendship with the South American nations.

The Reagan administration's foreign policy on Latin America gave preeminence to the strategic situation in the Caribbean Basin. The U.S. policy intended to help countries in the Basin improve their economic conditions, in the belief that "genuine stability can only be based on economic prosperity." In addition to economic aid, the United States pledged to help those countries defend themselves from Communist aggression by providing no-strings-attached military aid and by focusing on the perceived source of the problem: Cuba. "Both Central America and the Caribbean are exposed to an effort of armed subversion by Cuba of great subtlety and sophistication," said assistant secretary of state for inter-American affairs Thomas O. Enders. The Cuban targets, the Reagan administration claimed, were Nicaragua, El Salvador, and Guatemala. "In each of these countries, Cuba has been systematically creating a machine for the destruction of established institutions and governments," Enders said. He avowed that the United States would defend its allies from Cuba's "covert war," bringing "the costs of that war back to Havana."[68]

Enders pointed to four major factors in the Caribbean Basin perceived as engendering a regional threat to hemispheric stability. First, the new Cuban strategy initiated in 1978, when Fidel Castro decided to sponsor the Sandinista insurgency in Nicaragua. Second, the widening gap between export commodities and imported oil on the one hand, and local manufactured products on the other hand, resulting in a serious regional economic crisis (Enders: "Coinciding as it does with the Cuban drive to unify the left and commit it to violence, economic crisis creates great potential political vulnerability throughout the area"). Third, the U.S. perception that Nicaragua was being used as a base for Communist penetration in Central America, thwarting the prospects for democratization in the region.[69] Major U.S. concerns were the growing Sandinista military power and Nicaraguan support for the Salvadoran rebels. Enders's fourth point was that the war in El Salvador had been "progressively transformed into a textbook case of indirect armed aggression by Communist powers through Cuba."[70] This was a strong U.S. belief. The Salvadoran conflict was perceived as critical in the outcome of the East-West global confrontation. "If after Nicaragua, El Salvador is captured by a violent minority, what state in Central America will be able to resist?" asked Enders. "How long would it be before the major strategic United States interests—the canal, sealanes, oil supplies—were at risk?"[71]

The Debate about a Course of Action

The problem of external intervention in the Western Hemisphere and the role of Cuba as a proxy force for the Soviet Union were leitmotifs in the Reagan administration's rhetoric. A December 1981 State Department report entitled "Cuba's Renewed Support for Violence in Latin America" offered a detailed analysis of "the degree to which Cuba is directly engaged in efforts to destabilize its neighbors by promoting armed opposition movements." The report addressed the role of the "Moscow-Havana Axis" in exploiting indigenous conflicts grounded "in historical, social and economic inequities" for Communist expansionist goals. "Cuba's policies abroad are linked to its relationship to the Soviet Union. By intervening in behalf of armed struggle in Latin America, Cuba injects East-West dimensions into local conflicts."[72]

Some senior officials in Washington talked about Central America in terms of the Cuban missile crisis of October 1962. Early in 1981, Haig began a strong rhetorical offensive against Havana: "I think we have made it very clear from the outset that this is a problem emanating, first and foremost, from Cuba and that it is our intention to deal with this matter at its source."[73] Haig instructed McFarlane, by that time his State Department adviser, to outline a series of feasible military actions to put pressure on Cuba and the Sandinistas. The resulting plan contemplated the prospect of "shooting down small Cuban aircraft, sinking small Cuban boats, smuggling arms and even instituting a naval blockade of Nicaragua and Cuba."[74]

Haig's relative position vis-à-vis the president was weak. His strategic agenda of "going to the source" found definite opposition in Defense Secretary Caspar Weinberger, Vice President George Bush, and Reagan's inner circle in the White House. In addition, the joint chiefs of staff recommended that the president reject Haig's proposal for a potential naval blockade of Cuba. Such open-ended measures entailed the risk of a blunt clash with Castro, a consequence incompatible with Reagan's design to bolster U.S. power in Central America without increasing the risk of a direct confrontation with the Soviet Union.[75]

Reagan's closest advisers favored covert action as an effective and prudent course to deal with the "Moscow-Havana-Managua Axis" in the hemisphere. On February 26, 1981, the CIA issued a policy paper suggesting "a very broad program of covert actions to counter Cuban subversion in Central America."[76] In a memorandum commenting on the CIA proposal, McFarlane wrote to Haig that "this is a very worthwhile beginning which I recommend you welcome and support." McFarlane urged the coordination of all agencies' strategies in a comprehensive program to neutralize Cuban influence in Central America. "The key point to be made now is that while we must move promptly, we must assure that our political, economic, diplomatic, propaganda, military, and covert actions are well coordinated."[77] That same day, McFarlane drafted for submission to Haig a report that underscored the need to orchestrate the State Department's Central America strategy with the strategies of the Defense Department and the CIA. "Bill [William] Casey's paper provides an excellent covert dimension to what must be a prompt comprehensive strategy for dealing with Cuba throughout Central America," the report read. McFarlane's draft raised a number of questions regarding key matters that the administration had to deal with in order to carry out a covert program in Central America. First, the problem of financing the operations. McFarlane suggested that part of the program could be funded by the Defense Department. Second, the key problem of preventing information leaks on the covert program when submitted to Congress for consideration. Finally, and most importantly, the possibility of getting help from third parties (presumably Argentina and Honduras) from whom the United States had received "a tentative offer."[78]

Both the Argentine and the Honduran governments wanted to cooperate with the United States in an anti-Communist campaign in Central America. They were particularly interested in support-ing a U.S.-backed anti-Sandinista army. Later in 1981, the United States formalized an agreement with Argentina and Honduras to facilitate Reagan's counterrevolutionary program in the region.

A draft presidential finding dated February 27, 1981, instructed Casey, the director of central intelligence (DCI), to "directly or in cooperation with foreign governments, engage in a regional effort to expose and counter Marxist and Cuban-sponsored terrorism, insurgency, and subversion in El Salvador, Nicaragua, Guatemala, Honduras, and elsewhere in Central America." The draft finding directed the Defense Department to assist the CIA in the imple-mentation of the counterinsurgency program.[79] On March 9, 1981, Reagan issued a finding authorizing the CIA to "provide all forms of training, equipment and related assistance to cooperating gov-ernments throughout Central America in order to counter for-eign-sponsored subversion and terrorism."[80] We can thus see that, as early as March 1981, the Reagan administration had laid out its strategy to regain U.S. influence in Central America and to pro-mote stability in the region by bolstering local counterinsurgency forces.

Aid to Nicaragua Is Ended

On April 1, the United States officially terminated all economic assistance to Nicaragua "given [its] involvement in activities sup-porting violence in El Salvador." The communiqué issued by the State Department acknowledged that the U.S. government had "no hard evidence of arms movements through Nicaragua during the past weeks." However, it remained concerned that "some arms traffic" from Nicaragua to the Salvadoran guerrillas might be going on. The statement ratified the U.S. decision to support "moderate" forces in Nicaragua against "Marxist domination."[81] Former U.S. ambassador to Nicaragua Lawrence Pezzullo viewed the administration's policy as grossly erroneous: "We dealt ourselves out of the game for no reason in April 1981, because of small-mindedness on our side."[82]

The central U.S. assumption was that no solution to the problem of instability in Central America could be attained as long as the FSLN stayed in power in Nicaragua. For the Reagan administration, the Sandinistas were defined by their orthodox Communist origin; their political and military training in Cuba, the Soviet Union, and other Communist countries; and their preference for "the power that comes from the gun."[83] According to the State Department, the suggestion that the Sandinistas had been "'driven,' even against their will, to seek Cuban and Soviet shelter in response to U.S. policies . . . does not receive empirical support."[84] The dominant, and rather distorted, conception of the Sandinista-led revolution adopted by the Reagan administration prevented it from taking into account all the available evidence regarding the conduct of the new government in Nicaragua. In turn, the Sandinista leadership, as some sources indicated, assumed that Reagan's election would result in a definite U.S. offensive aimed at subverting the revolution, regardless of Nicaragua's efforts to conform to U.S. political and security demands.[85]

Moderates among the senior officials in Washington advocated a dialogue with the FSLN on the basis that Nicaragua did not represent a critical threat to U.S. allies in the region. But the hard-liners (particularly Casey, Kirkpatrick, and White House aide Edwin Meese) assumed that the Sandinistas, being Soviet surrogates, could not be trusted; hence, diplomatic efforts conducive to a security accord were considered worthless. For these officials, who did not support Haig's proposal of overt action against Cuba and Cuban allies in the region, the only alternative course was the paramilitary option.[86] Strategically positioned in the president's inner circle, these hard-liners succeeded in shaping the Nicaraguan policy. However, they could not rule out the negotiations approach. "Few people thought that the Sandinistas would talk to us seriously," confided a senior official, "but we had to try."[87]

Accordingly, U.S. Central American policy began to follow a "two-track" approach. While playing the diplomatic game to persuade Congress about the administration's belief in a negotiated solution, the White House unleashed the CIA to conduct paramilitary operations against Nicaragua.

Covert Action

The Reagan administration came to office and decided to adjust the agency's "highly moral" role imparted by Carter to a new mandate defined by an unambiguous ideology of energetic anti-Communism. Even though Reagan's restyling of the CIA was mainly superficial, he succeeded in restoring the agency's morale and enthusiasm. The appointment of Casey, Reagan's former campaign manager, as DCI was critical in making the CIA a can-do government bureaucracy.[88]

During his tenure as DCI in the 1980s, Casey contributed to an intensification of distrust of Congress in the key Directorate of Operations. Considered by many critics "the most secretive and . . . the most hidebound of the agency's four main directorates," that group ran the anti-Sandinista program in conjunction with the Argentine military. CIA officials in that section, which covertly collected intelligence and sought to influence foreign affairs, shared a "culture of obsessive secrecy."[89] This was translated into a disposition to withhold information from Congress regarding CIA ties to foreign individuals, agencies, or governments involved in illegal activities or human rights abuses. Agency officials serving in covert roles shared a mind-set that refused to concede that withholding, omitting, or delaying pertinent information was a serious act of deception.[90]

Central America was one of two places (the other was Afghanistan) where the Reagan administration faced the challenge of defining the United States' new role as a world power. In Central

America, the CIA served as an effective vehicle to implement covert programs to roll back "Communist expansionism." In Nicaragua the agency was instructed to promote an indigenous counterrevolutionary army under the guidance of Argentine advisers.

Why a Role for Argentina?

The operations by proxy responded to a number of constraints that made direct U.S. involvement impossible. The most important of those limitations were (1) the CIA's restricted capacity for covert action (there were few such specialists in the agency), (2) the CIA's vulnerability to congressional scrutiny, and most importantly (3) Congress's dislike for any kind of action that could invoke the "ghosts" of Vietnam; i.e., a progressive U.S. intervention that forced the United States to become directly involved in a war in Central America.[91] The CIA's decision to prop up an exile indigenous army trained by a third country provided an effective solution to those problems. The CIA left the day-to-day military management of the operation to the Argentine advisers. Aid to the Nicaraguan Contras was concealed in assistance monies for Argentina. Given the ample prerogatives enjoyed by Casey, it was possible for the CIA to set up the covert program in Central America without major interferences from Congress.

From January to August, 1981, while the efforts to build up an anti-Sandinista insurgency force gained momentum, Assistant Secretary Enders explored the possibilities for a negotiated agreement with Nicaragua. Secret talks between Enders and the FSLN leadership sought common ground. The United States wanted Nicaragua to terminate all support for revolutionary movements in the region and to reduce its links to the Communist bloc drastically. In turn, Nicaragua demanded U.S. assurances that the Reagan administration would not seek to destabilize the Sandinista revolution. In mid-August, while the CIA was formalizing an anti-Sandinista collaborative effort with Argentina and Honduras, Enders met with junta coordinator Daniel Ortega and foreign minister Miguel D'Escoto in Managua. Failing to reach a basis for a minimal consensus, bilateral talks ended soon after.[92]

With respect to the paramilitary option, DCI Casey would declare later that the United States was "buying into" an existing Argentine program.[93] "It was convenient to run the operations through the Argentines," a senior CIA official said. "We didn't have to ask questions about their goals that we couldn't escape asking about our own goals when we took over."[94] The tripartite relationship among the United States, Argentina, and Honduras was tailored to Washington's scheme of destabilizing the Sandinista regime without placing additional U.S. troops in Central America.[95]

On November 12, 1981, Haig refused to assure the House Foreign Affairs Committee that the United States was not involved in any attempt to overthrow the Sandinista government in Nicaragua. In a heated dispute with Democrat representatives, Haig would do no more than restate Reagan's assertion that the United States had no intention to employ U.S. troops in military action anywhere in the world. "I think the President's statement should stand," Haig said. "Based on your responses," Representative Michael Barnes, a Maryland Democrat, contended, "if I were a Nicaraguan, I'd be building my bomb shelter."[96]

On November 23, 1981, Reagan approved National Security Decision Directive (NSDD) 17, empowering the CIA to create a paramilitary group of five hundred men that would complement an existent thousand-man force under Argentine command. An initial amount of $19.95 million was allocated to the program, acknowledging that "more funds and manpower will be needed."[97] Actually, the Argentines were already training an anti-Sandinista force of about fifteen hundred men; NSDD 17 only formalized the operation. The Argentine military was actively engaged in training Contra rebels before Reagan took office. According to 1987 reports that could not subsequently be corroborated or disproved, when the Reagan administration decided to arm an indigenous anti-Sandinista force, it secretly paid Argentina $50 million to develop the Contra program.[98]

Secretary of State Haig disagreed with the administration's decision to pursue a covert action approach in Central America. "Covert operations can be ancillary to a foreign policy," Haig later said, "but they can't be the policy."[99] He viewed Casey's plan as a "cheap shot" that pretended to translate into action the president's anti-Communist rhetoric while assuring Congress that U.S. troops would not be engaged in a war in their own backyard. For Casey, covert action in Central America was the only alternative to direct U.S. involvement in the region. A main reason for his stance was that the United States did not want to be accused of gunboat diplomacy in the hemisphere.[100]

On December 1, Reagan signed a finding that authorized the CIA to "support and conduct paramilitary operations against the Cuban presence and Cuban-Sandinista support infrastructure in Nicaragua and elsewhere in Central America."[101] The agency would "work with foreign governments, organizations and individuals to build popular support that will be nationalistic, anti-Cuban and anti-Somoza." It would also "support and protect the opposition by developing and training action teams that will engage in paramilitary and political operations in Nicaragua and elsewhere."[102] The Reagan administration embraced the proxy alternative with enthusiasm. "It is much easier and much less expensive to support an insurgency than it is for us and our friends to resist one," Casey was quoted as saying in a news report about eighteen months into the operation. "It takes relatively few people and little support to disrupt the internal peace and economic stability of a small country."[103] As the presidential finding was signed and the head of the Latin America Division of the CIA's Operations Directorate Duane "Dewey" Clarridge was called into action, the covert program entered a new phase.[104]

In late 1981, Enders briefed the Senate and House Select Committees on Intelligence on the CIA's covert program in Central America. Enders told congressmen that the CIA was secretly supporting with training, money, and weapons a resistance force of exiled Nicaraguan guardsmen that was carrying out armed incursions into Nicaraguan territory from bases in Honduras. At the secret briefings, Enders said that the CIA was using Nicaraguan political dissidents, former guardsmen, ethnic minorities, and exile groups in the United States to provoke a situation of widespread unrest in Nicaragua. While the United States provided the funds for the secret operations, Enders said, military advisers from Argentina were responsible for implementing the program.[105]

Some congressmen voiced concern about the agency's capacity to control the operation. The Argentine counterinsurgency experts and the former members of Somoza's national guard were known for their unorthodox and brutal methods of repression. Responding to these complaints, Enders assured the members of the intelligence committees that the U.S.-backed operation would be firmly controlled and emphasized that the United States would not tolerate human rights violations. However, as some legislators observed, it was difficult to understand how the CIA could bolster democracy in Nicaragua helped by the Argentine military regime, at that time a "symbol of right-wing dictatorial rule," and the remnants of Somoza's national guard, infamous for their ruthlessness and corruption.[106]

Casey assured Congress that the CIA's covert operation was not intended to overthrow the Sandinista regime. The clandestine effort, Casey told the oversight committees, had the sole objective of interdicting arms trafficking from Nicaragua to El Salvador while persuading the Sandinistas to avoid further allegiance to the Cubans and the Soviets.[107] However, the presidential finding contained the essential elements to attempt a clandestine destabilization of the revolutionary government in Nicaragua. By guaranteeing that the opposition force was to be anti-Somocista, the finding lied from the very beginning about the significant presence of Somoza's former guardsmen in the new armed movement. By stating the open-ended nature of the operation, the presidential finding anticipated that the "interdiction" effort was to evolve into a large-scale counterrevolutionary venture (the December 1982 Boland amendment would prohibit any U.S. policy oriented to overthrow the Nicaraguan government). Finally, even though the presidential document acknowledged the role of foreign governments in the operation, Casey's report to Congress played down the fact that the Argentine military, which had recently implemented a vast campaign of extermination and terror in its own country, was a key component of the U.S. venture.[108]

Argentina as a U.S. Ally

The election of Ronald Reagan was a turning point for U.S.-Argentine relations. Reagan had strongly criticized Carter's policy toward Argentina and praised the Argentine military for the annihilation of the Marxist threat. Based on the broad coincidence of their ideologies and perceived national security interests—largely defined by intense anti-Communism—the administrations of the United States and Argentina swiftly moved into a relationship of mutual understanding and cooperation. This ideological concurrence led to a new model of partnership in which Argentina assumed the role of U.S. surrogate in Central America.

It was not surprising that Reagan's victory had a significant and immediate impact on U.S.-Argentine relations. In late 1980, Argentine military leaders had initiated informal talks with some of Reagan's top Latin American advisers, seeking to enter a partnership with the United States in case of a Republican triumph in the November elections. The new administration unconditionally abandoned the Carter policy of pressuring the military to rectify its domestic behavior and swiftly moved toward an alliance with Buenos Aires focused on the containment of Communism in Latin America.

The rhetoric that had been used in the campaign against Carter and his human rights policy had a strong impact on right-wing military regimes throughout the hemisphere. They perceived that the election of Reagan was to bring about broad U.S. support for a renewed, fierce offensive against Communism. A central role in this process was played by a team of freelancers, primarily staffers in the office of Republican Senator Jesse Helms, who went all over Latin America giving clear signals that the Reagan administration had decided to endorse a forceful military crusade to save the world from Communism. As a result of this campaign, human rights abuses stepped up significantly following the election of Reagan. In a four-month period, El Salvador, and some other countries, experienced some of the worst human rights abuses in their history. Military and paramilitary forces were unleashed to escalate massive repression to counteract the advance of international Communism.[109] In Argentina, the army expanded its missions to Guatemala, El Salvador, and Honduras in order to step up training and intelligence operations in the region.[110]

In February 1981, President Reagan sent Walters, the retired general, on a Latin American tour with the mission of gathering support for U.S. policy toward Central America (prior to this appointment as ambassador-at-large, Walters had helped organize the first groups of anti-Sandinista rebels). As recalled by Edgar Chamorro, "Walters himself arranged for all the bands [of exile national guardsmen] to be incorporated within the 15th of September Legion, and for the military government of Argentina to send several army officers to serve as advisers and trainers."[111] A main objective of Walters's trip was to explore the possibilities for military cooperation in Central America between the United States and the armed forces of Argentina, Honduras, and Guatemala.[112] In Buenos Aires, Walters said that his government's foreign policy was to respond to manifest friendship. He discussed with military leaders the U.S. strategic view of Soviet-sponsored interventionism in the hemisphere and offered details on the

64

Marxist Latin American network centered in Cuba and Nicaragua, with attention to the role of Argentine political exiles in insurgent operations.[113]

"I have encountered an understanding that exceeded my most exaggerated hopes," stated Gen. Roberto Viola after his visit to the United States in March 1981. A few months later, Jorge Aja Espil, retiring Argentine ambassador in Washington, said, "Reagan is a friend of Argentina and of President Viola, and this sets a course toward future possibilities."[114] Reagan and Viola concurred that "hemispheric security is crucial for the global geopolitical strategy." They acknowledged that the Caribbean Basin and the South Atlantic were fundamental nuclei of the hemispheric security system. After his mission in Washington, Viola assured the Reagan administration that "Argentina will give all necessary support to the Western cause."[115]

Later that year, the army commander in chief, Gen. Leopoldo F. Galtieri, met with Reagan's top foreign policy advisers in Washington, D.C. From the U.S. perspective, Galtieri appeared as the "most cooperative" of the generals regarding the potential for a full-fledged Argentine involvement in Central America. Galtieri ratified an agreement by which the Argentine army would receive U.S. funds and intelligence to help them cut off alleged Cuban-Nicaraguan assistance to the guerrilla movements in El Salvador and Guatemala.[116] In addition, the Argentine navy sent patrol boats to police the Gulf of Fonseca, supposedly a main route in the Nicaraguan arms pipeline to the FMLN guerrillas.[117]

One of Reagan's initial gestures of friendship toward the Argentine military regime was to request Congress to repeal the embargo on military assistance to Argentina. On April 1, 1981 (the same day the Reagan administration officially suspended all U.S. aid to Nicaragua), a joint hearing of the House Subcommittees on Human Rights and International Organizations and on Inter-American Affairs was convened to discuss "whether the human rights conditions in Argentina have improved sufficiently to lift the restriction." The administration's resolution to substantially improve U.S. relations with Argentina was strongly contested by Democrats, who argued that the United States could not cultivate harmony with an authoritarian regime responsible for gross violations of human rights.[118]

Reagan's "pragmatism" was perceived by the Argentine regime as a sound basis for mutual understanding. There were still discrepancies in the views of the two countries, but their coincidences on international policy nurtured a flexible bilateral relationship. The Argentines were relieved that the conflict of the Carter days was over. "In spite of our mutual disagreements," explained General Mallea Gil, "it became much easier for Argentina to gain access to the U.S. [foreign policy] decision-making core. Our ambassador had a much better rapport with the State Department." Argentina's novel interest in Central America coincided with the new U.S. foreign policy design. "A fundamental U.S. objective was to overthrow the Sandinista regime. Thus . . . when two countries have a common goal, they understand each other much better."[119]

It was almost twenty years since Argentina had openly backed the United States on the Cuban missile crisis (1962)—showing a decided anti-Communist stance and allegiance to the Western leader. The country now entered a new phase of agreement and cooperation with U.S. hemispheric objectives. The close, though brief, U.S.-Argentine alliance was perceived within influential Argentine military circles as the beginning of a new era in which Argentina was to obtain international recognition for its victory over the Communist foe.

"The fight against subversion in Central America marked a period of honeymoon between Argentina and the United States," said a retired navy officer. On the occasion of a visit by a Pentagon delegation to Buenos Aires in 1981, the Argentines felt, for the first time in years, that they were being treated as U.S. allies. "I recall a very favorable proclivity of the U.S. officers toward Argentina, because we had helped the United States to solve its problems in Central America," said this officer. "It was a time of great prestige for Argentina."[120]

In early 1982, the Reagan administration probed the Argentine military leadership about the possibility of infiltrating combat forces into Nicaragua. Argentina, as well as Chile, Colombia, Paraguay, and Uruguay, received a proposal from the Pentagon to create a combined force that could be deployed in Central America to roll back the guerrillas in El Salvador and, eventually, to establish a military blockade of Nicaragua.[121]

The CIA and Argentina

When, soon after his appointment as DCI, Casey learned that Argentine advisers were training an anti-Sandinista force, he immediately understood that the Argentine military could help the Reagan administration to implement its containment policy in Central America. The United States could easily buy into an existing Argentine program. "Bill [Casey] was absolutely delighted," the CIA deputy director, Adm. Bobby Ray Inman, said later. "He knew that the Argentines' hope was to unseat the Sandinistas. And that was farther than the U.S. Congress was ready to let us go."[122]

Casey instructed the CIA station chief in Buenos Aires to advance a proposal to General Galtieri indicating U.S. interest in the Argentine military program in Central America. The United States was willing to finance the operation, relieving the Argentines of that difficulty in being the leading force behind the anti-Sandinista rebels. Galtieri was captivated by the U.S. offer. A leader of the hard-line faction within the military institution, he viewed an alliance with the United States in Central America as an avenue to reestablishing friendly relations with the leader of the West. Presumably, such an improvement in U.S.-Argentine relations could help to advance Galtieri's personal political project at a time of heightened tensions within the military.[123]

Key sectors in the Argentine military perceived the interest of the CIA in the Argentine operations as an endorsement of the counterinsurgency methodology implemented in the 1970s. "It is possible that the U.S. military and intelligence services saw that what they could not achieve in Central America had been accomplished by the Argentine, Chilean, and Uruguayan armed forces in their own countries . . . using a successful counterinsurgency model, which was later questioned and discarded as a result of the debate on the disappeared ones," said the Argentine navy officer quoted in the preceding section. "The United States was losing the war in Central America. It was a war that the Americans could not win by themselves. Had they remained alone, there would have been another Vietnam." He went on to describe the men in the field:

> Argentina, which was coming out of its antisubversive war, was interested in the Central American conflict and became involved in it with some four hundred men who were moving in and out of the region. . . . They were just a few, but they were excellent advisers who got adapted very well to that terrain. They trained combat forces and became very influential. . . . The Argentine personnel implemented counterinsurgency techniques that they had learned in the Tucumán *monte* and began to obtain effective results in the war in Central America. . . . The Argentine advisers carried out the difficult task that the Americans had failed to perform.[124]

As a result of the CIA's covert action program in Central America, the United States began using veterans of Argentina's dirty war to fight a regime perceived as a threat to U.S. values and liberal democracy. Argentine military and paramilitary personnel involved in the Contra operation served in Army Intelligence Battalion 601 and other security agencies that had played a major role in the regime's program of state-sponsored terror. Argentine operatives working in Central America also came from the Argentine Anti-Communist Alliance (Triple A) and other ultranationalist terrorist organizations.[125] Many of these "experts" had tortured and killed prisoners in the clandestine internment camps of Argentina's dirty war.

The Impact on the Malvinas/Falklands Campaign

An intriguing feature of the Argentine covert involvement in Central America was its impact on the military junta's decision to try to recover the Malvinas/Falkland Islands. The influence of the extraterritorial intelligence program on U.S.-Argentine relations contributed to shaping the military leadership's strategic decision to undertake the conventional military operation in the South Atlantic.

However, it is important to note that the Argentine military involvement in Central America was not designed to be a quid pro quo for U.S. neutrality in case of a major conflict with the British: Argentina's participation in the anti-Sandinista operation was a result of a gradual military expansion throughout the region. Nevertheless, as Argentina increased its participation in the Contra program, a sector of the armed forces led by Galtieri viewed the Argentine covert involvement in Central America as a viable source for U.S. support in the Malvinas/Falklands issue.[126]

Key motives for the military leadership's interest in extraterritorial operations were (1) a belief that Argentina could expand its influence in Bolivia and Central America by taking advantage of the counterinsurgency capabilities developed in the dirty war; and (2) an interest in increasing sales of Argentine arms to those countries and to the anti-Sandinista forces. But the importance to the United States of the involvement of Argentine advisers in Central America (and possibly of the Argentine influence in Bolivia) was erroneously perceived by the military high command. They thought the United States would remain neutral in case of an Argentine confrontation with Britain.[127]

It is not the objective here to analyze the political-strategic decisions that led to the Malvinas/Falklands venture, but it must be noted that the Argentine resolution to occupy the islands was based on three major assumptions.[128] First, the generals supposed that Britain would not react militarily to recover the Malvinas/Falklands; second, they expected to obtain the support of the U.N. Security Council in the dispute; and third, they expected that if the British, because of domestic constraints, were to react with military force, the United States would mediate, impede a war, and, if a military conflict were to occur, remain neutral.

It has been suggested that Enders's visit to Buenos Aires in early March 1982 was perceived by the Argentine military leadership as Washington's green light for a takeover of the islands. One of my informants corroborated the thesis advanced by an Argentine investigation, according to which General Mallea Gil, Argentina's military attaché to the United States, had communicated to President Galtieri his belief that "the Argentine presence in Central America was of vital importance for the putsch that the Americans were organizing in Nicaragua."[129] However, Mallea Gil denied this account. "The U.S. government did not send any . . . signs regarding the Malvinas," he told me. According to Mallea Gil, following the Argentine invasion to the islands, Reagan told Galtieri that the United States wanted to mediate in the dispute. Subsequently, said Mallea Gil, Secretary of State Haig told Argentina's ambassador in Washington: "We are willing to mediate as President Reagan said . . . however, if the mediation fails . . . we will have no choice other than supporting Britain."[130]

Mallea Gil's account coincides with Haig's. In a 1984 book, Haig wrote, "The United States had not paid a great deal of attention to the Falklands situation. During a visit to Buenos Aires in early March, Thomas O. Enders . . . had urged the Argentineans to continue negotiations; he reported that they were non-committal on this point, but not negative." As with respect to the Malvinas/Falklands conflict, Haig said: "While my sympathy was with the British, I believed that the most practical expression of that sympathy would be impartial United States mediation in the dispute. The honest broker must, above all, be neutral."[131]

Argentina's military action in the South Atlantic in April 1982 eventually led to the end of its secret alliance with the United States in Central America.[132] At the time of the outbreak of the Argentine-British war, the Contra forces under Argentine command consisted of approximately 2,500 men,[133] but the U.S. decision to cooperate with Britain in the Malvinas/Falklands conflict affected Argentina's commitment in Central America. Thereafter, the Argentine military reduced its involvement in the Contra program.

Nevertheless, the Argentines stayed in control of the day-to-day anti-Sandinista operations throughout 1982. A group of Argentine officers continued training Contras until late 1984—presumably working for the CIA and not subject to command by military authorities in Buenos Aires. It took the CIA well into 1983 to attain operative control over the anti-Sandinista program in Honduras.[134]

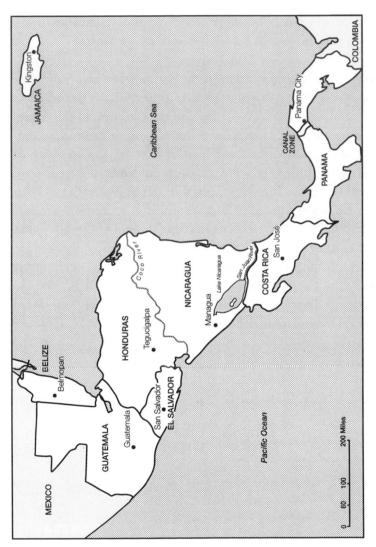

Central America

Chapter 3

Argentina in Central America

THE SANDINISTA REVOLUTION gave crucial stimulus to popular mobilization and radical tactics of resistance throughout Central America. In the early 1970s, faced with growing state-sponsored violence in response to their demands for social and economic reform, left-wing organizations in El Salvador and Guatemala had chosen armed struggle as a strategy for social change.[1] By 1979, the Salvadoran and Guatemalan rebel movements had grown substantially; they were able to challenge the forces of the incumbent military regimes.

The U.S.-trained Salvadoran and Guatemalan armed forces responded with broad counterinsurgency programs based on the premise that unconventional methods were preferable to traditional military tactics. Guided by a new operational code promoted by the United States in the 1960s, the armed forces' primary military objective was the eradication of domestic opposition.[2] In alliance with the highly conservative upper classes, the armed forces of El Salvador and Guatemala used systematic terror against the civilian population as a political tool. The importation of repressive technology (primarily from the United States, Argentina,

Chile, and Israel) turned El Salvador and Guatemala into testing grounds for counterrevolutionary techniques. The result, during the late 1970s and early 1980s, was tens of thousands of political killings and disappearances. Even in Honduras, where there was no significant insurgency threat, the military regime introduced an unprecedented program of state terror.

The Argentine military played a major role in this cycle of state-sponsored violence. Based on the assumption that it had achieved a high level of professionalism in internal security, the Argentine military transferred its counterinsurgency expertise to the Central American armed forces. Assistance was provided through military training, intelligence, and arms sales. That support conformed to both the armed forces' geopolitical view of an East-West confrontation and to a market position assumed by the Argentine government. There is no doubt that Argentine support to the Central American military regimes was essentially a short-term response to domestic social unrest in the region and to the U.S. retreat, under President Carter, from its role as enforcer of hemispheric security.

Given the generalized instability in the region and the Carter policies, the Argentine military offered the Central American counterinsurgency states a viable "parainstitutional" model designed to control their internal fronts. Immediately after the revolutionary triumph in Nicaragua, some fifteen hundred national guardsmen sought refuge in Honduras, one thousand in Guatemala, and five hundred in El Salvador.[3] The Argentine military presence in those countries greatly facilitated the creation of an anti-Sandinista army organized and commanded by former members of the Nicaraguan national guard.

A knowledge of this scenario is a key to understanding the Argentine role in the creation of the Nicaraguan Contras. There was an Argentinean military presence in Nicaragua before the Sandinista revolution and Argentine involvement in the anti-Sandinista effort was a logical result of its encroachment in the region. The flow of military aid from Argentina to other Central American governments started only after 1979. However, Argentina's connections with the Salvadoran, Guatemalan, and Honduran military and paramilitary forces—as well as its long-standing links with Somoza's national guard—eased the unfolding of the counterrevolutionary program in Central America.

The Argentine military took part in both domestic counterinsurgency activity and covert action against the Sandinista regime. This chapter traces the features of the Argentine advisory role in Nicaragua under Somoza, El Salvador, Guatemala, and Honduras.[4] It offers a profile of the Argentine military missions in Central America, their technical capacity, and their coordination with local security forces. This account of the extraterritorial military role of Argentina in Central America indicates how the resources for state violence, no longer needed in Argentina for domestic control, were used to strengthen state security in other Latin American countries—countries perceived as ideological allies by the Argentine military regime.

Nicaragua under Somoza

Argentine Military Assistance

After the armed forces seized power in Argentina (March 1976), they developed a close relationship with the regime of Anastasio Somoza Debayle (1967–1979). Officers in the Nicaraguan national guard received specialized instruction in Argentine military and police academies; Argentina also sold military equipment to Nicaragua and provided Somoza's security forces with advice on counterinsurgency. And as popular rebellion against the Somoza regime escalated, Argentina increased its support. This early friendship continued until the very last days of Somoza's rule and was extended into the period of Argentina's support for the remnants of the national guard.

By 1975, the Nicaraguan national guard was the most heavily U.S.-trained military establishment in Latin America. As part of their studies at the Nicaraguan Military Academy, fourth-year cadets received military training at the School of the Americas, Fort Gulick, in the Panama Canal Zone.[5] Up to the early 1970s, some guardsmen had occasionally completed their instruction in other Latin American training facilities (such as Argentina's military academy, *Colegio Militar de la Nación*, and police academy, *Escuela de Policía Coronel Ramón L. Falcón*). The escalation of insurgency assaults and the end of U.S. public safety programs drove Somoza to seek new outside security assistance.[6] Argentina was one of the countries that provided Somoza with expertise on unconventional warfare in the early fight against the Sandinista guerrillas.

In the wake of President Carter's human rights foreign policy, growing numbers of Latin American officers (from Nicaragua, Guatemala, El Salvador, Venezuela, Ecuador, Bolivia, Chile, Paraguay, and Uruguay) turned to Argentina for counterinsurgency training.[7] Argentine experts, such as Army Col. Mohamed Alí Seineldín, taught Latin American officers commando courses (a full range of special forces skills) and advanced courses in military intelligence.[8] An ultranationalist with a messianic sense of historic mission, Seineldín later trained the Panamanian Defense Forces under Gen. Manuel Noriega and, in the late 1980s, emerged as a leader of the military rebellions undertaken by the *carapintadas* (the painted faces) after Argentina returned to civilian government.

As recalled by a former Nicaraguan national guard officer trained in Argentina—who would become head of psychological warfare of the Nicaraguan Democratic Force (FDN) and a CIA favorite[9]—Seineldín was perceived as "a strong, great leader, who used to tell us that it was imperative to fight Communism with God." Seineldín had a strong impact on this officer and others who similarly underwent commando instruction under his supervision. He was highly effective in convincing his counterparts in

Central America that religion was vital to legitimizing the war against Marxist penetration in the region.

The Argentine courses in military intelligence consisted of political and ideological instruction (the birth of ideologies, political parties, and subversive movements; the coordination of subversive organizations in Latin America; the transfer of counterguerrilla experience between countries) and technical instruction (the management and organization of the intelligence section; the role of the intelligence chief). The training included visits to the army intelligence headquarters in Buenos Aires, the Córdoba base of the Third Army Corps, and the "theater of operations" of the Tucumán campaign.[10]

The Argentine army was seen by the Central Americans as highly qualified for counterinsurgency warfare. "The Argentines are first rate professionals: most of us have taken courses with them at the School of the Americas," noted the officer quoted above. "The Argentine army had the experience of suppressing the guerrilla movement in Tucumán and we wanted to learn from that."[11] However—notwithstanding the Argentines' ostensible credentials—the Nicaraguan guardsmen trained in Argentina soon realized that their instructors' background was primarily in urban counterinsurgency. The core of the 1975 Operativo Independencia in Tucumán Province had been centered in the cities, where the army conducted a brutal, unconventional secret war.[12] As would be confirmed by the Contra war, the Tucumán experience was hardly useful in the Nicaraguan mountains.

At the 1977 Conference of American Armies (Conferencia de Ejércitos Americanos, CEA) held in Managua, Gen. Roberto Viola and Adm. Emilio Massera secretly guaranteed the Somoza government extensive support for their antiguerrilla effort; the Nicaraguan dictator had confided that a larger and reorganized guard would defeat the Sandinista insurgents.[13] After Carter cut off military assistance to Nicaragua in early 1979, Argentina filled in for the United States—along with Israel (which became Somoza's prime military supplier), South Africa, Brazil, El Salvador, and Guatemala. The Argentine military regime attempted to thwart Somoza's fall by providing him with covert military support until the eve of the revolutionary triumph.[14] A selected group of Argentine officers served as advisers to the elite force known as the Basic Infantry Training School (Escuela de Entrenamiento Básico de Infantería, EEBI), commanded by Anastasio *el Chigüín* ("the Kid") Somoza Portocarrero, the dictator's son.[15] Argentine support for the Somoza regime came primarily from the ultranationalist faction of the army led by Gen. Ramón Genaro Díaz Bessone and from the navy high command led by Admiral Massera. The involvement in Nicaragua was a profitable operation for those groups.[16]

Argentine military sales to Nicaragua in the period 1977–1979 included 9-mm submachine guns, rocket launchers, high-impact bombs, ammunition, and armored personnel carriers.[17] The military regime's association with Somoza was denounced by the Sandinistas following the triumph of the revolution. Referring to the $7.7 million debt contracted by the Nicaraguan Defense Ministry with an Argentinean firm, Special Developments Enterprise (Empresa de Desarrollos Especiales, EDESA), (debt of which the Somoza government had amortized only $2.5 million), Daniel Ortega said: "We think that greater [proof] of the complicity of the crimes committed against the [Nicaraguan] people cannot exist. There just cannot be greater evidence. The answer of this Government of National Reconstruction is that it is not paying a single cent of this debt."[18] EDESA was owned by high-ranking navy officers and managed by the navy general staff. EDESA sold military equipment not only to Nicaragua but also to Guatemala and other Latin American countries.[19]

After Somoza's fall, Brig. Gen. Rubens Graffigna, commander in chief of the Argentine Air Force, said that the loss of one country to Marxism represented a serious threat to hemispheric security. Graffigna underscored that Argentina, victorious against subversion, should lead the defense of the Western Hemisphere: "It is a fact that there is no domestic policy without extraterritorial projection."[20] In view of what they perceived to be U.S. abdication of responsibility, the Argentine armed forces decided to launch an ambitious program of continental expansionism aspiring to place Argentina in the international political forefront. On the other side, some radical Left Argentines became involved with the revolutionary Sandinista National Liberation Front (Frente Sandinista de Liberación Nacional, FSLN) in the late 1970s in its struggle to overthrow Somoza's dictatorship.

Internationalist Dissidents in the Fight against Somoza

In early June 1979, a dissident group of approximately fifteen members of Argentina's People's Revolutionary Army (Ejército Revolucionario del Pueblo, ERP) in exile joined the Sandinista forces in the final offensive against Somoza. Led by Enrique Haroldo Gorriarán Merlo, the group had censured the ERP, the armed offshoot of the Revolutionary Workers' Party, for showing "an irresponsible lack of solidarity with the FSLN." This handful of ERP veterans asserted that armed struggle remained the major strategy to promote revolution, and because Argentina did not offer the appropriate conditions for that quest, they decided to become involved in the Nicaraguan struggle.[21]

The Argentines joined the Colombian Socialist Workers' Party's Simón Bolívar Brigade in the southern front, Benjamín Zeledón. Commanded by Edén Pastora and strengthened by many internationalist fighters from Latin America, the front to the south in El Naranjo, Peñas Blancas, and Sapoá fought a fierce and protracted battle against the guard's elite EEBI units. The largely conventional war in the Benjamín Zeledón front was a novel experience for the Argentine combatants.[22]

Following the overthrow of Somoza, several Argentine guerrillas remained in Nicaragua as part of the Sandinista security apparatus. Most of the Argentines worked at the Ministry of the Interior in the area of international affairs.[23] Gorriarán Merlo and his group were recruited into the Fifth Directorate, an elite unit organized by Cuban Col. Renán Montero, under Lenin Cerna's General Directorate for State Security (Dirección General de Seguridad del Estado, DGSE). The group, known as the Nucleus of Steel, became the Fifth Directorate's strike force.[24] Its baptism of fire was the 1979 capture and execution of a former national guard major, Pablo Emilio Salazar, who was influential in the early attempts to organize an anti-Sandinista force. Salazar's counterrevolutionary efforts were supported by an influential network of Nicaraguan exiles in the United States with access to U.S. rightist political sectors.

On September 17, 1980, an Argentine dissident commando team killed Somoza in Asunción, Paraguay.[25] To quote *Barricada,* the FSLN newspaper, Nicaragua became a "sea of happiness"; popular euphoria engulfed the whole country.[26] The day after the operation, one member of the squad, Hugo Alfredo Irurzún, was captured by the Paraguayan police. A former commander of the Compañía de Monte Ramón Rosa Jiménez in Tucumán, Argentina (1974–1976), Irurzún died in the torture chamber.[27]

In 1982, the Nucleus of Steel group participated in the kidnapping (in San José, Costa Rica) and interrogation of an Argentine military operative, Héctor Francés.[28] Gorriarán Merlo and his associates were also involved in the creation of highly effective Sandinista army counterguerrilla units (*batallones de lucha irregular*) used against the Contras.[29]

Montonero Participation

Argentina's other major guerrilla organization, the Montoneros, supported the Nicaraguan insurrection with professional combatants, a health brigade, military equipment (mainly explosives), and a donation of more than U.S.$1 million.[30] Although Montoneros and Sandinistas had much in common (a pragmatic Marxism and a nationalistic and highly emotional approach to their movements) their relationship was far from congenial. But the Sandinistas held Rodolfo Puiggrós, a key Peronist-Montonero intellectual guide, in high esteem, and, according to one source, when the Montonero leadership met in Cuba with Daniel and Humberto Ortega and Jaime Wheelock in late 1977, pressed by the Cubans, the Montoneros eventually agreed to contribute some money to the Sandinista anti-Somoza struggle. However, there was a condition: that the Sandinistas would report that Montonero leader Mario Firmenich was directly involved in the revolution.[31]

Firmenich, who did not participate in combat during the insurrectionary period, was in Managua at the time of the revolutionary triumph. "A study of the Sandinist struggle shows us quite an original combination of urban insurrection and rural guerrilla warfare," Firmenich told reporters. "The strategic encirclement of cities by the rural guerrillas was combined with the insurrection of the masses inside the cities." The Nicaraguan revolution, Firmenich held, "shows that there is a new situation in the world, permitting us to surmise that for our continent the 1980s will be the decade of liberation and the counteroffensive of the Latin American people."[32]

Stressing that "the Montoneros are not dead," Firmenich asserted that Argentina would follow the Nicaraguan revolutionary path.[33] His lieutenant, Fernando Vaca Narvaja, boasted that Firmenich would return to his country in the wake of a Montonero triumph to be received by the masses as "a new Perón."[34] Ensuing events turned out to be very different. In late 1979, the Montoneros launched a "strategic counteroffensive" in Argentina and, as a result, more than a hundred exiled Montoneros (who had been sent back to Argentina) were killed by the security forces. By December of that year, the Montonero guerrilla counteroffensive against the Argentine military regime had been definitely crushed.[35]

According to journalist Martin Andersen, Firmenich was a double intelligence agent. The Montonero leader, Andersen argued, had been working for Army Intelligence Battalion 601 since the early 1970s. According to Andersen's main source, a retired U.S. diplomat assigned to Argentina in the 1970s, Firmenich's handler was an army colonel (later general), Alberto Valín, who played a key role in domestic and extraterritorial intelligence operations during the dirty war.[36] Firmenich's double role as guerrilla leader and military intelligence operative, Andersen noted, was "well known in the U.S. intelligence community."[37]

The Junta Sends Commandos

In 1978, the Argentine military sent operatives to Nicaragua to identify Argentine guerrillas fighting in the Sandinista ranks. Working in conjunction with Somoza's Office of National Security (Oficina de Seguridad Nacional, OSN), the military's Argentine commando team aimed at capturing exiled ERP and Montonero cadres.[38] Said an Argentinean adviser to the national guard: "In Nicaragua I carried out the same tasks as in Argentina . . . intelligence tasks . . . struggle against Communism through unconventional means. Those were tough jobs, disappearances, activities that could not be conducted in legal ways."[39]

The Argentinean team in Nicaragua was headed by Carlos Dürich, a former Triple A member who served in the Task Force 3.3.2 that operated out of the Navy Mechanics School (Escuela de Mecánica de la Armada, ESMA) in Buenos Aires.[40] The prime liaison with Somoza's security forces was Lt. Col. Emilio Echaverry Mejía, the national guard's deputy chief of personnel.[41] A graduate of Argentina's Colegio Militar (class of 1961), Echaverry would become a favorite of the Argentines in the general staff of the main Contra group, the Nicaraguan Democratic Force (Fuerza Democrática Nicaragüense, FDN), and would be directly involved in the recruitment of Argentine advisers for the Contras in 1981.

Survivors from the ESMA in Argentina reported that at least one political prisoner had been captured in Nicaragua by the Argentinean extraterritorial squad collaborating with the Somoza regime. The detainee was executed in the torture center at the ESMA in mid-1979, before the arrival in Buenos Aires of a delegation of the Inter-American Commission on Human Rights of the Organization of American States.[42]

When Sandinista forces took over Managua's Inter-continental Hotel on July 19, 1979, they captured three Argentinean military officers, who at the time were working with Somoza's security apparatus. They were later released as part of a secret deal with Videla's government in exchange for Argentinean grain.[43]

El Salvador

Terror Training from Argentina

Counterinsurgency cooperation between Nicaragua, El Salvador, and Guatemala stepped up in the final year of the Somoza regime. Following the Sandinista triumph, exiled Nicaraguan guardsmen and Guatemalan security personnel participated in counterinsurgency operations in El Salvador, assisted by Argentine operatives from the army intelligence service and Army Intelligence Battalion 601.[44]

The chronology of events and the cooperation between paramilitary forces in late 1979 indicate that the nucleus of the Nicaraguan Contra armed movement was formed in that year as a result of the collaboration among irregular forces from Nicaragua, El Salvador, Guatemala, and Argentina. As noted earlier, one source suggested that the transnational counterrevolutionary project was sanctioned by the CIA under the Carter administration.[45]

In the summer of 1979, the Argentine army sent advisers to El Salvador at the request of the regime of Gen. Carlos Humberto

Romero (1976–1979), who asked Argentina for intelligence experts specialized in interrogation techniques and analysis of information.[46] Reportedly, the Argentines were involved in advising death squads: White Warrior's Union (Unión Guerrera Blanca, UGB) and Anti-Communist Armed Forces of Liberation–War of Elimination (Fuerzas Armadas de Liberación Anticomunista–Guerra de Eliminación, FALANGE).[47] Following Romero's replacement by a joint civilian-military junta in October 1979, and as the junta was taken over by hard-liners and the civil war escalated, Argentina expanded its military presence in the country. Although most of the major involvement of Argentine military in El Salvador came about during the Reagan administration, Argentine military advisers were already in that country in the late 1970s.[48]

Post-1979 state violence differed from that under Romero, both in terms of scale and repressive coordination. Political assassinations and disappearances multiplied throughout 1980. By early 1981, Amnesty International reported that more than six thousand civilians died as a result of government-sponsored repression. Evidence compiled by Amnesty indicated that "the majority of victims of torture and death at the hands of the security forces have not generally been proven to have any direct involvement in armed insurrection."[49] As in most of the other Latin American military establishments, regular army units were integrated with police and paramilitary forces for counterinsurgency operations. By deploying the army in the state terror effort, the military leadership forced young officers to become directly involved in atrocities against civilians, thus strengthening intramilitary solidarity.[50]

In collaboration with the National Security Agency of El Salvador (Agencia Nacional de Servicios Especiales de El Salvador, ANSESAL), the Argentines trained officers in the use of psychological procedures for interrogation. The Argentine mission promoted a system of interrogations as a counterinsurgency tool.[51] They wanted to reproduce the countersubversive method employed in Argentina's dirty war—the destruction by paramilitary operations of opposition organizations, working from the periphery (noncombatants) inward to the organizational core (leadership). The procedure followed a pattern: the summary execution of prisoners after interrogation, even when their political affiliation was negligible or incidental.[52]

From October 1979 to May 1981, the United States, in cooperation with Argentina, Chile, and Uruguay, secretly trained some three hundred Salvadoran officers in the Panama Canal Zone. According to one document:[53] "The most solid bloc of support for the current government and its counterinsurgency efforts comes from the southern cone military regimes. Among these Argentina, Chile and Uruguay provide training, advisers on intelligence, urban and rural counterinsurgency, and logistics. Argentina has become the second largest trainer of Salvadoran officers after the U.S." As in the case of Guatemala, Argentine expertise was instrumental in the state-sponsored effort to destroy the insurgents and to quiet and atomize the population. "The Argentines are the only ones in the world who fought an urban guerrilla war and won it," said a member of a Salvadoran death squad. "So, they're just naturally recognized as the best."[54]

In early 1980, the guerrillas' base of power was in the cities, especially in the capital, San Salvador. Thus the Salvadoran armed forces focused their counterinsurgency effort on the annihilation of political and military urban bases. Their success against the guerrillas and their allied political organizations was accomplished via a ruthless program of state terror. During José Napoleón Duarte's year as president of the civilian-military junta (1981), some fourteen thousand noncombatants were killed by the Salvadoran armed forces.[55] "We don't like to admit it," said a U.S. adviser appointed to El Salvador, "but the horrible lesson of the early eighties is that terrorism works [as a counterinsurgency device]."[56]

In January 1981, the Salvadoran guerrilla umbrella organization Farabundo Martí National Liberation Front (Frente Farabundo

Martí de Liberación Nacional, FMLN) launched a "final offensive" against the Salvadoran government. Despite the FMLN's thousands of combatants, the insurrection was put down by the armed forces. The background of collective military rule in El Salvador, fundamentally different from the Nicaraguan personalist state of the Somozas, in strong alliance with a unified elite class provided a formidable barrier to the guerrilla offensive. While autocratic rule in Nicaragua had been essentially dynastic, political power in El Salvador had been dominated by the coffee elite and the military officer corps. The unity within and between both groups proved to be crucial for the stability of the regime.[57] In addition, the guerrilla offensive suffered from lack of widespread popular support. This was a result of, among other factors, fear of retribution by the armed forces and lack of trust on the FMLN's ability to guarantee the protection of the population.

It must be noted that the guerrillas' setback in urban areas after the January 1981 offensive occurred before the United States reestablished meaningful military assistance to the Salvadoran government.[58] (In 1977, El Salvador, along with Argentina, Brazil, and Guatemala, had rejected proposed U.S. military aid in protest over the Carter administration's denunciation of their human rights records.) That situation highlights the relevance of Argentina's military support to the Salvadoran counterinsurgency program in the period 1979–1981.

Pipelines for Argentinean Know-how

One of the key liaisons to the Argentine military mission in El Salvador was Maj. Roberto D'Aubuisson, who had been secretly reassigned by the Salvadoran high command to ANSESAL following the reformist coup of 1979. "They were here a very short time," D'Aubuisson has been quoted as saying, referring to the Argentines. "But that time was very helpful [because] they tried to transmit their experiences, inform people and suggest to them, act this way and that, use this system, coordinate information and analyze it this way."[59]

D'Aubuisson played a central role in the Latin American anti-Communist network. Trained at the Washington, D.C. International Police Academy, the U.S. School of the Americas, and police academies in Uruguay and Taiwan, D'Aubuisson became a major political figure in El Salvador as leader of the ultraright Nationalist Republican Alliance (Alianza Republicana Nacionalista, ARENA). An admirer of Taiwan's counterinsurgency techniques, D'Aubuisson was implicated in the 1980 murder in San Salvador of Archbishop Oscar A. Romero. He was also linked to the principal conspirators of the assassination of two U.S. labor advisers and the Salvadoran land-reform director in 1981.[60] D'Aubuisson was among the delegates to the September 1980 conference of the Latin American Anti-Communist Confederation (Confederación Anticomunista Latinoamericana, CAL) in Buenos Aires, Argentina (see chapter 5).[61]

Raúl Midense, a Guatemalan paramilitary expert (nephew of Guatemala's "godfather of the death squads" Mario Sandoval Alarcón), was another intermediary between the Argentines and the Salvadorans. He operated with Argentine naval intelligence informant Carlos Dürich, adviser to Somoza's secret police and leader of the Argentine hit team in Nicaragua, and Alfredo Zarattini, a 601 Battalion agent who coordinated the dispatching of Argentine advisers to El Salvador in 1979.[62]

Military Assistance—and a Denial

From 1979 on, Argentina supplied military equipment to the Salvadoran armed forces. This activity was based on the rationale that these transactions would "strengthen our relations with that country and would also contribute to toughening its position in the struggle being waged against subversion in conjunction with other countries in the area."[63] An example of these transactions can be found in a document dated February 1982; therein, Argentina's Central Bank, following orders from the army commander in chief, authorized the General Directorate of Military Industries to export light and heavy arms, ammunition, and replacement parts for military equipment to El Salvador in the amount of $20 million.[64] Another document stated that the transaction was primarily based on "strategic and political reasons." Similar arms transfers had been made to Guatemala, Honduras, Uruguay, Bolivia, and Peru.[65]

Funds from Roberto Suárez Levy, Bolivia's prime cocaine trafficker and partner of Gen. Luis García Meza, the Bolivian military dictator who seized power in 1980, helped to finance Argentine military operations in El Salvador. Argentina had provided key military support to the Bolivian military coup d'état of July 1980. The full-fledged Argentine participation in the brutal coup that brought García Meza to power had been funded by drug money. The Argentine army high command then used those funds in the Salvadoran theater of operations (see chapter 1).[66]

"The Argentines," noted one political analyst, "were particularly useful to the Reagan administration . . . because, during most of 1981, the latter was engaged in a pitched battle with Congress over military aid to El Salvador. . . . Argentina (along with Israel, Taiwan, South Africa, and possibly South Korea) became fallback sources of military aid in the event of a congressionally mandated cut-off."[67] In a March 1981 official visit to Washington, D.C., Argentine President-designate Viola confirmed his country's pledge to support El Salvador's counterinsurgency effort. The Salvadoran army chief of staff, Col. Jaime Abdul Gutiérrez, visited Buenos Aires in the spring of that year to finalize the details of Argentina's military assistance to his country. An immediate result of Gutiérrez's visit was an increase of Argentine counterinsurgency personnel in El Salvador to one hundred military and civilian advisers.[68]

In the fall of 1981, Vernon Walters, the retired lieutenant general and Reagan's ambassador-at-large, requested the Argentine military high command to increase its assistance to the Salvadoran armed forces (see chapter 2).[69] At that time Walters stated that "Argentina should be ready to send troops as part of an inter-American force, to be organized if the government of José Napoleón Duarte requested such military aid."[70] The Argentine generals ratified an agreement by which they would receive U.S. intelligence and logistic support for a paramilitary covert operation to cut off alleged Cuban-Nicaraguan arms support to the guerrillas in El Salvador and Guatemala.[71]

When another Salvadoran army colonel, Rafael Flores Lima, paid an official visit to Buenos Aires in February 1982, the Argentine Foreign Ministry announced that Argentines would participate as observers in El Salvador's constituent assembly elections— meanwhile denying Argentine involvement in counterinsurgency operations in that country.[72] In an official statement, Army Gen. Antonio Vaquero said: "The strengthening and consolidation of the relations now linking our armies have great importance. The Argentine Army—which along with the Navy and the Air Force, supported by the Argentine nation, defeated terrorism—understands and values the struggle of the Salvadoran Armed Forces and people and will provide its assistance, as much as feasible, to a friendly nation in a difficult situation." In El Salvador, Vaquero said, "two concepts of ways of life are at stake . . . on one hand, respect for the dignity of mankind—God's creations—and on the other, terrorism, men at the service of an atheistic, omnipotent state."[73]

Vaquero's remarks had been foreshadowed months earlier when, in referring to the antiguerrilla war in El Salvador, Gen. Alfredo Saint Jean had stressed that "the Argentine armed forces have acquired internationally-renowned experience in unconventional warfare and they are willing to offer training and all kind of cooperation to allied countries."[74] As the state's use of violence in El Salvador increased, the aid, as we have seen, was forthcoming. El Salvador had become suitable ground for the transfer of Argentine counterinsurgency technology.

Guatemala

Indiscriminate Massacre

El Salvador was not the only country ripe for Argentinean involvement. From the emergence of U.S.-promoted counterinsurgency in the 1960s to the scorched-earth war in the early 1980s, Guatemala had emerged as an "ideal testing ground" for counterrevolution. The great waves of state terror of 1954, 1967–1971, and 1978–1983 were the response of the Guatemalan ruling class to growing popular participation and armed struggle. Disappearances and torture had been a standard "counterterror" methodology since the Zacapa military campaign of 1966. Aimed at paralyzing the population's capacity for mobilization, both selective and mass state terror resulted in thousands of civilian victims. The campaigns particularly targeted peasants, workers, and members of the dependent middle class. Most political killings were perpetrated by the Guatemalan army and government-linked death squads.[75]

The Argentine presence in Guatemala coincided with the third wave of terror, which hit the nation under the regime of Gen. Romeo Lucas García (1978–1982).[76] Labor and student unions, peasant leagues, and other grassroots organizations were targeted for annihilation by the Lucas García regime. In response to the guerrillas' military offensive, the army launched an unprecedented counterinsurgency campaign aimed at destroying the powerful indigenous revolutionary movement.[77] Under Lucas García, state violence grew dramatically as selective repression turned into indiscriminate massacres.[78]

Military Assistance

From 1963 to 1977 the United States played a major role in the creation and support of the Guatemalan counterinsurgency state. Formal U.S. security assistance to Guatemala was significantly cut back under the Carter administration and the regime of Gen.

Kjell Laugerud (1974–1978) unilaterally rejected U.S. military aid linked to human rights provisions as external meddling in Guatemala's domestic affairs. Guatemala stepped up military purchases from Argentina, Israel (which had been Guatemala's main supplier of counterinsurgency technology since 1975, when the United States sided with Britain in the dispute over Belize), South Africa, Italy, Belgium, and Yugoslavia.[79]

Argentina became one of the principal trainers of Guatemalan elite army units. In October 1981, Guatemalan and Argentine military authorities signed a secret agreement increasing Argentine participation in the counterinsurgency effort. As part of this assistance program, some two hundred Guatemalan army and police officers were sent to Buenos Aires to receive advanced intelligence training, including the use of "interrogation techniques."[80]

Circumstantial confirmation of Argentina's military aid (in cooperation with Israel) dates back to June 1977 when an Argentine plane in mechanical difficulty on route to Guatemala landed in Barbados. Alerted by British intelligence, the Barbados authorities confiscated twenty-six tons of Israeli arms and ammunition. The plane belonged to River Plate Air Transport (Transporte Aéreo Rioplatense, TAR), a private firm owned by high-ranking Argentine air force officers. This type of operation, one that combined anti-Communism with personal profit, was characteristic of the Argentine armed forces during the military regime.[81]

In 1982 and 1983, Argentina sold more military equipment to Guatemala under secret agreements with the Lucas García and Efraín Ríos Montt (1982–1983) governments. Sales included MAG 60-20 submachine guns, M60 machine guns, 105-mm mortars, 105-mm HEAT (high-explosive anti-tank) ammunition, incendiary projectiles, and high-impact bombs. The initial $30 million agreement assured Guatemala that Argentina would continue producing replacement parts for that equipment up to 1993 and it contemplated future arms transfers to Guatemala on preferential conditions.[82]

Involvement in the Urban and Rural Offensives

In early 1980, in response to a request by the Lucas García regime for advice in counterinsurgency warfare, an Argentine military mission composed of army and navy officers arrived in Guatemala. In collaboration with military advisers from Israel and Chile, the Argentines instructed Guatemalan elite forces in advanced intelligence techniques. Argentine military personnel worked with government-sanctioned death squads, specifically the Secret Anti-Communist Army (Ejército Secreto Anticomunista, ESA).[83] Numerous assassinations carried out by army and police forces in the early 1980s were attributed to the ESA, a paramilitary unit closely associated with Lucas García himself. Death-squad activity was reportedly coordinated by Guatemala's Regional Telecommunications Center, a presidential security agency established with U.S. assistance in the early 1960s. Under Lucas García, the regional center received substantial technical advice from Argentina and Israel.[84]

In July 1981, the Guatemalan military launched a vast counteroffensive against the guerrillas. The military action met with considerable success in Guatemala City, where it dismantled the guerrillas' rearguard. Using expertise gained from the Argentines and Israelis, the military targeted and destroyed a network of safe houses run by the Organization of People in Arms (Organización del Pueblo en Armas, ORPA). Argentine advice to the G-2 intelligence branch of the Guatemalan army was decisive in the military success against the urban guerrilla infrastructure. Reportedly, the Argentines introduced the use of "computerized review of telephone calls, and electricity and other bills for suspect houses."[85] That technique helped identify guerrilla safe houses based on, for example, exceptionally high consumption of electricity.[86]

The Argentines also participated in the rural offensive initiated in August 1981 under the command of the army chief of staff, Gen. Benedicto Lucas García. The operation introduced an extermination campaign against the indigenous population unparalleled in Guatemalan history. The scorched-earth war of 1981–1983 resulted in the destruction of more than 440 highland villages, the killing of more than 100,000 civilians, and the forced relocation of nearly one million people.[87] It is worth noting that, since late 1981, the expression *guerra sucia* (dirty war), by that time widely identified with Argentina's campaign of state terror, became a standard term in press briefings by Guatemalan military staff. Guatemalan army officers used this term when they explained to the press that the killing of civilians in counterinsurgency operations was an unavoidable feature of the unconventional military campaign to annihilate the guerrillas.[88]

A Base for the Contra Legion

Following the triumph of the Sandinistas in July 1979, a group of Nicaraguan guardsmen exiled in Guatemala organized the Nicaraguan Revolutionary Front (Frente Revolucionario Nicaragüense, FRENICA). The group was led by Col. Ricardo Lau, a notorious torturer in Somoza's Office of National Security, who had received military intelligence training in Argentina in the early 1960s.[89]

In mid-1980, FRENICA joined with other exiled guardsmen and formed the September 15 Legion (Legión 15 de Septiembre). From the initial confusion following Somoza's collapse to the first steps in the organization of an anti-Sandinista force, the leaders of Guatemala's neofascist National Liberation Movement (Movimiento de Liberación Nacional, MLN), Mario Sandoval Alarcón and Lionel Sisniega Otero, provided crucial support to the Nicaraguan guardsmen.

The new Contra organization, led by Col. Enrique Bermúdez (who had served as Somoza's last military attaché in Washington, D.C.), carried out criminal activities in Guatemala such as robberies, kidnappings, and assassinations with the consent of the Guatemalan authorities.[90] In addition to the funds collected via

those activities, the legion received money from Luis Pallais Debayle, Somoza's cousin, with the goal of creating an armed movement against the Sandinistas.[91] According to a former guardsman,
Argentina gave a large sum of money to Bermúdez in the early
phase of the Contra effort. My informant recalled several conversations in which the Argentine advisers complained about
Bermúdez's misuse of those funds.[92]

The term *Contra* began to be used in Nicaragua immediately
after the collapse of the Somoza regime. It was employed in reference to the *contrarrevolucionarios*—those individuals who opposed
the revolution. With the emergence of armed groups of counterrevolutionaries, the term Contra began to designate those armed
organizations that fought against the Sandinista regime.

By the end of 1980, Argentine operatives started to organize
and train the dispersed and ill-equipped bands of Nicaraguan
guardsmen exiled in Guatemala.[93] In addition, a squad from Intelligence Battalion 601 based in Guatemala (and operating also in
El Salvador and Honduras) collaborated with the military regime
in the repression of leftist organizations. Led by a retired lieutenant colonel, Santiago Hoya, the Argentine task force had direct
responsibility for the killing and disappearance of Guatemalan
peasants and political dissidents. The central mission of the squad
was the abduction of Argentines alleged to be subversives exiled in
Central America. Its membership, which consisted of veterans of
Argentina's dirty war, included Juan Martín Ciga Correa, former
adviser to the Nicaraguan EEBI, and Zarattini, liaison with the Salvadoran security forces and member of the Argentine commando
team that operated in Nicaragua during Somoza's last months.[94]

Reportedly, the Argentine group worked with former guardsmen Ricardo Lau and Hugo Villagra, Néstor Sánchez (CIA chief
of operations for Latin America), and Israel's Mossad agents in
Guatemala.[95] One of Hoya's lieutenants was Héctor Francés, who
in late 1982 disclosed key details of the Argentine covert operations,
after being kidnapped by the Sandinistas.[96] Posing as employees of

Argentine firms Bridas and El Ganadero, the Battalion 601 operatives remained in Guatemala until the end of 1981.[97] After moving to Honduras, they were replaced by another group of Argentine advisers; later, intelligence personnel who operated in Central America were responsible for extortion, kidnapping, and other criminal activities in Argentina under the democratic regime inaugurated in 1983.[98]

The Argentines helped the September 15 Legion set up a training base in a farm outside Guatemala City. Known as Detachment 101, the base was one of the first Contra posts in the region. Under Argentine supervision, and with the participation of Guatemalan army officers, the Nicaraguan guardsmen received technical and ideological counterinsurgency instruction.[99] The legion's baptism of fire was the aforementioned December 1980 attack on the shortwave radio station Radio Noticias del Continente in Costa Rica (see chapter 1). The operation, which received CIA support, failed miserably.[100]

In spring 1981, Argentine officers oversaw the move of the legion's headquarters from Guatemala to Honduras.[101] Col. Gustavo Alvarez Martínez, head of the Honduran Public Security Force (Fuerza de Seguridad Pública, FUSEP), had offered CIA Director William Casey an anti-Sandinista base of operations in his country. With U.S. assistance, Honduras would become a "secure sanctuary" for the Contra combatants. Honduras was to serve as platform for the counterrevolutionary war against the Sandinista regime in Nicaragua.[102]

Honduras

An Apt Pupil of the Argentine Method

The presence of Argentine advisers in Honduras between 1980 and 1984 coincided with the development of the doctrine of national security under the aegis of Argentine-trained General Alvarez Martínez (Colegio Militar, graduating class of 1961).[103] The so-called Argentine method—clandestine detention centers, disappearances, and summary executions by government-sanctioned secret task forces—began to be systematically implemented following the appointment of Alvarez Martínez (then a colonel) as commander of the Public Security Force in August 1980.[104] "The paramilitary squads were already operating out of FUSEP [the security force] before Alvarez took it over," noted a Honduran political analyst, "but what he did was to professionalize the setup by bringing in the Argentine advisors."[105] Even though state terror in Honduras remained at a very low level compared to that of El Salvador and Guatemala, post-1980 repressive practices marked a substantial departure from Honduras's previous record.

During his tenure as head of FUSEP, Alvarez Martínez used ample state resources to professionalize the military for its role as guardian of national security.[106] A primary aspect of that professionalization involved the development of technical expertise—an area in which the Argentine armed forces offered key assistance. Alvarez Martínez publicly advocated the effectiveness of the Argentine method for a countersubversive campaign. In his view, the Argentine armed forces, guided by "their own national security doctrine," had waged a legitimate war against the Marxist enemy in the late 1970s. Reproducing the discourse of his Argentine counterparts, Alvarez Martínez frequently asserted that "the so-called 'disappeared ones' are probably off in Cuba or Nicaragua training in terrorism to subvert the Fatherland."[107]

Alvarez Martínez's designation as commander in chief of the Honduran armed forces in January 1982, his promotion to the rank of brigadier general, and the forced relocation of rival officers to posts abroad, strengthened his control over the security apparatus.[108] The emergence of a national security regime in Honduras in the early 1980s, distinguished by the active cooperation of the armed forces in the defense of U.S. strategic interests in the region and the undisputed leadership of Alvarez Martínez, resulted in a program of selective repression aimed at beheading popular organizations.

In the first years of the constitutional government of Roberto Suazo Córdova (1982–1986), the rapid escalation of security-force violence (under the direct supervision of the Argentines) coincided with the consolidation of U.S. military control over Honduras ("our Central American whore," in the words of a U.S. State Department official).[109] Under the Reagan administration, the U.S. counterinsurgency strategy sought the eradication of popular dissent in Honduras, the relocation of Salvadoran refugees away from border areas, the cooperation between the Honduran and Salvadoran armed forces in the struggle against the FMLN, and the establishment of Honduras as a military base in support of the CIA covert war against Nicaragua.[110]

Military Death Squads

Battalion 3-16, a clandestine paramilitary unit responsible for the disappearance and extrajudicial execution of hundreds of Honduran civilians in the 1980s, was originally trained and equipped by the FBI and CIA, Argentina, and Chile.[111] The brainchild of Alvarez Martínez, Battalion 3-16 (a small-scale version of Argentine Army Intelligence Battalion 601) operated in collaboration with FUSEP and the National Investigations Directorate (Dirección Nacional de Investigaciones, DNI) in the elimination of "those individuals that caused problems for the Armed Forces of Honduras and who were incorrigible communists."[112]

Under the Carter administration (August 1980), twenty-five Honduran army officers were secretly flown to U.S. training facilities in Houston, Texas, to receive a six-month course in interrogation techniques, and Argentine and Chilean instructors trained Honduran death squads and special forces (the Cobras and a unit known as TESON) at the Police Training Center (Centro de Instrucción Policial, CIP) outside Tegucigalpa.[113]

In 1981, Alvarez organized, with Argentine assistance, the Command of Special Operations (Comando de Operaciones Especiales, COE), an elite counterinsurgency unit, within FUSEP, that coordinated repressive activities. The Argentines trained Honduran army personnel (including numerous members of Battalion 3-16) in combat maneuvers, explosives, and interrogation techniques at the Contra base in Lepaterique.[114]

Argentine military advisers in Honduras participated in operations of capture, interrogation, and execution of Honduran labor and student leaders, suspected Sandinista sympathizers, and Salvadoran refugees. As veterans of Argentina's dirty war, they were experts in death-squad activities.

One of the Argentine advisers working with paramilitary groups in Honduras was Battalion 601 agent Ciga Correa.[115] A former Triple A member, Ciga Correa had collaborated with the Chilean National Information Directorate (DINA) in the September 1974 assassination in Buenos Aires of Gen. Carlos Prats, Chile's commander in chief under President Salvador Allende (see chapter 1, "Operation Condor"). Ciga Correa served as instructor to Somoza's EEBI and then as paymaster for Battalion 601 in Central America. He was a member of the Argentine task force that operated out of Guatemala City with the objective of capturing suspected Argentine guerrillas in the so-called Iron Triangle (Guatemala, El Salvador, and Honduras). Ciga Correa was later identified as one of the Argentine army officers that trained a Honduran paramilitary unit known as the Group of Fourteen, a predecessor (along with the Group of Ten) of Battalion 3-16.

The repressive pattern that emerged in Honduras in the early 1980s paralleled that employed in Argentina during the 1970s. According to a 1982 report by Americas Watch, "perhaps the decisive factor in disappearances [in Honduras] is also borrowed from the Argentine experience: the total ineffectiveness of *habeas corpus* writs to locate detainees, secure their release or verify the legality of their arrests."[116] The techniques of unconventional warfare applied in both countries were strikingly analogous: compartmentalized task forces (intelligence, interrogation, kidnapping, and executions) directly subordinated to military structures; heavily armed plainclothesmen using unmarked cars; operations in broad daylight without interference by regular security forces; secret detention centers and clandestine cemeteries; and, finally, the method of disposing of political prisoners by dumping them from military helicopters and airplanes (in Honduras, into the Sumpul River; in the Argentine case, into the Atlantic Ocean) (see chapter 1).[117]

In Honduras, the Argentines worked in direct collaboration with Capt. Alexander Hernández, head of Battalion 3-16.[118] A graduate of the U.S. Office of Public Safety's police training program, Hernández was directly responsible for running the day-to-day operations of the battalion. He also acted as liaison between Alvarez Martínez and the exiled Nicaraguan guardsmen in Honduras. In late 1982, Hernández was removed from his post, as a result of public denunciations by Honduran Col. Leónides Torres Arias (himself a key player in the incorporation of Argentina into the Contra program) and sent as a military attaché to Buenos Aires. Hernández remained in Argentina, presumably working in the Contra operation, until the constitutional government of Raúl Alfonsín declared him persona non grata in late 1984. (At that time, coincidentally, the last Argentine advisers left Honduras and the CIA took total control of the Contra program.)

Official Links

The participation of Argentine advisers in the development of an internal security apparatus in Honduras and their mission, from late 1980 onward, to organize the remnants of the defeated Nicaraguan national guard into an effective fighting force against the Sandinistas was an operation approved by the Argentinean, Honduran, and U.S. governments.[119] Argentina's military attachés in Honduras, El Salvador, and Guatemala ran the day-to-day operations out of the Argentine embassies in those countries.[120] The Honduran armed forces were in direct command of the clandestine repressive network and, with support from the CIA, actively promoted the organization of armed anti-Sandinista groups throughout 1980.[121]

In April 1980, Argentina's military authorities agreed to supply counterinsurgency assistance to Honduras. Throughout that year, U.S. agencies (the CIA and FBI) provided specialized intelligence training to Honduran paramilitary forces in the southwestern United States and collaborated with the Argentine intelligence unit that operated out of Miami and Fort Lauderdale, Florida. (See chapter 5 on the role of the Argentine task force based in the United States.)[122]

Early in 1981, the Honduran foreign minister, Col. César Elvir Sierra, offered to cooperate with the United States to handle the issue of arms smuggling from the Nicaraguan revolutionary regime to the Salvadoran guerrillas.[123] Later that year, after a meeting between Colonel Sierra and his Argentine counterpart, Oscar Camilión, the military command in Buenos Aires authorized a $10 million loan to Honduras for the purchase of military equipment. Both countries had issued a public condemnation of "terrorism and subversion," claiming that their goal was to maintain stability in Central America.[124] At that time, representatives from Argentina, the United States, Honduras, and the Nicaraguan opposition established a formal accord on the anti-Sandinista armed movement. A document from Argentina's General Directorate of Military Industries stressed that the sale of "secret military equipment" to Honduras responded primarily to "political and strategic reasons."[125] Arms exports to Honduras included 81-mm and 120-mm mortars, antipersonnel and antitank mines, hand grenades, and ammunition. By the end of 1981, more than 150 Argentine officers and troops were stationed in Honduras.[126] Secret military sales to Honduras continued throughout 1986; that March, the Brazilian police seized a ship in the Rio de Janeiro harbor carrying six tons of arms, ammunition, and war-oriented medical supplies being sent from Argentina to Honduras for the Contra forces.[127]

General Alvarez Martínez's dominant role in the Honduran military establishment eased the participation of the Argentine army in the counterrevolutionary operation by formalizing ties with the United States and supporting anti-Sandinista armed activities in Honduras. Indeed, the initial plan promoted by the Honduran leader was to utilize a U.S.-backed anti-Sandinista force to cause a military confrontation between Honduras or Costa Rica and Nicaragua, thus legitimating U.S. direct intervention in the region.[128]

Argentine advisers became directly involved in the organization and training of former guardsmen in base camps along the Nicaraguan border. Argentine officers also operated in the Gracias a Dios Province, in eastern Honduras, where thousands of Miskitos who had fled Nicaragua were living in refugee camps. Anti-Sandinista Miskito combatants led by Steadman Fagoth received military instruction from Argentine advisers in training camps set up under the supervision of Honduran military authorities (see chapter 4, "Miskito Counterrevolutionaries").[129]

The Contras and Domestic Repression in Honduras

Some fifteen hundred enlisted men of the defeated Nicaraguan national guard fled to Honduras following the Sandinista triumph of July 1979. For many months, the ex-Somocista guardsmen engaged in petty jobs and criminal activities for a living, while high-ranking national guard officers in Miami and Washington tried to obtain support for the counterrevolution. Some of the guardsmen formed small bands and began attacking Sandinista patrols in the Honduran-Nicaraguan border regions.[130] Initially, the Honduran security forces were hostile to the Nicaraguan exiles and sought to control their criminal activities, but with the appointment of Alvarez Martínez as head of FUSEP, the situation changed rapidly. Honduran-based Nicaraguan exiles became protégés of the regime of Gen. Policarpo Paz García (1978–1982). Armed incursions into

Nicaragua by ex-guardsmen increased as FUSEP began providing arms (M-3 and FAL automatic rifles) and military infrastructure.[131]

Following Somoza's fall, exiled guardsmen developed a network of contract killers in Honduras, El Salvador, and Guatemala. One of its most notorious leaders was Ricardo Lau, the former OSN torturer trained in military intelligence by the United States and Argentina. As head of the FDN intelligence section in Honduras, Lau commanded the campaign to eliminate suspected Sandinista agents and Salvadorans targeted as arms traffickers for the FMLN. The relationship between the Honduran clandestine repressive structure and the Contra assassination network was given formal status in late 1981 when the Argentine military advisers suggested that Lau's Contras be used to execute prisoners held by Battalion 3-16 in clandestine detention centers. Reportedly funded by the CIA, Lau's gunmen were responsible for many of the political killings in Honduras from 1981 to 1984.[132]

Throughout the early 1980s, the Honduran state terror program and the Contra operation were interwoven ventures. The Argentines provided the technical and organizational resources to keep the counterrevolutionary effort running. The bulk of the operations, on the Argentine side, was assumed by Army Intelligence Battalion 601, which served as the axis of a complex clandestine network comprised of the Honduran army intelligence section (G-2), the FUSEP, the DNI, Battalion 3-16, the CIA, and the FDN general staff, with support from the Guatemalan and Salvadoran army intelligence services.[133]

Conclusion: The Web of Technology Transfer

Argentina's military cooperation with the Somoza regime and its subsequent support for the counterinsurgency states of El Salvador, Guatemala, and Honduras is a critical factor in the analysis of the Argentine-U.S.-Contra enterprise. This chapter has shown that Argentina operated as an independent actor in its early involvement in the Central American imbroglio. The decision to fill in for the United States in the hemispheric struggle against Communism indicates the determination of the Argentine military to project its influence throughout Latin America under a foreign policy agenda strongly determined by cold war geopolitical perceptions.[134] Substantial profits from sales of military equipment to the Central American countries, sometimes conducted by private firms owned by high-ranking military officers, explain additional motivation for the Argentine armed forces' interest in "the defense of the Western system." Argentina's de facto regime undertook its ambitious military expansionist design when subversion was no longer perceived to be a serious threat in the domestic realm (the guerrilla organizations had been annihilated and the program of state-sponsored terror had achieved the goal of disarticulating most of the popular organizations). The deployment of counterinsurgency techniques in Central America was conducted through the same intelligence network that played a main role in the dirty war in Argentina, primarily the infamous Army Intelligence Battalion 601.

While mass rebellion gained momentum in Central America, some of the hemisphere's most violent ultraright elements (from Argentina, Chile, Nicaragua, El Salvador, Guatemala, and Honduras) cooperated in a ruthless antidissident program sanctioned by U.S. government agencies, specifically the CIA, under the administrations of Carter and, especially, Reagan. One of its most dreadful features was the "professionalization" of security-force death squads and the dissemination of the notorious Argentine method throughout the region.

Personal connections played an important role in the counterrevolutionary venture, mainly because of intense personal loyalties resulting from shared military educational experiences. For instance, Central American officers from Nicaragua, Honduras, Guatemala, and El Salvador, many of them key players in their local counterinsurgency wars, had been trained in Argentina's military academies in the early 1960s. The U.S. School of the Americas in the Panama Canal Zone, where the Argentines excelled as counterinsurgency instructors, was a hub for the development of transnational military links during the 1960s, 1970s, and early 1980s. Main actors in the establishment of national security states throughout Latin America received some training at the School of the Americas; namely, Gen. Leopoldo Galtieri (Argentina), Gen. Augusto Pinochet (Chile), Gen. Hugo Banzer Suárez (Bolivia), Gen. Policarpo Paz García (Honduras), Gen. Manuel Antonio Callejas y Callejas (Guatemala), Gen. Manuel Antonio Noriega (Panama), and Maj. Roberto D'Aubuisson (El Salvador). In addition, four of the five officers accused of organizing the infamous Battalion 3-16 in Honduras received counterinsurgency training at the School of the Americas, as did nineteen of the twenty-seven Salvadoran army officers implicated in the brutal murder of six Jesuit priests in November 1989.[135]

Understanding the Argentine military role in Central America requires an emphasis on the issue of technology transfer. This chapter has identified several of the countersubversive methods exported to the region and the general conditions under which they were implemented. As this account of the Salvadoran, Guatemalan, and Honduran cases shows, Argentine counterinsurgency technology was particularly effective in the military success against the guerrilla organizations in urban areas. The Argentine expertise in urban combat would prove inadequate for the Contra guerrilla war in the Nicaraguan countryside. Even though the Argentine army had used the rural setting of Tucumán as a testing ground for some of the more "successful" techniques of unconventional warfare, the counterinsurgency expertise developed during the Argentine dirty war did not fit the needs of a rural guerrilla movement such as the Contras. However, the Argentine advisers succeeded in their early role as military trainers and leaders of the disbanded

Nicaraguan guardsmen, mostly because of their anti-Communist zeal and ruthlessness. As an Argentine army officer explained, "At the commando courses one began to think that torture was, if not a legitimate method, a common procedure in counterinsurgency war. After some time, the Argentines became experts in counterinsurgency matters. This fact drove them to become trainers of the Contras, because they had proven their success in Argentina."[136]

With the decisive support of the CIA from late 1981 onwards, the nascent anti-Sandinista armed movement organized and trained by the Argentine army eventually evolved into a large-scale military operation that would take an immense human and economic toll on Nicaragua. The infamous Argentine professionals in counterinsurgency warfare would play a major part in the transnational effort to roll back what was perceived to be a Marxist threat in Central America. This enterprise was undertaken in no small measure because of the tendency on the part of the Reagan administration to ascribe societal unrest largely to the machinations of international Communism, ignoring local factors such as endemic poverty, extreme inequality, and state-sponsored repression.

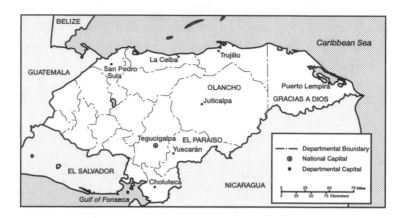

Honduras

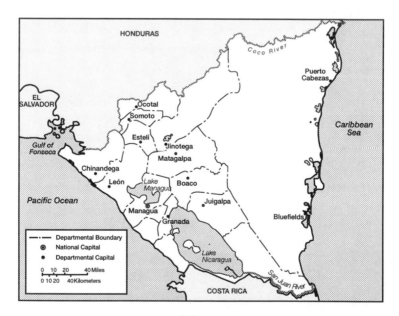

Nicaragua

Chapter 4

Argentina and the Nicaraguan Contras

THIS CHAPTER EXPLORES the relationship between Argentina and the Nicaraguan counterrevolutionary forces, the so-called Contras, in the period 1979–1984. As noted earlier, the Argentines initiated their involvement in the Central American imbroglio during the Nicaraguan civil war (1977–1978), giving military support to Anastasio Somoza Debayle up to the collapse of his regime. Following the Sandinista triumph in 1979, the Argentines provided counterinsurgency assistance to other Central American military governments. This early presence in the region was crucial to Argentina's key participation in the organization of the Nicaraguan Contras. The involvement in Central America's military and paramilitary network facilitated the anti-Sandinista operation and the establishment of Contra camps along the Honduran border with Nicaragua.

Under President Carter (particularly during the first half of his administration), the United States had largely given up its role as military enforcer in the hemisphere. Carter's commitment to a U.S. foreign policy based on human rights represented a major shift in U.S. traditional approach to the region—one often based on violence. This novel foreign policy was perceived by many actors concerned about revolution in Latin America as an abdication of the long-standing U.S. role as hemispheric leader. As already noted, the Argentines were to some extent filling the vacuum left by the United States in Central America in the late 1970s.

When Reagan came to power, the United States rapidly reverted to its strong-arm role in Latin America. With the Argentines already operating in Central America, the United States became decisively involved in counterrevolutionary reaction in the region. For a brief period, the United States would work closely with the ruthless Argentine military in what might be called the dirty war in Central America.[1]

The organization and training of the first Contras by Argentine advisers evolved in the early 1980s into a vast, covert operation supported by the CIA. The Reagan administration perceived the Sandinista regime to be a Communist-inspired threat to regional stability and attempted to overthrow it by means of supporting an armed movement largely formed by aggrieved peasants (see "The Nature of the Counterrevolution") and led by former national guard officers and political allies of Somoza.

The collaboration between Argentina and the United States with respect to the Contras was the result of a gradual process that involved the coincidence of the national security interests of the two nations. As already stated, in 1981, the United States became the main force behind Argentina's Central American military program. In all likelihood, by assuming the role of U.S. surrogate in the region Argentina expected to improve its relations with Washington. In addition, U.S. support of the Contra effort assured the Argentine military that the operation would acquire major dimensions. A former national guard lieutenant colonel told me, "The Argentines made an initial investment to see if the project was viable. They took that risk to see if there were any responses for a potential joint venture with the United States. It worked, because the Americans bought into the Argentine project in 1981."[2]

The Nature of the Counterrevolution

A revolution[3] entails the redistribution of political power away from old elite groups to new groups.[4] There is an inherent authoritarianism in revolution, because the reordering of society often occurs by violence, dispossessing the previous rulers of their privileges. Inevitably, a revolution involves a disintegration of central authority, which makes possible the dislodging of the old elite. Opposition to revolutionary regimes comes from, in addition to old elite groups, various parts of the original revolutionary coalition or neutral groups. These groupings attempt to prevent the revolution from embracing transformations that lie outside their desires or intentions.[5]

In the Nicaraguan case, politico-military action against the Sandinista revolutionary government began almost from its inception in July 1979. Sectors from the business class, the rich and middle peasantry, and indigenous communities soon felt disaffected from the FSLN-led project and embarked on a counterrevolutionary venture that converged with the efforts of old-regime groups that had lost their political, economic, and social power to the Sandinistas; namely, the members of the defeated national guard and the Somocista political bureaucracy and landowner elite.[6]

The counterrevolution in Nicaragua was the result of a convergence of foreign and domestic actors interested in halting revolutionary processes, rather than a pursuit of the restoration of the Somoza regime.[7] The initial counterrevolutionary movement evolved into a large-scale U.S.-backed insurgency centered in rural Nicaragua and launched from neighboring Honduras and Costa Rica.

The concurrence between foreign and domestic forces on an armed effort to shape Nicaragua's political arena was by no means a new phenomenon in that country's history. For instance, early in this century the United States openly supported the Nicaraguan conservative elite against the Zelayista liberals—supporters of President José Santos Zelaya (1894–1909)—in a conflict that led to direct U.S. military intervention in Nicaragua for more than two decades.[8] A significant number of the people making U.S. foreign policy in this century have seemed to share the view that "the American military interventions were often at the invitation, indeed at the pleading, of a host Central American government for the explicit goal of returning stability during a particularly dangerous moment in its history."[9] However, the case of the low-intensity warfare against Sandinista Nicaragua indicates that U.S. policy was dictated by the goal to reinstate in power supportive elites who would assure pro-U.S. stability in the hemisphere, no matter what their commitment to democratic practices and respect for human and civil rights. The U.S. concern with the maintenance of these elements in power was translated into a preference for military solutions to the Central American conflict in the 1980s, which contributed to the escalation of violence in the region.[10]

Opposition Inside Nicaragua

The resolute efforts of the United States to kill off the Sandinista regime and the refusal of the Soviet Union to provide Nicaragua with full-fledged support were unquestionably major reasons for the outcome of a decade of revolution—defeat of the Sandinistas at the polls in 1990. In addition to these external factors, the FSLN's economic and political decisions contributed to the erosion of the legitimacy of the revolutionary regime and to heighten the appeal of the Contras. In particular, these decisions strengthened the counterrevolutionary business sector and alienated peasants and ethnic minorities. The business class, despite its active role in the ouster of Somoza, had no interest in the success of the revolution beyond ending the old regime, although there were elements that accepted the Sandinista government.[11] Supposedly junior partners in the anti-Somoza coalition, the members of the business class were the sector best organized in autonomously pursuing their own interests. They were able to press their case to the government in matters of economic policy and maintain a level of autonomy that permitted the playing of a double game: internal opposition and external assault.

The Peasantry

Although the Sandinistas embarked on an ambitious agrarian reform shortly after coming to power, their relations with the peasantry, a key sector in a largely agrarian country, were disappointing to both peasants and the government. The peasantry's welfare was undermined by economic policies that resulted in a stark decline in terms of trade for the countryside (which in turn frustrated income redistribution policies in the rural sector) and by the unintended effects of centralizing in urban areas the distribution of credit and consumer goods.[12] The peasants were also antagonized by the state-promoted policy of agricultural collectivization that focused attention on large, state-managed rural units of production (considered vital for the reactivation of the economy), overlooking the demands of private peasant producers.[13] The attempt to impose an organizational model that did not correspond to historical patterns of rural organization of production resulted in the disaffection of a large sector of the peasantry. The pressure on peasants to enter into forms of collective farming in order to gain access to land, and the state's goal of destroying the traditional individualistic peasant economy of production and replacing it with cooperative production, were also major causes of peasant alienation.[14]

Other important reasons for the increasing appeal of the Contras among rural inhabitants were ideological and religious dissent and ethnic conflict.[15] U.S.-promoted anti-Communist propaganda and fear of a one-party Marxist state by Nicaragua's Roman Catholic Church hierarchy, which also opposed the identification between Sandinismo and Christianity, permeated the core of the Nicaraguan peasantry. Anti-Sandinista views were strong among some poor sectors of the population in both rural and urban areas.[16] Furthermore, the mistakes committed by Sandinista officials in their relations with the ethnic minorities of the Atlantic region (Miskitos, Sumus, and Ramas) accentuated a historical legacy of conflict between the coastal people and western Nicaraguans. Early Miskito-Sandinista tensions resulted in spiraling Contra activity on the Atlantic coast.[17]

The rich and middle peasantry, who were among the first to organize anti-Sandinista armed bands following the triumph of the revolution, played a major role in the recruitment of rank-and-file troops for the Contra forces. In terms of the Nicaraguan rural social structure, the rich and middle peasantry may be defined as a landed group (ten to fifty *manzanas*—one *manzana* = .7 of a hectare) whose main activity is the production of crops for the domestic market. In addition, the rich and middle peasantry produces subsistence crops and participates, to a limited degree, in agro-export production. This class grouping represented 21.6 percent of Nicaragua's agricultural economically active population in 1978.[18] As a strategic link between the agrarian bourgeoisie and the poor peasantry, rich and middle peasants articulated interests that cut across class alignments.[19] The rich and middle peasantry had been a long-standing influential figure in peasant communities: they controlled communal resources and functioned as a liaison with the market and the local and national political apparatus.[20] The revolutionary state's strong intervention in the agrarian sector via control over market and prices disaffected rich and middle peasants, who responded to a logic of simple commercial exchange and whose identity was closely linked to the goods they produced. The economic restrictions and socialist restructuring imposed by the Sandinista regime threatened that class grouping's traditional network of commercialization.[21] Land confiscations by the state heightened resentment among rich and middle peasants, driving many of them to the counterrevolution.[22]

The Sandinista government's efforts to centralize power and group the population into mass organizations clashed with a strong tradition in Nicaragua for high levels of local autonomy. Regional identities, to some extent threatened by the revolutionary policies, were intertwined with ingrained religious beliefs. In addition, the Sandinistas' attempt to build a coalition ample for national liberation conflicted with the country's deep class tensions. The ideological rigidity of important sectors of the revolutionary vanguard intensified the misunderstanding between Sandinistas and peasants.[23]

The Elitist Agenda

Although it was for a peasant insurrection that outside mobilizers provided resources, the struggle was shaped solely in terms of elitist interests; namely, the goal to regain the elites' prerevolutionary socioeconomic and political privileges. These counterrevolutionary actors, both domestic and foreign, with independent but complementary agendas were able to gather strength when influential peasant groups became highly dissatisfied with state policies.[24] Peasant discontent was thus channeled through armed resistance into a movement that consistently ignored the peasantry's demands and identity. Accordingly, the negotiation process that accompanied the transition from FSLN to UNO rule in 1990 favored elites' interests and disregarded rank-and-file demands.[25] Contrary to their expectation of immediate benefits from the National Opposition Union (Unión Nacional Opositora, UNO) electoral victory, the Contras were marginalized in the process of consensus building.[26] As a result, groups of former Contras (*recontras*) took up arms to demand the Chamorro government supply them with land and support services as promised by the demobilization accords. Rural violence by rearmed groups sky-rocketed in 1992.[27]

The Contras: From Bandits to a U.S.-Backed Army

At the strategic-military level, the Contra war went through stages, each directly linked to the organizational and material resources made available to the anti-Sandinista rebels and to the strategy defined by the external actors in command of the Contra effort; namely, Argentina's Army Intelligence Battalion 601 and, most significantly, the CIA.

At first, the counterrevolutionary insurgents emerged as a series of isolated and ill-equipped bands that operated in the mountain regions and northern border areas of Nicaragua. Gradually, these bands grouped into a few insurgent organizations that would constitute the foundation of the Contra army. Following the creation of the U.S.-backed Nicaraguan Democratic Force (Fuerza Democrática Nicaragüense, FDN) in late 1981, the counterrevolutionary forces entered a new phase, multiplying their manpower and military capabilities and assuming the strategic offensive against the Sandinista army. By late 1983, the Contra forces had established solid operational bases in Honduras and Costa Rica, secured the support of a large sector of the peasantry, and initiated military operations inside Nicaragua aimed at undermining the Sandinista army's rearguard.[28]

After the failure to "liberate" Nicaragua's north-central region in 1984, it was evident that the Contra forces could not achieve a military victory over the Sandinistas. Therefore the Pentagon and the CIA led the anti-Sandinista insurgency into a program of "low-intensity conflict" that combined guerrilla warfare (military operations designed to "wear down and inflict casualties upon the enemy, damage supplies and facilities, and hinder and delay enemy operations") and subversion (politico-military operations, mainly sabotage, devised to obstruct the decisions and actions of the Sandinista government).[29]

The counterrevolutionary war in Nicaragua was a conflict of immense proportions for such a small country. The Contras evolved into a large, semiconventional military force: more than 22,000 men were officially demobilized following the inauguration of Violeta Chamorro in 1990. The Sandinista Popular Army (Ejército Popular Sandinista, EPS) reached some 75,000 troops. The military conflict was centered in the rural areas of the country: Estelí, Madriz, and Nueva Segovia (designated by the Sandinista government as First Region), Boaco, Chontales, Zelaya's municipalities and San Juan River (Fifth Region), Matagalpa and Jinotega (Sixth Region), northern and southern Zelaya, and San Juan River (the Special Zones). These geographical areas contained nearly one-third of Nicaragua's total population.[30] By 1987, property destruction and losses in production as a result of the war reached $1.15 billion.[31] War deaths on both sides, including civilians, amounted to nearly 31,000 in the nine years of military confrontation.[32]

Growing Insurrection: The MILPAS

In the first months following Somoza's ouster, groups of small farmers, cattlemen, and tradesmen in north-central Nicaragua began to rise up against the Sandinista regime. Many of those rebels had participated in the 1978–1979 Sandinista-led insurrection and a number of them had become EPS soldiers or militiamen after the triumph of the revolution. "The Marxist system," said a member of one of the original groups, "did not offer the opportunity to fight against it through civic channels, so the only alternative was an armed struggle."[33]

These counterrevolutionaries formed armed bands, calling themselves MILPAS (Popular Anti-Sandinista Militias/Milicias Populares Anti-Sandinistas)[34]—a designation that had been used earlier (before July 1979) for the Popular Anti-Somocista Militias

(Milicias Populares Anti-Somocistas), insurrectionary groups linked to the pro-Maoist Popular Action Movement (Movimiento de Acción Popular, MAP). During late 1979 and 1980, a number of centers of MILPAS activity unfolded in Matagalpa, Nueva Segovia, Jinotega, and other northern regions.[35] It was not until months later that the MILPAS began to collaborate with the bands of former guardsmen operating in northern Nicaragua.

The first three groups identified as MILPAS responded to the leadership of Pedro Joaquín González, a disaffected Sandinista guerrilla commander, considered by many "the founder of the anti-Sandinista armed struggle."[36] A second leader of the early anti-Sandinista MILPAS was another former Sandinista commander, Encarnación Valdivia, who had been sent by the EPS to track down González's band after its takeover of the town of Quilalí in July 1980.[37] The third earliest leader of the MILPAS was Oscar Sobalvarro, the son of a coffee producer and *juez de mesta* (a rural judge) in northern Jinotega.[38] (Under the Somoza dynasty, these rural judges often served as spies and source of social control via their ties to the national guard and the corrupt Liberal Nationalist Party—Partido Liberal Nacionalista, PLN.)[39]

At first, the MILPAS engaged in petty robberies and propaganda activities; later they began to attack Sandinista military and civilian targets.[40] They were armed with pistols, revolvers, and hunting rifles, and a very few Galils, M-16s, and Uzis captured from the Sandinista forces. Soon they began to receive support from the peasantry.[41] The structure of the MILPAS was similar to that of the Popular Sandinista Militias—citizen volunteers (not part of the standing army) who, increasingly after 1981, were given old weapons and received a week or two of drilling to defend local villages and installations. The MILPAS were supported by a network of collaborators that included rich and middle peasants as well as poor peasants attached to the former by strong, patrimonial links.[42] As figure 4.1 shows, an analysis of the class structure of a Jinotega-based anti-Sandinista militia in 1979–1980 reveals that nearly half of its membership came from the rich and middle peasantry.

Having emerged immediately after the revolutionary takeover, well before the Sandinistas initiated their agrarian policies (except for confiscations of Somocista property), the rebel groups in northern rural areas were a reaction to the collapse of a traditional pattern of local authority and its sudden replacement by a revolutionary military command that lacked understanding of the specific sociopolitical dynamics of rural communities. Numerous peasants joined the rebel bands claiming to have suffered abuses by Sandinista local authorities.[43] In early 1980, price and market controls were enforced throughout the country: these measures, and the coercion needed to implement them, disaffected the middle peasants, who (as noted earlier in this chapter) experienced that process as an infringement upon their economic identity.[44]

Figure 4.1. Analysis by class of collaborators and rank and file with a MILPAS anti-Sandinista militia, Yalí, Jinotega, 1979–1980

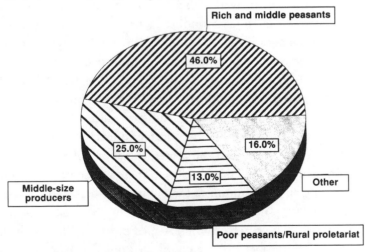

The analysis is of the rank and file and the network of collaborators (total = 110). **Data source:** CIERA, "Caracterización de las primeras bandas contrarrevolucionarias," November 1980, in CIERA, *La reforma agraria en Nicaragua, 1979–89*, vol. 6 (Managua: CIERA, 1989), p. 253.

The political discourse of the MILPAS leadership, which paid particular attention to establishing a frequent interaction with poor peasants, was characterized by four main elements; namely, a defense of private property vis-á-vis the socialist state; a promise of land distribution (specifically, land already confiscated by the state); an emphasis on the liberation of Nicaragua from the FSLN's "Communism," and a religious overtone opposed to the FSLN's "atheistic" political project. In order to recruit young ex-guerrillas in rural areas, these groups underscored the distinction between Communist and anti-Communist Sandinistas, while posing the need to build up a national liberation movement in alliance with Somoza's former guardsmen. The MILPAS perceived the FSLN's original social programs (for instance, the National Literacy Crusade, which mobilized thousands of volunteer teachers to rural areas in 1980) as an attempt by the Sandinista regime to "tame" the peasantry and spread Communism throughout the countryside.[45]

By late 1980, some MILPAS had crossed the border into Honduras, where they merged with other anti-Sandinista groups based in the area of Las Trojes. Honduran authorities allowed the bands to operate clandestinely in the mountains and put them in contact with supportive local populations. As recounted by a leader of one of the MILPAS operating in Honduras, a few weeks later they were contacted by a former national guard colonel, Enrique Bermúdez, and an Argentinean military officer, Santiago Hoya. "The exiled guardsmen had been in Honduras for months, setting up an organization," said the aforementioned Sobalvarro, one of the original MILPAS commanders. "There was some U.S. interest in creating an anti-Sandinista force, but the Americans looked for Argentine support. Colonel Villegas [Hoya's alias] handed us $2,000 to buy food. That money helped us survive during the first months. By October 1981 we established our first base camp near Capire, Honduras, and escalated our infiltrations into Nicaragua. Our group, some sixty men, later became part of the September 15 Legion."[46]

Initially, the MILPAS encountered strong animosity among the Honduran peasantry, because "they confused us with Somoza's guardsmen, who had an infamous reputation as assassins," Sobalvarro told me. "We had to win the peasants' trust, which we did, gradually. After a while, the Honduran people were supplying us with food and other essentials because the initial Argentine aid did not last long." A few months later, Sobalvarro's group moved to another camp near Las Trojes, where they joined the September 15 Legion and began to receive a steady flow of sustenance aid via Bermúdez.[47]

The transition from the ill-equipped and badly trained MILPAS to the September 15 Legion (and later FDN) was accomplished via the unification of the military command, the selection of objectives according to a predesignated politico-military operation, and, above all, the implementation of a training program aimed at imposing military order to the ragtag militias. The Argentine advisers and the former guardsmen played a critical role in this process.[48]

The MILPAS, lacking the independent capacity to overcome their military weaknesses (training, strategy, and military equipment), found that their survival and growth were dependent on external actors: the former guardsmen, Honduras, Argentina, and the United States.[49] But the anti-Sandinista groups were central to the counterrevolutionary movement because they supplied its original popular base, which would expand into a large peasant insurrectionary army throughout the 1980s.

Politico-military Organizations

A few months after the Sandinista takeover, small and scattered bands of former guardsmen began to operate in the Honduran-Nicaraguan border areas. The collapse of the national guard had forced thousands of guardsmen into exile: officials from rank of colonel and up and the Somocista political class flew to the United States; most rank-and-file guardsmen escaped to Honduras and Costa Rica. "National guard officers and the Somocista political leadership abandoned the *guardias* to their own fate. So they decided to organize into an anti-Sandinista force," said one former Contra leader.[50] Former guardsmen such as Capt. Hugo Villagra, Sgt. Pedro Ortiz Centeno, and Sgt. José Efrel Martínez Mondragón were among the first to organize armed bands in Guatemala and Honduras, well before Bermúdez arrived in Central America to lead the anti-Sandinista forces.[51]

Beginning in 1980, armed groups of former guardsmen, led by Francisco Ruiz Castellón, Juan Ramón Rivas, and other exiles, began to attack EPS posts along the Honduran border, steal cattle, kill and torture literacy campaign volunteers, and terrorize Sandinista supporters in rural areas. The growing movement of former guardsmen in Honduras helped to spread reports about a mounting anti-Sandinista movement, which encouraged disillusioned peasants to join the MILPAS that were emerging spontaneously in the north-central region.[52]

A number of politico-military organizations (exiled guardsmen, independent farmers and cattle ranchers, and members of the business and landed upper class) emerged in 1980 after initial contacts with U.S. conservatives:[53] they were the Nicaraguan Democratic Revolutionary Alliance (Alianza Democrática Revolucionaria Nicaragüense, ADREN), whose founders included two former national guard colonels, Enrique Bermúdez and Guillermo Mendietta, as well as Eduardo Román, José Robelo, and Frank Arana; the Nicaraguan Democratic Union–Nicaraguan Revolutionary Armed Forces (Unión Democrática Nicaragüense–Fuerzas Armadas Revolucionarias Nicaragüenses, UDN-FARN), one of the best-organized groups, whose original leadership included José Francisco Cardenal, David Stadthagen, Max Vargas, Edmundo Chamorro, Enrique Bolaños, and later, Fernando Chamorro; and the Revolutionary United Force (Fuerza Unida Revolucionaria, FUR), the least influential group at the time, which included Julio Pataky, Juan Bautista Sacasa Gómez, and Arístides Sánchez, an exiled Nicaraguan businessman who would be recruited by the CIA in 1981 to work closely with Bermúdez and the Argentines in the FDN.

Some of these organizations established the first links with Argentine military intelligence and served as liaison between the old regime's political and military bureaucracy and the civilian MILPAS. Other organizations sought to strengthen links with U.S. policymakers. Among the right-wing contacts made by the Nicaraguan exiles in the United States was Lt. Gen. (retired) Gordon Sumner, one of the authors of *A New Inter-American Policy for the Eighties* (the Santa Fe Document), the policy analysis that served as a blueprint for the Reagan administration's Latin American policy. The 1980 report argued that the United States could not tolerate the presence of a Sandinista regime in Nicaragua and advocated a reestablishment of U.S. continental leadership to "protect the independent nations of Latin America from Communist conquest."[54]

Other counterrevolutionary groups[55] were the Democratic Armed Forces (Fuerzas Armadas Democráticas, FAD), with direct links to the Nicaraguan Federation of Cattle Ranchers (Federación de Ganaderos de Nicaragua, FAGANIC); the Anti-Communist Armed Forces (Fuerzas Armadas Anticomunistas, FARAC); the November 11 Movement and the Anti-Communist Forces of León–Popular Anti-Communist Organization (Fuerzas Anticomunistas de León–Organización Popular Anticomunista, FALOPAC). The FAD received economic assistance from Jorge Salazar, former vice president of the Superior Council of Private Enterprise (Consejo Superior de la Empresa Privada, COSEP). Salazar, who was killed by Sandinista security forces in November 1980, led an early attempt to create a politico-military counterrevolutionary front in Nicaragua (the Sandinista Democratic Army/Ejército Democrático Sandinista) based on an alliance between the independent business sector and exiled guardsmen (headed by Colonel Bermúdez) and supported by the government of El Salvador. The FAD also operated in Bluefields, seeking the support of the Atlantic coast's ethnic communities. The November 11 Movement was soon absorbed by the UDN-FARN. Its leadership included Fernando Chamorro, a self-exiled Social Democratic Party (PSD) leader, and Vicente Rappaccioli of the Democratic Conservative Party (PCD).[56] The group received support from the Argentine Army Intelligence Battalion 601 to finance travel and military training costs in Honduras and Argentina.

The Sandinista government quickly reacted to counterrevolutionary activities in Nicaragua and neighboring countries. In 1980, the Ministry of the Interior (Ministerio del Interior, MINT) created a special division under the General Directorate for State Security (Dirección General de Seguridad del Estado, DGSE) to gather intelligence on opposition groups, infiltrate them, and establish networks of civilian informants to support MINT-DGSE operations. At the same time, the EPS created unconventional units led by experienced Sandinista guerrillas that conducted special missions in rural areas where the Contras operated. In spite of the new regime's fast, and strong, response, local counterrevolutionary networks outlasted the Sandinista counteraction and continued to provide combatants and support to the Contra rebellion.[57]

The Legion

The emerging opposition organizations sought to develop both "internal and external fronts" with the objective of gaining legitimacy and resources for their cause. In 1980, a group of former national guard officers (Bermúdez and Lau, among others) created the September 15 Legion (Legión 15 de Septiembre) in Guatemala. The legion united most of the existing counterrevolutionary groups into a single organization led by a military junta and, most importantly, attempted to absorb the dispersed MILPAS. The legion set up three operational bases on the Honduran-Nicaraguan border—Ariel, Zebra, and Sagitario—and initiated a style of warfare marked by small ambushes and hit-and-run attacks.[58] The legion consisted of nearly five hundred former guardsmen, including some of the most ruthless representatives of the Contra ethos: Leonte Arias, who ordered the execution of Sandinista prisoners in 1985; Marcos Navarro and Armando López, commanders of the Zebra camp accused of numerous assassinations of recruits and prisoners; José Benito Bravo Centeno, a vicious Contra commander involved in several murders and one of the legionnaires trained in Argentina in 1981; and Ricardo Lau, a notorious torturer and assassin who also received intelligence training in Argentina.[59]

The Church

The Roman Catholic Church hierarchy played a significant role in the anti-Sandinista effort. In March 1979, Monseñor Miguel Obando y Bravo, Archbishop of Managua (later a cardinal), and Monseñor Pablo A. Vega, bishop of Juigalpa, promoted the creation of a civil organization, the Comité de Reflexión Patriótica, to block the ascension of the Sandinistas to power.[60]

Immediately after the collapse of the Somoza regime, the Argentine military junta began to support Obando's anti-Communist activities through financial assistance and contacts at the "highest levels" in Latin America, Europe, and the United States. "We had a common enemy: subversion had taken power in Nicaragua, allowing Montonero and ERP guerrillas to operate freely in that country," a high-ranking Argentine military officer told me. "Cardinal Obando was a great fighter. We introduced him to key international circles where he could explain what was happening in Nicaragua."[61] In addition to the aid provided by the Argentine military regime, by 1981 Obando was receiving ample financial support for his Managua-based Commission for Social

Promotion in the Archdiocese (Comisión para la Promoción Social de la Arquidiócesis, COPROSA), which coordinated the conservative church's counterrevolutionary activities, from the U.S. Agency for International Development (AID), Misereor and Adveniat (agencies of the West German bishops), and other international organizations.[62]

Argentina's Role in Detail

By the end of 1980, Argentine advisers started to organize and train Nicaraguan guardsmen exiled in Guatemala.[63] In April 1981, Colonel Bermúdez met with high-ranking intelligence officers in Buenos Aires. Bermúdez told them that Argentina could play a major role in Central America, facilitating U.S. involvement in the region.[64] The Argentines decided to support Bermúdez as military leader of the anti-Sandinista movement and, soon after, started funneling money to the Contra rebels.

On November 23, 1981, President Reagan approved National Security Decision Directive (NSDD) 17, authorizing the CIA to create a five-hundred-strong paramilitary force to "interdict" an alleged flow of arms from Nicaragua to the Salvadoran guerrillas (see chapter 2). This group would complement an existent thousand-strong force under Argentine command. An initial $19.95 million was allocated to the program, with an observation that more funds and military personnel would be needed.[65] As already noted, the Argentine military, which was actively engaged in training Contra rebels well before Reagan took office, thus assumed the role of U.S. surrogate.

Argentine military intelligence placed its personnel in critical areas so that it could operate effectively in the uncertain Central American setting. Nicaraguan rebels were trained in Buenos Aires, Guatemala, El Salvador, Honduras, and the United States. Even though the Argentine-led counterrevolutionary venture was initially mounted with limited resources, the operation rapidly gained momentum with the resolute support of the United States.

Anti-Sandinista Training in Buenos Aires

In the early part of the Argentine effort (early 1981), Argentina began providing counterinsurgency training to select groups of Nicaraguans in Buenos Aires. The purpose of this instruction was to have a number of well-trained personnel who would be able to serve as instructors in Honduras-based training camps and as field commanders for the mission of penetrating into Nicaragua to set up the conditions for an anti-Sandinista insurrectional environment.[66]

Three groups of some twenty men each were flown to Buenos Aires in spring 1981 for intelligence and military training. Selected on the basis of their military expertise and commitment to the rebel cause, the trainees were former guardsmen and civilian combatants of the earliest anti-Sandinista bands. The secret journey was coordinated by Colonel Bermúdez. "He said we were going to undertake a training course abroad," a former guard sergeant, Mariano Morales, told me, "but he did not say where it would take place." The rebels were taken to clandestine military facilities in suburban Buenos Aires for a six-week course to prepare them for secret assignments in Central America.[67]

The Nicaraguans, most of them members of the September 15 Legion and the UDN-FARN, received training in intelligence, counterintelligence, psychological operations, leadership, camouflage, demolition, explosives, sabotage, kidnapping, and interrogation techniques.[68] The instruction, which included both urban and rural guerrilla and counterguerrilla warfare, was provided by advisers from Argentina's Army Special Forces.[69]

The Argentines who provided the training were veterans of the dirty war; some had been involved in the instruction of Triple A operatives in the mid-1970s.[70] The human rights records of several

of the Nicaraguan trainees would come to match those of their instructors. For instance, Morales, chief of the Nicaraguan rebel
army's military police from 1985 to 1987, would be accused of torture and rape by the State Department–funded Nicaraguan Association for Human Rights.[71]

According to the Argentines, the training offered to the anti-
Sandinista combatants was based on the trainers' successful experience in fighting domestic insurgent organizations, particularly
the Montoneros.[72] The Argentines claimed that military intelligence had evidence that the Sandinista government was training
and supporting Montonero guerrillas in Nicaragua for terrorist
operations in Argentina.[73] Reportedly, such a threat strengthened
the Argentines' commitment to the anti-Sandinista effort.[74]

Early in this phase, the Argentines attempted to impose a distinct anti-Communist accent to the Contra movement, interna-
tionalizing and Sovietizing the Nicaraguan conflict. "The
Argentinean officers' ideas had an important influence over the
early ideological development of the *contra* movement," a former
FDN official, Edgar Chamorro, said. "Much like that of the
Cubans in Miami, the Argentinean influence gave a more ideological tone to the group, a tone of anti-Soviet, anti-Cuban, anti-
communist goals. They began to transform what had originally
been nationalistic goals tailored to Nicaragua's particular historical, social, and cultural situation."[75] The Argentines stressed that
the revolutionary war was an ideological confrontation, "the
legacy of World War II," with the goal of conquering the population's "hearts and minds."[76] According to the Argentines, the Soviet Union, whose initial strategy had been centered on conventional wars for national liberation in Africa and Asia, had opened
a front in Latin America, adapting its strategy to the specific conditions of the region.[77] That aggression demanded an unconventional politico-military response that justified any methods to
secure success. Interestingly, that view mirrored the U.S. doctrine
of "low-intensity conflict" (LIC), which replaced "counterinsur-

gency" as the guiding rationale for U.S. intervention abroad.[78] (In evaluating the poor results—in terms of U.S. national interest— of low-intensity conflict doctrine as applied by the United States in El Salvador, a RAND report concluded in 1991 that the U.S. government and military overestimated the Communist threat in that country and failed to understand that revolt was predominantly locally rooted rather than Soviet instigated.)[79]

Following the instruction in Buenos Aires, the Nicaraguans were assigned to Honduras, Guatemala, Costa Rica, Panama, and Miami, where other anti-Sandinista rebels received training in Cuban-American paramilitary camps[80] (a group of Argentine officers was transferred to Miami to train anti-Sandinista forces).[81] Most of the Nicaraguans trained in Argentina went to camps on the Honduran border, where they provided military instruction to several groups of combatants, including many Contra field commanders, such as Encarnación Valdivia, Israel Galeano, Tirzo Moreno Aguilar, and Oscar Sobalvarro. Later some of the Argentine-trained rebels entered Nicaragua commanding their own troops to conduct operations in the north-central region. Other Nicaraguans were sent to the Honduran Gracias a Dios Province to instruct anti-Sandinista Miskito forces and a few commando teams trained in Buenos Aires were dispatched to Managua on infiltration missions.[82]

"The Argentines emphasized their anti-Communist zeal and their total support for our cause," Morales told me. "They blamed the United States for failing to prevent Nicaragua's fall into Communism." Morales stressed the professionalism of the Argentine instructors in Buenos Aires, who were of higher rank than those who trained Contra forces in Honduras. The course's accent was on military skills, but the Argentine officers also frequently briefed the Nicaraguan trainees on political and ideological warfare. "They told us to awaken the Nicaraguan people so that they understood that it was imperative to rescue our nation from Communism," Morales said.[83] His account was confirmed by another account, that of former EEBI officer Martínez Mondragón, who received specialized instruction in Argentina in 1981 and a year later joined the Argentine-trained commando team that blew up the bridge on the Río Negro in northern Chinandega.[84]

The Argentine Army General Staff, which was directly involved in the recruitment of advisers to the Contras in collaboration with former Nicaraguan guard officers, paid attention not only to the military capabilities of the Argentine advisers to be sent to Central America but also to their political ideas. For instance, an expert Argentine commando officer considered for the position of adviser to the Contras was rejected by the general staff because he suggested implementing in Nicaragua a socioeconomic system similar to that of Argentina's 1940s Peronism in the event of an anti-Sandinista victory.[85]

The Argentines may have been involved in the production of *El Legionario*, the newsletter of the September 15 Legion, which discussed concepts of national strategy, national power, national objectives, and geopolitics. The Legion newsletter of June 1981 owed much to publications by Argentinean military think tanks, particularly the writings of a leading Argentine geopolitical thinker, Gen. Juan Guglialmelli.[86] "Third World countries," *El Legionario* read, "are highly vulnerable to socialist ideologies because of a number of features that strongly influence their development: colonialist heritage, low levels of economic growth, foreign dependence, lack of interest group representation, inequality, instability, significant urban-rural gap, low levels of education, absence of an industrial base, and inadequate military capabilities." In order to confront the vulnerability of Third World countries to ideologies based on the "irrationality of the masses," the Contra publication advocated the formula of security and development "to achieve economic growth with social justice."[87]

The Legion newsletter defined the Nicaraguan guardsmen as "democrats," emphasizing that "they have experienced a significant change, because they are not Somocistas nor do they intend to initiate an armed struggle on behalf of the national guard. They think in terms of liberating their fatherland from the Communist yoke . . . [and] accept that the liberation struggle cannot be won without the participation of all Nicaraguans united against Communism."[88] Special attention was given to the coordination of Latin American guerrilla movements, a key theme in the training courses offered by the Argentine military.[89] Ampié Quiróz, the FDN intelligence chief, told me, "The Argentines stressed the fact that all guerrilla movements in Latin America were coordinated under a central command. The FSLN played a major role in organizing and promoting insurgent operations throughout the hemisphere."[90]

Formation of the FDN

In early 1981, two independent operators with strong connections to the Argentine military, Francisco Aguirre, a powerful member of the Nicaraguan exile community in the United States, and Nat Hamrick, a businessman with excellent contacts on Capitol Hill, introduced Enrique Bermúdez to the heads of Argentine military intelligence.[91] Aguirre played a central role in the organization of an anti-Sandinista movement backed by Argentina and the United States. He linked key elements in that venture, including former national guard officers, UDN-FARN leaders, Argentine army intelligence chiefs, and U.S. State Department officials, including the assistant secretary for inter-American affairs, Thomas Enders.

The Argentine program in Central America was supervised by the same command structure that led the urban counterinsurgency warfare in Argentina's dirty war. Primarily an intelligence operation, the program of support to the Contras was overseen by Valín, who, having served as advisor to Somoza's national guard during the insurrectional period in Nicaragua, had the experience needed to assume overall control of the Argentine counterrevolutionary activities in Central America. He ran the anti-Sandinista program from Buenos Aires throughout 1981. In early 1982, he was appointed ambassador to Panama with the mission of coordinating the operation at firsthand.[92]

The early support of the Argentine military was critical for the development of the Contra forces. Bermúdez acknowledged in the late 1980s, contrary to the generalized view that the Contra movement was initially supported by the United States, "The Argentines were the ones who gave us the necessary sponsorship to begin our military struggle against the Sandinistas."[93]

In early August 1981, a UDN delegation visited Buenos Aires to discuss with the chiefs of Argentine military intelligence the terms of its incorporation into the FDN. A member of the group, William Baltodano Herrera, said, "We held a meeting with General Valín . . . and his top aide, Col. Mario Davico, who wanted to know the meaning of UDN, what political goal it was seeking and its purposes. At our third meeting with these people, they handed over the amount of $50,000. . . . It was delivered by Colonel Davico who said: 'Gentlemen, this is the beginning, to get this thing going.'"[94]

That same month, representatives from the September 15 Legion and the UDN held a unity conclave in Guatemala City to establish a single anti-Sandinista organization, the FDN.[95] "The meeting was arranged and the documents were prepared by the CIA," asserted disaffected anti-Sandinista leader Edgar Chamorro.[96] The FDN incorporated the September 15 Legion, UDN-FARN, FUR, and other dissident groups.[97] However, until 1984 many of the rebels in the field continued to operate under their original groups. The new umbrella organization was cosmetic in nature.[98]

However, one of the first efforts of the September 15 Legion organized as FDN was to incorporate the MILPAS into its military force. Dissident Sandinistas were sent into Nicaragua to gather the independent small groups operating in the north-central region, take them to Honduras for military training, and lead them again into Nicaraguan territory. By early 1982, that action greatly expanded the number of combatants and the popular base of the anti-Sandinista forces.[99] Figure 4.2 shows the rapid increase of Contra combatants in the early 1980s.

Later in the same month as the meeting in Guatemala City (August 1981), representatives from the CIA, Argentine military intelligence, and the Honduran military forces met in Tegucigalpa to establish a three-sided accord, *"la tripartita."*[100] The agreement determined the role of each partner in the counterrevolutionary program: the Argentines would provide the organization, administration, and military training; the CIA would supply covert aid; and the Honduran government would provide the territory for the operational bases.[101] The U.S. people, Bermúdez explained,

Figure 4.2. Nicaraguan Democratic Force (FDN) military forces, 1981–1987

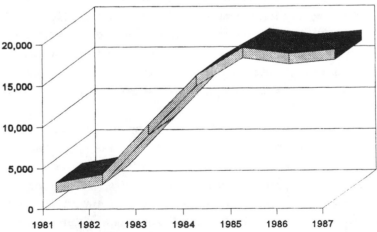

Data sources: U.S. Department of State, *Documents on the Nicaraguan Resistance: Leaders, Military Personnel, and Program* (Washington, D.C.: Bureau of Public Affairs, 1986), p. 3; Jaime Morales Carazo, *La Contra* (México, D.F.: Planeta, 1989), p. 57.

"wanted to do something but at that time they didn't know how to do it. And the Argentines eased the way for United States involvement."[102] According to Bermúdez, "it was not until November 1981 that we started to receive U.S. aid, and that happened when we got indirect assistance to set up the September 15 Radio."[103] Following the establishment of the tripartite enterprise, the Argentine junta approved the sale of "secret military equipment" to Honduras in the amount of $10 million.[104] As a result of the creation of the FDN—notwithstanding its cosmetic nature—the Contra program entered a new phase because of the decided financial and logistical support of the CIA.

In late 1981, the first FDN combat units were dispatched into Nicaraguan territory, primarily to carry out hit-and-run attacks. In March 1982, the FDN conducted its first major military actions when Argentine and Nicaraguan commandos, with CIA operational support, blew up the bridges at Río Negro and Ocotal in northern Nicaragua.[105] "The Argentine advisers," disclosed Battalion 601 operative Héctor Francés, "instructed in the United States for carrying out these operations and who transmitted this knowledge to Nicaraguan counterrevolutionaries, brought with them highly technical elements such as programmed explosives . . . detailed maps of Nicaragua developed for them by the Pentagon, special scale maps and diagrams of targets, [and] also satellite photographs."[106]

The Argentine general staff that oversaw the Contra forces was headed by José Osvaldo Ribeiro, political head of operations, and Santiago Hoya, chief of logistics and military operations. Ribeiro, regarded by his peers as "one of the best cadres" of Argentine military intelligence, conducted the Contra war from the Argentine headquarters at the Hotel Maya in Colonia Nueva Palmira, Tegucigalpa; Hoya was often working in the field.[107] Ribeiro "became a prominent figure in Tegucigalpa, living in a large house, distributing American money and dispensing what CIA officials viewed as unsound military advice," said a U.S. newspaper report. "For example, since his own experience was in urban rather than rural combat, he advised the Contras to mount a program of urban terrorism. The CIA wanted to cultivate a popular insurgency in the countryside."[108]

Ribeiro, praised as "probably the best strategist on guerrilla warfare in this hemisphere" by an aide to Republican Senator Jesse Helms, had been involved in the organization and operation of an infamous clandestine detention center at Campo de Mayo military base outside Buenos Aires during the dirty war.[109] In the first years of the authoritarian regime, Ribeiro had served as army intelligence chief in Mendoza Province under the command of Gen. Jorge A. Maradona, being involved in numerous violations of human rights. He also operated in Bahía Blanca as intelligence chief of the Fifth Army Corps. As a member of Army Intelligence Battalion 601, Ribeiro was under the direct authority of Colonel Muzzio.[110]

Hoya, who served as liaison with the CIA station chief in Honduras, controlled the flow of military equipment and funds from the CIA to the Contra forces.[111] Hoya "authorized the disbursement of military equipment and CIA monies for the FDN forces. The CIA agent in charge of supervising the day-to-day operations in Honduras worked closely with him," said a senior FDN operative in charge of logistics.[112] Hoya had worked closely with anti-Sandinista political and military leaders to constitute the FDN in August 1981.[113] He also played a decisive role in the reorganization of the FDN military general staff in December of that year, placing pro-Argentine Nicaraguan officers (Bermúdez, Lau, and Emilio Echaverry Mejía) in key positions.[114] Hoya and Ribeiro sought to control the Contra operations through a cohesive relationship with the Hondurans and the Nicaraguan rebels.[115]

The Argentine staff supervised the FDN military operations, leaving the specific management of the armed organization to the Nicaraguan former guardsmen. From the beginning, the Contra military structure was corrupt, lacking control and effective ad-

ministration, a trend that worsened when the CIA took over training and logistics (early 1984). "The Argentines were very effective
in preparing military leaders for the resistance movement," a former Contra leader said. "However, they underestimated the in-
competence of the FDN military command structure to establish
an efficient internal administration."[116] According to some Contra
commanders, the change of leadership had a negative impact on
the counterrevolutionary military organization: "The Argentines
were more demanding, they provided better training, and required
more compartmentation and better planning of the operations,"
FDN intelligence chief Ampié Quiróz told me.[117]

The FDN Leadership

When the FDN was formed in August 1981, merging the September 15 Legion and the UDN-FARN, the CIA created a political junta consisting of José Francisco Cardenal, Mariano Mendoza
Juárez, and Arístides Sánchez. UDN leader Cardenal had been
persuaded by the CIA (and particularly by Vernon Walters) to join
forces with Somoza's former national guardsmen to help remove
the Sandinistas from power.[118] Mendoza Juárez was a Nicaraguan
labor leader working for the CIA-backed American Institute for
Free Labor Development (AIFLD), and Sánchez, a former associate of Somoza, was a close collaborator of Bermúdez and the Argentine general staff in Honduras.[119] He was also directly linked
with a Costa Rica-based cocaine ring that operated in the San
Francisco Bay Area of the United States in the early 1980s.[120] Even
though there was no hard evidence to prove a connection between
Sánchez's drug-trafficking activities and those of Carlos Suárez
Mason, a key actor in Argentina's extraterritorial program, the
abundance of links between the two men and the cocaine business
under the umbrella of anti-Communism suggested the existence
of such connection.

The original FDN military general staff consisted of Bermúdez, Lau, Orlando Bolaños, Raúl Arana, Justiniano Pérez, and Carlos Rodríguez. In December 1981, it was reorganized: Bermúdez was chief of staff, Echaverry Mejía, a former national guard major, was chief of operations, Lau was head of intelligence, Edgar Hernández was chief of personnel, and Manuel Antonio Cáceres was head of psychological operations. Francisco Rivera was in charge of logistics.[121]

Bermúdez, backed by the Argentines and other key political actors, took over as supreme commander of the new anti-Sandinista force.[122] After receiving a six-week guerrilla warfare course in Argentina in June and July 1981, Bermúdez established himself in Honduras to run the FDN military operations.[123]

During the Argentine leadership period, Echaverry Mejía, a graduate of Argentina's Military College (1958–1961), was a powerful actor in the FDN military structure. "The Argentines made a serious mistake that almost caused the breakup of the resistance movement in its early stage," Ampié Quiróz told me.[124] "They gave too much power to Echaverry [in accordance with Alvarez Martínez]. He was very authoritarian and did not know how to deal with rank-and-file combatants and the peasantry. There were a number of revolts against Echaverry and Bermúdez led by field commanders, who did not want to accept their leadership."[125] Bermúdez endured in his post because of CIA pressure, but Echaverry was ousted from the Contra forces in 1983 when the Argentines and Alvarez Martínez lost their leverage in the operation.[126] A CIA-backed investigation found serious irregularities in Echaverry's handling of FDN funds.[127]

Miskito Counterrevolutionaries

The conflict between the Sandinista regime and the indigenous organization that united Miskitos, Sumus, and Ramas rapidly escalated in the period from late 1979 to early 1981. Serious incidents of confrontation between the Sandinista army and this organization, sometimes involving the region's Moravian Church, had vast repercussions in the area. Miskito leaders became involved in separatist and counterrevolutionary activities, establishing connections with groups of former guardsmen exiled in Honduras. Many young people defected to the expanding counterrevolutionary movement. Soon the resentment of the ethnic communities of the Atlantic coast with respect to Sandinista policies and practices incorporated a distinct anti-Communist tone—a combination of anti-foreigner and anti-Cuban feelings—exacerbating local disaffection.[128]

In early 1981, some three thousand Miskitos from communities along the Coco River, under the leadership of Steadman Fagoth, migrated to Honduras. Subsequently, Fagoth—a former informant for Somoza's infamous OSN—organized a small armed group and began attacking indigenous communities in the Nicaraguan border areas.

Fagoth was soon joined by another Miskito leader, Brooklyn Rivera; however, tensions between these leaders increased rapidly.[129] The Honduran government actively supported Argentine-protégé Fagoth in his dispute with Rivera for leadership of the Miskito rebels in the war against the Sandinista regime. After being denied access to refugee areas in Mokorón, Rivera was summarily expelled from Honduras by military authorities.[130]

With the support of the Honduran army, Fagoth and his group established training camps in Mokorón (headquarters) and surrounding areas of Gracias a Dios Province by September 1981. Initially, instruction was provided by former guardsmen exiled in Honduras. Soon afterward, a group of about fifty Argentine advisers was deployed in the area to organize and train a counterrevolutionary army of Miskito exiles.[131] Training included guerrilla and counterguerrilla warfare and interrogation techniques (the Argentines established informal rules for dealing with prisoners, tolerating the practice of killing them after interrogation).[132] The Argentine advisers sought to transfer the lessons from the Tucumán campaign in the 1970s to Central America. (Operation Independence Commander Gen. Acdel Edgardo Vilas depicted the army's unconventional methodology as follows: "How many people are there in Río Colorado? Seven hundred? Okay. Quarantine everybody. We will find out later who is a guerrilla and who is not.")[133]

Miskito units were sent back to Nicaragua to establish support networks in their communities and secretly recruit and train young combatants. In late 1981, Miskito rebel forces launched their first major offensive against Sandinista army outposts along the upper Coco River. In addition to these military targets, the offensive involved several villages, where the forces led by Fagoth committed atrocities against the population, particularly against Miskitos regarded as Sandinista sympathizers.[134] There was a consistent pattern: disappearance, torture and rape, and summary execution.

These attacks preceded a major CIA-sponsored counterrevolutionary separatist plan called Operation Red Christmas.[135] The plan sought to provoke a state of emergency in northern Nicaragua so as to isolate the Miskito population of the Atlantic coast from the rest of the nation and promote a general insurrection against the regime. The objective was to secure control of the region down to Puerto Cabezas and declare the area liberated territory so as to install a provisional government and request international recognition. "The captured MISURA pastor who confessed the plan reportedly said the U.S. intended to use the area as a beachhead from which to attack the revolution on the Pacific," noted an expert on Nicaragua's Atlantic region.[136] The CIA-backed operation, which was to involve Argentine advisers, Honduran military intelligence officials, and former guardsmen, was thwarted by the Sandinista security forces in February 1982.[137] However, as a result of the increasing counterrevolutionary threat in the area, the Sandinista government resettled indigenous communities from the Coco River and imposed strict controls on regional travel and the press.

Backed by Argentina and the United States, Fagoth's organization joined the FDN; Rivera united with Edén Pastora and Alfonso Robelo's Democratic Revolutionary Alliance (Alianza Revolucionaria Democrática, ARDE) in 1982.

As noted, MISURA launched major counterrevolutionary operations by late 1981. The objective was to create Vietnam-style strategic hamlets throughout the Atlantic coast region that could function as supply networks for FDN forces. At the same time, they would facilitate the recruitment of combatants and collaborators into the anti-Sandinista movement. Miskito forces increased to about four thousand men by 1982–1983. With the decisive support of the Honduran military and the United States (which conducted various naval and air exercises in the area in conjunction with Honduras, for instance, *Halcón Vista* in 1981 and Big Pine I in 1983), MISURA forces increased their attacks against economic targets in the region. Strategically, the goal was to establish a powerful military presence in the area while exacerbating the confrontation between local communities and the central administration.[138] The incorporation of the ethnic minorities into the venture permitted the FDN to open another front along the Honduran-Nicaraguan border in the Miskito region of Gracias a Dios.[139] Argentine advisers continued training MISURA forces throughout 1983.[140]

The Style of Argentine Training

The Argentine-led training of anti-Sandinista forces was centered on guerrilla warfare and a few elements of semiconventional operations, such as techniques in the use of explosives and demolition. As the military confrontation escalated, the instruction began to focus more on semiconventional tactics and less on small ambushes and hit-and-run attacks. However, soon after that shift the Argentines were replaced by U.S. advisers. "We combined their [Argentine] instruction with our experience in the mountains and gradually moved into more army-style and less guerrilla-type operations," a former Contra commander told me. "The Argentines trained us more specifically on guerrilla and sabotage actions. They transferred to us their background in counterguerrilla warfare while they learned from our guerrilla experience in the Nicaraguan mountains."[141]

The training provided by the Argentines included guerrilla and counterguerrilla tactics and strategy (hit-and-run attacks, mobile warfare, and war by ambush), sabotage, some forms of offensive operations, psychological warfare, the use of light arms (such as rifles and small-caliber machine guns) and some heavier weapons (larger-caliber machine guns, 81-mm and 82-mm mortars, and light artillery), the use of explosives, demolition, directional finding techniques, river navigation, mapping, survival techniques, the attributes of command, movement of troops, administrative and military leadership, and military intelligence.

Each course was focused on a set of specific military skills, tailored to suit the group of trainees. Courses varied in terms of theoretical or practical emphasis. Teams of up to ten Argentine officers provided the courses, which lasted from three to six months. They were held in Honduras-based training camps (Sagitario, Quinta Escuela, Lepaterique, and others) throughout early 1984, when the Argentines were replaced by U.S. instructors, most of them Vietnam veterans, and Latino advisers, mainly Cuban Americans.

The Argentine experience in the dirty war played a critical role in the instruction of the Contras. As Sobalvarro told me, "they were very honest about their experience in fighting rural and urban guerrillas in Argentina. They acknowledged their mistakes so that we would not repeat them. Most of their errors, the Argentines said, had been a result of overconfidence, particularly in urban areas, where the guerrillas could easily sabotage military and police installations."[142]

Special Forces and Psychological Warfare

The Argentine operation in Central America had a substantial direct and indirect impact on the anti-Sandinista armed movement. Argentine advisers were directly responsible for the training of more than two thousand Contra combatants and they also trained many of the leading Nicaraguan instructors and field commanders, as well as Honduran special forces, the Cobras and Tesones (see chapter 3).[143]

In early 1982, a team of Argentine advisers at the Lepaterique base offered specialized courses on the use of explosives and demolition. They organized a special commando team for the first major sabotage operations inside Nicaragua. The select group, under Argentine leadership, conducted several actions designed to destroy military and civilian infrastructure in Nicaragua.[144] The first action took place in March 1982, when the Contra team blew up the bridges at Río Negro and Ocotal in northern Nicaragua to impede the movement of tanks and heavy machinery to Chinandega.[145] The Argentines designed these early operations with CIA intelligence. As a former Contra commander put it, "based on the appropriate information, the Argentine advisers trained the commandos, supervised the preparations, and led the infiltration missions."[146] After the Argentines left the field in early 1984, one of the objectives of instruction by U.S. advisers was built on the guerrilla warfare courses given by the Argentines as well as on their training and guidance in the use of explosives and demolition.[147]

A key feature of the Argentine instruction was an emphasis on psychological warfare. "The Argentines prepared us primarily for sabotage and psychological operations. They talked about the origins of Communism and the fact that the Sandinista regime was the cornerstone for Communism in Central America, and Nicaragua the basis for its expansion throughout the region," Sobalvarro told me. "They stressed the importance of psychological action and sabotage to defeat the enemy. We were taught that it was crucial to detect the enemy's weaknesses as a basis for a comprehensive politico-military strategy."

The strategy was to be centered on different types of operations; namely, quick and decisive attacks designed to cause major human and material losses to the enemy, and propaganda and counterpropaganda actions designed to gain the support of the population and, at the same time, instill fear among rural inhabitants. "The Argentines," Sobalvarro said, "told us to show peasants our military capabilities and to introduce fear among them by talking about murders and torture committed by the Sandinista military, and by stressing that if they continued to support the Sandinista government, they would lose their homes and land, thus becoming state vassals."[148] Great emphasis was placed on infusing anti-Communist sentiments among the peasantry:

> "If we don't stop the Sandinista aggression now," we told the local population, "we'll soon have to fight against the Honduran and Costa Rican people." We said that the Sandinistas did not want peace: the proof of that was their support to the Salvadoran guerrillas. We also showed the peasants Soviet-made weapons captured from the EPS as proof that the Sandinistas were Soviet proxies and that the Cubans were invading Nicaragua to impose their political system.[149]

Under Argentine leadership, there was a decisive attempt to give the anti-Sandinista movement an ideological tone. Such effort to impose a conscious ideological purpose on the armed struggle through indoctrination at all levels was lessened when the United States replaced the Argentines as main advisers to the Contras. Several Contra civilian field commanders pointed out that the main problem of the opposition was that it grew into a military force and not into a politico-ideological guerrilla movement like the Sandinistas. "One of our key weaknesses was the lack of ideological cadres," said a Contra leader. "Most of the field commanders were men involved only in military operations, without any training to disseminate their cause among the population. There had been minimal ideological training provided by the Argentines, but only to the military command structure."[150]

Tensions at the local community level usually determined a population's decision whether or not to join or support the counterrevolution: "A majority of the rank and file did not know what they were fighting for. Most of them joined our forces because of resentment over specific incidents, such as the murder of a relative or the rape of their mother or sister. We failed to build up a commonly accepted set of beliefs upon that initial resentment."[151] It is important to point out that most of the former guardsmen in leadership positions saw no need to indoctrinate the peasants because, in their view, the peasants were already expressing their voice by volunteering as anti-Sandinista combatants.[152]

Millions of Dollars Not Accounted For

After Argentina's return to democracy in December 1983, its support for the Contras waned. U.S. involvement became pervasive. In sum, by deploying a relatively small number of expert advisers in the area, the Argentines had created the core of what became one of the most powerful counterrevolutionary armies in the Third World.

At the time the CIA took effective control of the program, approximately one-third of all the positions in the FDN command structure were held by former national guardsmen or civilians who had received training from Argentine advisers or from Nicaraguan, Honduran, Guatemalan, or Salvadoran personnel instructed by Argentines.[153] Most of the key military strategic positions in the FDN, including the strategic commander, were held by Argentine-trained former national guardsmen.

In addition, Argentine military personnel were directly and indirectly involved in the instruction of several field commanders at different levels of the Contra military structure: regional commands (500 to 1,200 combatants), task forces (250 combatants), companies (120 combatants), groups (60 combatants), and detachments (20 combatants). Argentine advisers also trained Miskito forces and former guardsmen (some of them in Buenos Aires) assigned to instruct MISURA troops in Honduras.

The Argentine involvement in the war against the Sandinista regime, initiated in light of a perceived U.S. abdication of responsibility in hemispheric security under the Carter administration, revealed a strategy designed to offer the Nicaraguan counterrevolutionaries an alternative source of military and political support. As the next chapter shows, the Argentine efforts were designed to attain major dimensions. In fact, officials appointed by the Raúl Alfonsín administration in 1983 found military records at Argentina's Defense Ministry revealing that millions of dollars had been secretly injected into the Central American operation without any financial accounting.[154]

In the 1980s, following Reagan's election as president, the collaboration between Argentina and the United States was grounded on concurrent views of the Third World as an arena of an East-West confrontation. Both the United States and Argentina claimed that such conflict demanded decisive military action to counteract perceived Soviet expansionism. Threats to national security were viewed as inspired by international Communism. The Reagan administration's option for covert action as the most effective way to destabilize the Sandinista government coincided with the Argentine objective of secretly organizing an exile army that could engage in guerrilla operations within Nicaraguan territory.

In conclusion, it can be noted that national security principles and the leading role of the intelligence apparatus were key features of the Argentine extraterritorial operations. The network of largely autonomous and powerful intelligence services that had emerged as an autonomous core within the Argentine authoritarian state developed a broad counterrevolutionary program in Central

America. In collaboration with the CIA, the Argentines organized a rebel army characterized by corruption and brutality. As part of this effort, the Argentine advisers provided the Nicaraguan Contras with their expertise in unconventional warfare. Such know-how, combined with the traditional ruthlessness of Somoza's former guards, led to gross violations of human rights, in a war that devastated Nicaragua and deepened that country's social tensions.

Argentine military junta members Jorge R. Videla, Emilio Massera, and Orlando Agosti (*from left to right*). (Courtesy Presidencia de la Nación, Secretaría de Información Pública)

Gen. Carlos G. Suárez Mason, a key actor in Argentina's anti-Communist crusade and its web of illegal transnational operations. (Courtesy *Página 12*)

Raúl Guglielminetti, head of Army Intelligence Battalion 601's Extra-territorial Task Force. (Courtesy *Página 12*)

Intelligence operative Leandro Sánchez Reisse (*center*) served as administrator of the Argentine task force based in Florida. (Courtesy *Página 12*)

Former National Guard Col. Enrique Bermúdez, commander of the Nicaraguan Democratic Force (FDN). (Courtesy *Barricada*)

Strongman Gustavo Alvarez Martínez (*center, background*) was responsible for the implementation of the "Argentine method" of repression in Honduras. (Courtesy *Barricada*)

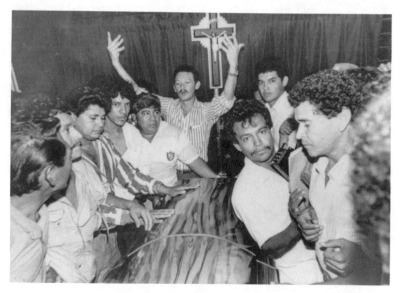

Oscar Sobalvarro (*background, raising his arms*) at the funeral of Bermúdez in February 1991. Sobalvarro was one of the first leaders of the MILPAS (Popular Anti-Sandinista Militias). (Courtesy *Barricada*)

Trained in Argentina in the 1970s, Rodolfo Ampié Quiróz (*left*) would become FDN's head of psychological warfare and a CIA favorite.

Former National Guard Sgt. Mariano Morales, one of the Nicaraguan Contras trained in Argentina in spring 1981. Morales, who would become chief of the FDN's military police, was accused of torture and rape by the Nicaraguan Association for Human Rights, a non-governmental organization funded by the U.S. State Department. (Photo by author)

Argentine-trained José Benito Bravo Centeno (*left*) with Argentine Lt. Col. (ret.) Santiago Hoya (alias Villegas) in a training camp in Honduras. Bravo, a former guardsman, was a vicious Contra commander involved in several murders. Hoya was chief of logistics and military operations of the Argentine general staff based in Honduras. (Courtesy *Patria Libre*)

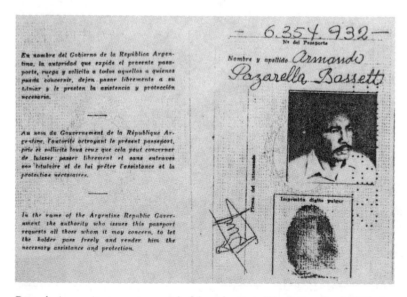

Bravo's Argentine passport with false identity. (Courtesy *Patria Libre*)

In March 1982, Argentine-led Contra commandos blew up a bridge on the Río Negro in northern Nicaragua. (Courtesy *Barricada*)

At a press conference, President Daniel Ortega shows a photograph of the bridge destroyed by the Contras. In response to the increasing pressure of the Contra war, the Sandinista government decreed a state of emergency. (Courtesy *Barricada*)

Honduran officers receiving military training at the U.S. School of the Americas in the Panama Canal Zone (1982). (Courtesy *Barricada*)

A Contra base camp near the Honduran-Nicaraguan border. (Courtesy *Barricada*)

Chapter 5

A Clandestine World: Central America in the Era of the Contras

THE CLANDESTINE NATURE of the cooperation between governments (and nongovernment interests) in the Central American counterrevolutionary effort drove these political actors to establish ad hoc transnational links. Grounded in shared perceptions of the situation, all the players hoped to improve their chances of influencing the political and security outcomes in the region. The unstable situation stimulated the convergence of governments and nongovernmental actors around the anti-Sandinista armed movement, creating a multifaceted network of interactions. These alliances played a key role in advancing the covert counterinsurgency program. The initial attempts to reorganize the remnants of the Nicaraguan national guard were aided by transnational political processes based on specific regional interests and attitudes.[1]

The cooperation between governments and pressure groups was centered primarily on the exchange of information, the mobilization of economic and military resources, and the coordination of operational plans. But the paramount result of these multiple interactions was the development of the informal transnational network itself. The support structure for right-wing actors, based on the principle of so-called anti-Communism, resulted in effective collaboration across national boundaries.

The groups involved, whether directly or indirectly, in the initial phase of the imbroglio were of various types. Nonstate actors played a major role in linking the domestic Contra movement to transnational networks. There were:

1. specific-issue groups (these were among the most important sponsors of the anti-Sandinista venture)—World Anti-Communist League (WACL) and its Latin American chapter, the Latin American Anti-Communist Confederation (Confederación Anticomunista Latinoamericana, CAL), Cuban exile organizations Omega 7 and Alpha 66, the Free Costa Rica Movement (Movimiento Costa Rica Libre, MCRL), and the Italian Masonic lodge Propaganda Due (P-2);
2. right-wing religious organizations, including the Reverend Sun Myung Moon's Unification Church and its political arm the Confederation of Associations for the Unity of the Societies of America (CAUSA), and the U.S.-based Gospel Outreach and the Moral Majority;
3. political parties—particularly, Guatemala's National Liberation Movement (Movimiento de Liberación Nacional, MLN), El Salvador's Nationalist Republican Alliance (Alianza Republicana Nacionalista, ARENA), and the U.S. Senate Republican Conference;
4. economic groups—companies and financial institutions, primarily from Argentina, such as Ingenio Ledesma, Bridas, Special Developments Enterprise (Empresa de Desarrollos Especiales, EDESA), and Transporte Aéreo Rioplatense (TAR).[2]

The source of strength of these groups could be found not only in their capacity, in some cases, to mobilize significant economic or coercive resources, but also in the intense personal commitment of their members. This resulted from political beliefs, expressed primarily as anti-Communism and loyalty to the Western and Christian order, and the lack of bureaucratic constraints. Members had the possibility of operating under unorthodox procedures, with greater flexibility and swiftness than governments, free from the obligation to obtain periodic approval from authorities.

The Intelligence Angle

Support to the Sandinistas since the late 1970s from various revolutionary and national liberation movements, and the involvement of external state actors in Somoza's counterinsurgency war during the same period, had given the Nicaraguan revolution a geopolitical dimension. The efforts of external actors to aid Nicaraguan rebel groups in their challenge to the Sandinista regime accentuated that element of the conflict. The rise of revolutionary activity in El Salvador and Guatemala, as well as the increasing involvement of Honduras and Costa Rica in regional conflicts, turned Central America, and particularly Nicaragua, into a surrogate for multiple geopolitical confrontations; namely, the Argentine military regime versus the revolutionary organizations Montoneros and People's Revolutionary Army (Ejército Revolucionario del Pueblo, ERP), Israel versus the Palestine Liberation Organization (PLO), and Cuban exiles versus the Communist regime of Fidel Castro.[3] In the case of Argentina, the military's concern was not focused on a possible Argentine guerrilla offensive out of Nicaragua—because both the Montoneros and ERP had been defeated by late 1979—but on the possibility of "subversive intelligence operations" against the Argentine military regime launched from Nicaragua.[4]

The collaboration among Latin American military intelligence services and their ties with domestic nongovernmental actors, particularly businessmen and anti-Communist organizations, helped to mobilize material and organizational resources in the initial phase of the counterrevolutionary effort. As already noted, per-

sonal connections played a decisive role in the alliance, mainly because of intense personal loyalties resulting from socialization and
recruitment. For instance, Central American officers trained in
Argentine military academies (Colegio Militar and Escuela Superior de Guerra) in the early 1960s played significant roles in the organization of the paramilitary opposition to the Sandinista
regime.[5] Also, the U.S. School of the Americas in the Panama
Canal Zone played a critical role in establishing continentwide
anti-Communist networks among Latin American officers,
trained there in intelligence techniques in the 1960s and 1970s.[6]

Spies, Guns, and Drugs: Argentina's Extraterritorial Apparatus

The internationalization of the Argentine counterinsurgency
apparatus required the development of autonomous intelligence
units. They had to operate out of bases outside the country and
establish connections with transnational networks.

Army Intelligence Battalion 601, a unit with extensive formal
and informal capabilities, established extraterritorial bases primarily in the United States. Key bases of operations were established
in Florida, where the Argentines had broad contacts. Their activities thus eased, the Argentine intelligence unit was able to operate
efficiently, maintaining its budget, plans, and personnel both secretly and autonomously. The establishment of headquarters in
the United States for operations in Central America also facilitated
the connection between Argentine agents and the U.S. espionage
apparatus.

The Task Force Headquarters in Florida

Having decided to play a role in countering the revolutionary
threat in Latin America, the Argentine military leadership knew
that, for the decisions of the central structure in Buenos Aires to
be carried out, a covert apparatus had to be established through-

out the hemisphere. This was the rationale for the organization of a special intelligence unit, the Extraterritorial Task Force (Grupo de Tareas Exterior), created as an extension of Army Intelligence Battalion 601.

The sensitive nature of the task force's activities, which included arms trafficking and drug-related money laundering, prompted the Argentine high command to establish the task force's headquarters in Florida, an exceptionally convenient location given the connivance of U.S. government security agencies regarding Argentine covert operations in the United States.[7]

The Carter administration was still in office when, in 1978, the Argentine military regime established operational bases in Miami and Fort Lauderdale with the objective of coordinating financial transactions, arms shipments, intelligence operations, and counterinsurgency training. According to testimony given to the U.S. Senate Foreign Relations Committee by Leandro Sánchez Reisse, a former Argentine army intelligence agent, the CIA authorized Argentine covert activities in the United States.[8] As noted earlier (see chapter 2), Sánchez Reisse said that he dealt directly with CIA agents when serving as administrator of the task force.[9]

The CIA's collaboration with Argentinean intelligence operatives before Reagan's inauguration indicates that, even during the Carter administration, the CIA was involved in an unauthorized operation. The CIA's involvement, under Carter, in a counterrevolutionary effort promoted by the Argentine military is a key illustration of the autonomy with which this agency operated. The role of the CIA in the early promotion of counterrevolutionary reaction in Nicaragua went well beyond Carter's much criticized attempt to preserve Somoza's ruthless National Guard after the collapse of the dictator's regime.[10]

The Argentinean task force was headed by a civilian intelligence agent, Raúl Antonio Guglielminetti. His immediate superiors in Buenos Aires were Battalion 601's Col. Raúl A. Gatica and two colonels in the First Army Corps, Roberto L. Roualdés and

Enrique C. Ferro.[11] A former Triple A member linked to the fascist Andes Group (a continentwide intelligence program aimed at detecting and capturing political dissidents),[12] Guglielminetti had been recruited into Battalion 601 in the mid-1970s. During the dirty war in Argentina, he operated in clandestine detention centers in Neuquén and Buenos Aires Provinces.[13]

Both Guglielminetti and Sánchez Reisse received intelligence training in the United States in 1976.[14] They worked for the Intelligence Advisory Committee (Comunidad Informativa), the interforce network that coordinated the clandestine repressive apparatus in Argentina. The Intelligence Advisory Committee had its core in Army Intelligence Battalion 601 and Police Federal Security (Coordinación Federal), with support from the intelligence services of the navy and the air force. Linked to Latin American military intelligence services, the United States Defense Intelligence Agency (DIA), and the CIA, this sophisticated Argentinean structure was professedly aimed at confronting "a systematic and integrated network of communist terrorist organizations in Latin America."[15] Actually, it became the hub of a vast ultraright network directly involved in illegal activities and supported by Latin American military regimes and U.S. government agencies.[16]

The Argentinean Front Companies

From 1978 to 1981, the Florida-based Argentine intelligence unit arranged foreign currency transactions and shipments of weapons and special military equipment to support the Argentine counterrevolutionary program in Central America. During that period, Argentine front companies handled more than $30 million from accounts in the United States, Switzerland, the Bahamas, the Grand Cayman Islands, Liechtenstein, and Panama.[17]

The Argentines set up dummy corporations in most of those countries, handling transactions in cash or wire transfer by code. This operation allowed them to purchase weapons and sophisticated equipment that could not be obtained through normal channels. The Argentines purchased arms and military equipment from sources as diverse as East Germany, Britain, Taiwan, Thailand, and South Korea.[18]

Guglielminetti's front business, the Silver Dollar, a coin and pawn shop in Miami, conducted traffic in weapons and served as a center of operations for the Argentine task force. Weapons were purchased mainly from Cuban American sources and then shipped to Central America and Panama with the knowledge of the U.S. government.[19] A key liaison in this venture was CIA operative John Hull, a U.S. rancher whose airstrip in Costa Rica was used for the Contra resupply network and cocaine trafficking.[20] Reportedly, Hull had worked for the CIA in Brazil between 1974 and 1976, being involved in clandestine operations that included kidnappings and assassinations.[21] Testimony was given about meetings between Guglielminetti and Hull dating back at least to 1980, when the two agents met in Costa Rica to discuss the impact of revolutionary Nicaragua in Central America and financial aspects of the Argentine enterprise.[22]

Sánchez Reisse's cover was a company called Argenshow, whose ostensible business was to book presentations for U.S. entertainers in Argentina. Argenshow, located in Fort Lauderdale, had been initially incorporated in New York in 1977 by Sánchez Reisse's attorney, Norman Faber, an associate in the law firm of William Casey, director of intelligence under President Reagan.[23]

The Argentines often utilized the services of the exchange firm Deak Perera and Crédit Suisse Bank.[24] In 1982, Deak Perera was involved in a financial scandal related to money laundering.[25] Reportedly, the corporation's general manager, Raúl del Cristo, was closely linked to Ramón Milián Rodríguez, a Cuban American money launderer for the Colombian drug cartels.[26] In turn, Crédit Suisse Bank played an important role in the Iran-Contra affair; "funds from all parties to the Iran arms sales flowed into and out of this bank, as did the majority of funds used in the Contra resupply operations."[27] The Iranian government, Iranian arms dealer Manucher Ghorbanifar, and several of the companies that made up Oliver North's Enterprise had accounts in Crédit Suisse Bank.[28]

The Florida-based Extraterritorial Task Force cooperated with the Argentine navy's Pilot Center in Paris.[29] Created in 1977, the center gathered data on Argentine opposition groups in Europe, infiltrated human rights organizations, and produced propaganda materials to improve the military regime's international image.[30]

The Underworld

The international network set up by Argentine military intelligence served as a conduit for drug and arms trafficking, money laundering, and terrorist activities, well beyond the original purpose of rolling back the Communist threat in the Western Hemisphere. In Argentina, the development of an autonomous intelligence apparatus with the capability to carry out vast secret operations had a strong impact on civil and political society; in fact, it became a threat to the democratic government inaugurated in 1983. The solidification of clandestine centers of power internally by the state created a strong informal apparatus that escaped control by governmental agencies or civil society.[31]

The operatives in charge of the financial activities of the Argentine extraterritorial intelligence apparatus, chiefly Sánchez Reisse and Guglielminetti, had been previously involved in the war against so-called economic subversion during Argentina's dirty war.[32] One of the targets of that effort was the financial empire headed by Argentine banker David Graiver.[33] The military accused Graiver of handling Montonero funds collected through kidnappings and extortion of Argentine businessmen. The investigation of the Graiver holdings and other corporations presumed to be linked to the guerrilla movement was conducted by Army Intelligence Battalion 601. Claiming to be fighting subversion, high-ranking Battalion 601 officers plundered the assets of several businessmen and stockholders who were abducted by security forces.[34] This criminal ring was significantly expanded when Battalion 601 internationalized its intelligence and financial operations in the late 1970s.

Other Actors, Other Agendas

The Argentine involvement in Central America was abetted by a number of actors who, the political situation in the region having become important to them, decided to engage in informal interactions across boundaries. In some cases, these players implemented their programs independently from the Argentines, as was the case of Israel, which was pursuing its own geopolitical agenda but immediately perceived the advantage of cooperating with the Argentines in the Central American counterinsurgency effort. In other cases, the Cuban-exile network for instance, the anti-Sandinista venture was seen as a necessary battle in the war against Castro's Cuba. Specific-issue groups (e.g., WACL-CAL) were the source of a strong ideological-conspiratorial movement committed to defeat what was perceived as a multifaceted international enemy threatening Western society. The anti-Communist network was intertwined with decision makers in the countries involved in the counterrevolutionary war. This network showed an exceptional capacity to mobilize nongovernmental resources throughout Latin America.

Israel

When the Carter administration suspended all military assistance to Argentina in 1978 because of the regime's gross violations of human rights, Israel emerged as an alternative arms supplier to the Argentine armed forces. From 1978 to 1983, Israel exported to Argentina military equipment worth more than a billion dollars, including Mirage-5 Dassault fighters, Mirage-3C (Dagger) fighters, U.S.-made A-4 Skyhawks, Gabriel missiles, and equipment for internal security. Mossad, Israel's foreign intelligence agency, sent advisers to Argentina to train army officers.[35] Israel also shared counterinsurgency intelligence with the Argentine army; for instance, intelligence on Montonero combatants training at PLO camps in Lebanon for "the final counteroffensive" against the military regime in Argentina.[36]

Israeli embassy and Mossad officials had close links with Gen. Albano Harguindeguy, Argentina's minister of the interior. Harguindeguy arranged for Israeli intelligence personnel to use federal police facilities for shooting practices; in exchange, the Israelis provided the task forces that operated out of the Ministry of the Interior with ammunition and sophisticated police equipment.[37] In addition to running repressive operations against "subversives," Harguindeguy commanded an extortion-kidnapping ring, using the operational capabilities of his ministry. Paradoxically, Jewish businessmen were preferred victims of such practices.[38] Israeli intelligence services actively cooperated with the Argentines in internal security during the years of the dirty war.[39]

Israeli officials in Argentina also had close relations with Intelligence Battalion 601. The Israeli ambassador and 601 operative Sánchez Reisse held several meetings in Buenos Aires (Argenshow, Sánchez Reisse's covert business in Fort Lauderdale, collaborated with the Israelis and, on many occasions, Battalion 601 agents provided "security" for Israeli diplomats). The Israeli embassy in San José, Costa Rica, supplied false passports to Argentine advisers working undercover in Honduras and assisted Central American anti-Communist extremists closely linked to the Argentines and the Nicaraguan Contras.[40]

Israeli military experts collaborated with the Argentine forces involved in the July 1980 cocaine coup in Bolivia. The Argentine military, particularly the army and the navy, played a major role in the coup d'état that installed a gangster state in that country under the command of Gen. Luis García Meza and his interior minister, Luis Arce Gómez (see chapter 1). Argentine military intelligence units, which operated out of the headquarters of the Bolivian high command, received assistance from Israeli advisers in the vast repressive campaign associated with the coup.[41]

But Israel seems to have had a two-track approach to the Argentine military regime. The Argentine junta was well known for anti-Semitism and particularly vicious treatment of Jewish political prisoners, and Israel subordinated its concern for the well-being of the Jewish community in Argentina to political and commercial considerations. However, the Israeli government also was secretly involved, via operations run by the Mossad, in saving hundreds of Jews, but not all, from being disappeared by the Argentine security forces.[42]

I have evidence in my files that the Argentine regime played a role in the U.S. program covertly to arm Iran with the help of Israel. The Argentine military's involvement in the Iran arms deal supplemented its extraterritorial activities in Central America and possibly strengthened its relations with the Reagan administration. In 1981, Israel and Argentina took part in a secret deal between the Israelis and the Khomeini regime involving the provision of 360 tons of U.S.-made spare parts for tanks and ammunition for the revolutionary forces in Iran. Argentina provided the air-cargo facilities for the operation.[43]

In spring 1981, an Israeli cover firm sold $27.9 million-worth of military equipment to Iran. The twelve planeloads of supplies were to be flown from Tel Aviv to Tehran via Larnaca, Cyprus, by an Argentine freight company, Transporte Aéreo Rioplatense (TAR).[44] The contract between the TAR airline and the British middlemen working for the Israelis read, "Charterer specifically declares that cargo involved is ammunition. . . . The parties hereto agree that the route to be operated under the terms and conditions of this agreement shall be: Ben Gurion (Israel)/Larnaca (Cyprus)/Tehran (Iran), and vice versa."[45]

The Argentine TAR freighter company, with offices in Argentina, Switzerland, Panama, and the United States, was owned by high-ranking air force officers retired from active service and closely linked to the air force high command. The freight company was allegedly controlled by an air force brigadier general, Rodolfo Aquilino Guerra, and his associates.[46] Identified as a dependable company for confidential cargo operations, TAR grew rapidly, drawing its profits mainly from arms trafficking. In the period 1979 to 1980, TAR had a gross income of $30 million. According to some reports, TAR served as a contract freight company for the CIA.[47]

On July 18, 1981, a TAR airline plane transporting military equipment to Iran crashed near Yerevan, in the former Soviet Union, after reportedly straying over the Soviet-Turkish border and being intercepted by Soviet jet fighters. According to an official from the Cyprus Civil Aviation Department, the Argentine CL-44 turboprop cargo plane had made four stopovers in Cyprus on trips between Tel Aviv and Tehran during the first half of 1981.[48] This incident was not the only hard proof of the involvement of the Argentine freighter company in secret Israeli arms dealing: as noted in chapter 3, in 1977, the government of Barbados had seized a TAR airline cargo plane carrying Israeli arms and ammunition to Guatemala.[49]

Israel's aggressive arms export drive in Latin America in the late 1970s, coupled with its self-perceived role as U.S. surrogate in the region, in a way similar to Argentina, were key sources of Israeli involvement in Central America.[50] Its existing role in the region at the outset of the Reagan administration strengthened Israel's rationale that "it could increase its leverage over Washington by performing indispensable functions for the United States in third countries."[51] In addition, Israel's growing concern over the use of Nicaragua as an operational base for PLO agents working in Central America drove it to increase its intelligence and advisory activities in the region.[52]

Israeli advisers collaborated in the development of a counterinsurgency strategy in El Salvador, Guatemala, and Honduras. Israeli police and internal security assistance was focused on improving the effectiveness of local security forces, mainly their competence in intelligence work. The Central American security forces, according to Israeli training personnel, were "very emotional and cause unnecessary deaths among their prisoners."[53] The Israelis taught them more effective methods of interrogation. When the Reagan administration came to office in 1981, Israeli experts in counterinsurgency became involved in the training of former Nicaraguan guardsmen in Honduras, possibly in collaboration with Argentine officers.[54] When Argentina officially pulled out of Central America after the Falklands/Malvinas war (and before the CIA assumed total control of the Contra program) the CIA attempted, unsuccessfully, to convince Israel to assume that role.[55]

Miami-Based Cuban Exiles

A number of Cuban exile organizations provided direct and indirect assistance to anti-Sandinista activities following the collapse of the Somoza regime. In the early phase of the counterrevolutionary effort, the Miami-based Cubans played a major role as intermediaries between the exiled Nicaraguan national guard officers and several individuals and organizations interested in rolling back the Communist tide in the Caribbean Basin. Veterans of the anti-Castro movement made initial contacts between the Nicaraguan guardsmen and the Argentine operatives in Florida. Those links were crucial for the development of an Argentine-supervised armed movement to oppose the Sandinista regime.

As disclosed by Battalion 601 operative Sánchez Reisse, the Cuban exile network, particularly terrorist organizations Omega 7 and Alpha 66, served as initial liaisons between the Argentines and the Nicaraguan guardsmen exiled in the United States.[56] Argentine operatives, Sánchez Reisse said, were "in contact with Alpha 66, Omega 7 . . . [and] some of the Contras were part of those organizations."[57] Some Contras downplayed the significance of the Cuban exile support for the anti-Sandinista venture. In their view, the Cubans did not fulfill their promises of providing combatants and financial support to the anti-Sandinista cause. "The Cubans tend to run at the mouth," said a former Contra. "They never put their money where their mouth is."[58]

The strong anti-Communism among Cuban exiles, who viewed Nicaragua as a bridge to the liberation of their country from Castro, helped to advance a broad front against the Sandinistas. Under such a coalition, the nationalistic objectives of many Nicaraguan dissidents were soon superseded by Miami's dominant anti-Communist ideology.[59] Anti-Communism was also a crucial bond between the Cubans and the Argentines. In the mid-1970s, Argentina's Triple A had developed strong ties with Cuban extremist terrorist groups. Ultraright Cubans also collaborated with the Argentine and other Southern Cone military regimes in the continentwide repressive enterprise known as Operation Condor.[60] A long-standing relationship between Argentine rightists and two leading members of the anti-Castro Cuban community, Jorge Más Canosa and Félix Rodríguez, eased the coordinating efforts of the anti-Sandinista operation. Rodríguez, a career CIA operative and major player in the Contra venture, had been secretly assigned to Buenos Aires in 1972 as special adviser to the First Army Corps on counterterror and low-intensity warfare.[61]

Like the Argentine military regime, Cuban exile extremist groups had advisers working with Somoza's national guard during the insurrectional period in Nicaragua. A team of Cuban exiles was directly involved in combat against the Sandinistas and some Cubans held high-ranking positions in Somoza's guard.[62] Following the Sandinista takeover in 1979, the Cuban community in

Miami was highly instrumental in providing exiled Nicaraguan guard officers with political and CIA contacts.[63]

During the early phase of the Contra venture, in which the Argentine task force in Florida handled the finances and arms shipments for the anti-Sandinista forces in Central America, the force maintained periodic contacts with Omega 7 and Alpha 66. Their collaboration was centered on exchange of information and arms trafficking.[64] Omega 7, a clandestine anti-Castro organization, had been involved in numerous terrorist acts against Cuban and pro-Cuban targets in the United States and Puerto Rico throughout the 1970s. The FBI considered Omega 7 "the most dangerous terrorist organization in the United States" at that time.[65] Three members of Omega 7 were indicted for the 1976 assassination of a former Chilean foreign minister and ambassador to the United States, Orlando Letelier, an action reportedly linked to Operation Condor. Two fugitives known as militants of Omega 7, José Dionisio Suárez and Pablo Paz Romero, were also accused of participating in the bombing murder of the former Chilean ambassador in Washington.[66] A former CIA agent offered evidence that Suárez worked in Guatemala (under Argentine auspices) helping to train anti-Sandinista rebels in 1980.[67]

Like Omega 7, the extremist organization Alpha 66 was charged with several terrorist acts in the United States.[68] The group was engaged in the anti-Sandinista military venture via its support of the guardsmen's training in the United States (the group reportedly controlled two training camps in Florida) and its involvement in the anti-Communist clandestine network in Costa Rica.[69]

Some evidence suggests a link between Argentine military intelligence and Mario Dellamico, a Miami-based Cuban exile arms dealer with multiple connections to the CIA, including a key CIA agent (and former adviser to Argentina), Félix Rodríguez.[70] Dellamico was the representative in Honduras of the U.S. arms dealership R. M. Equipment, which exported weapons from Miami to the Contras. The company was allegedly also involved in drug trafficking. One of its partners, Col. James L. McCoy, had been a former U.S. defense attaché in Managua during the final years of the Somoza regime.[71]

In 1980, Nicaraguan guardsmen began training in Cuban American camps in Florida. A year later, there were at least ten Nicaraguan paramilitary organizations undertaking commando training in the area.[72] Argentine officers were recruited in 1981 to train combatants in those U.S.-based camps.[73]

Most of the Nicaraguans trained in U.S.-based Cuban exile facilities joined the ranks of the National Liberation Army (Ejército de Liberación Nacional, ELN) and the Nicaraguan Democratic Union–Nicaraguan Revolutionary Armed Forces (Unión Democrática Nicaragüense–Fuerzas Armadas Revolucionarias Nicaragüenses, UDN-FARN).[74] These two anti-Sandinista groups merged into the Nicaraguan Democratic Force (Fuerza Democrática Nicaragüense, FDN) in late 1981.

The links between the Argentines and the Cuban exiles strengthened after the Reagan administration came to office. Eventually, when the United States bought into the Argentine Central American program in late 1981, it was a group of Cuban American businessmen linked to Omega 7 who purchased Guglielminetti's front business in Miami for arms-trafficking operations.[75]

The Anti-Communists

Argentina's extraterritorial program received financial support from the World Anti-Communist League (WACL) via the Latin American Anti-Communist Confederation (CAL).[76] Since its creation in 1966 "as public relations arm for the governments of Taiwan and South Korea," the WACL evolved into a powerful transnational network, operationally connected to multiple intelligence services worldwide. The league's South and Central American chapters experienced a significant growth in the late 1970s. Drawing its membership mainly from government officials, these chapters acquired extensive power capabilities, linking authoritarian regimes such as those of Argentina, Paraguay, Guatemala, El Salvador, and Honduras.[77]

General Suárez Mason, commander in chief of the Argentine First Army Corps and later head of the Joint Chiefs of Staff, was the visible liaison between the Argentine high command and CAL.[78] A key promoter of the Andes Group (see "The Task Force Headquarters in Florida" earlier in this chapter), Suárez Mason played a critical role in Argentina's military expansion throughout Latin America (particularly in the triangular narco-military operation Argentina-Bolivia-Central America).[79]

Using the principle of ideological frontiers (see chapter 1, "National Security and the Transition to Globalism"), the head of the powerful First Army Corps, in alliance with other hard-line officers who had been directly involved in Argentina's dirty war, launched an ambitious program of continental expansionism—armed, as they were, with autonomous power capabilities.[80] Having advocated the annihilation of all political dissent toward the military regime in Argentina, these hard-liners soon discovered the financial potential of the anti-Communist venture. Suárez Mason, said one analyst, "privatized the anti-Communist business."[81] He collected funds from diverse organizations and individuals identified with the anti-Communist cause, and secured the appropriate national and international channels to link the principle of ideological frontiers to the business of trafficking in drug and arms.

After retiring from active service, Suárez Mason was appointed director of the state oil monopoly, Yacimientos Petrolíferos Fiscales (YPF), where he played a central role in a multi-million-dollar clandestine business centered on the adulteration of gasoline and motor oil.[82] The fraudulent operation, which allegedly contributed to fund the Central American program, was carried out through a private company, Sol Petróleo S.A., and involved not only YPF but also two other state-owned enterprises, Fabricaciones Militares (Military Industries) and Petroquímica General Mosconi. In a two-year period (1980–1982), Sol Petróleo produced profits of nearly $1 billion, being at the time "the most lucrative illegal business after drug-trafficking."[83] Suárez Mason's aide in the operation was Maj. Hugo Raúl Miori Pereyra, secretary of the 1980 WACL-CAL convention in Buenos Aires and courier for the salaries of Argentine officers stationed in Central America. Sol Petróleo possibly served Suárez Mason and his entourage to launder drug money from the Bolivia–Central American operation.[84]

In September 1980, CAL held its Fourth Congress in Buenos Aires. Officially endorsed by the military governments of Argentina, Chile, Paraguay, Uruguay, and Bolivia, the convention's resolutions deplored the Sandinista takeover in Nicaragua and denounced President Carter's betrayal of Somoza. The delegates blamed the Carter administration for "favoring the advance of Marxism in Latin America and the so-called policy of human rights, using it as a political weapon against those governments who combat with efficiency communist subversion in all its forms."[85] The geopolitical views expressed at the meeting reflected those explicitly held by the Argentine military government, which claimed to be waging an ideological war without borders against Marxism, alongside the armed forces of the Southern Cone.[86]

The congress was chaired by Suárez Mason and financed by WACL and the Argentine army general staff.[87] Among the delegates to Buenos Aires were WACL president Woo Jae Sung, Paraguay's defense minister, Gen. Marcial Samaniego, death-squad leaders Mario Sandoval Alarcón (Guatemala) and Roberto D'Aubuisson (El Salvador), Italian terrorist Stefano delle Chiaie, and representatives from Alpha 66 and the Italian Masonic lodge Propaganda Due (P-2).[88] In his keynote address, Suárez Mason delineated a program for "halting the Brazilian *abertura*, blocking Uruguay's projected 'democratic' plans, wiping out the *ligas agrarias* in Paraguay, giving wholehearted support to the García Meza regime in Bolivia, [and] . . . [launching] a destabilization campaign against the [Fernando] Belaúnde Terry administration in Peru."[89] Following the July 1980 Argentine-backed coup in Bolivia, Peru had emerged as the new target in Argentina's geopolitical scheme for South America. Reportedly, Argentine military intelligence had found that Montonero guerrillas were establishing a new operational base in Peru, in collaboration with local revolutionary forces, thus creating what was perceived to be a potential threat to Argentina.[90]

John Carbaugh, a staffer to Republican Senator Jesse Helms and a central player in the U.S.-Argentine-Contra venture, and Margo Carlisle, legislative aide to another Senate Republican, James McClure, and staff director of the Senate Republican Conference, participated in the WACL-CAL congress in Buenos Aires as observers. Both U.S. delegates would play a critical role in repackaging the image of Salvadoran death-squad leader D'Aubuisson for the U.S. public. Carbaugh worked closely with D'Aubuisson to shape the idea of a viable anti-Communist party in El Salvador (ARENA) and provided him with important right-wing contacts in Washington. For her part, Carlisle met in Buenos Aires with Ricardo Valdivieso, one of D'Aubuisson's lieutenants, and arranged on his behalf several meetings with influential individuals in U.S. right-wing circles.[91]

The Reagan administration formally sanctioned these informal processes when it bought into the Argentine operation in Central America in 1981. When U.S. Rep. Michael Barnes, a Democrat, learned about the CIA plan to use Argentina in the organization of an anti-Sandinista armed movement, he communicated concern about the plan to Thomas Enders, assistant secretary for inter-American affairs. All the players in the operation, particularly the Argentines, were notorious for their ruthlessness. Enders assured Barnes that the operation would be strictly controlled and that there would be no human rights violations.[92]

The Costa Ricans

The ultrarightist Free Costa Rica Movement (MCRL), an anti-Communist paramilitary group with close links to WACL, as-sisted the Argentines in the organization of the anti-Sandinista program in Costa Rica. The extremist MCRL, which received economic assistance from the U.S. embassy in San José, demanded political tolerance in Nicaragua for anti-Sandinista exile organiza-tions and secretly abetted the Contra forces. The Costa Rican paramilitaries collaborated with the CIA and Argentine advisers in planning the attack on Radio Noticias del Continente in 1980 (see chapter 1, "The First Attack in Central America").[93]

Battalion 601 agent Héctor Francés was based in Costa Rica with the responsibility of establishing information networks and creating conditions for military actions against Nicaragua. Under the supervision of the Argentine general staff in Honduras and "the permanent oversight and direction of the CIA," Francés was assigned to set up FDN cells in Costa Rica, with the intention of building a viable anti-Sandinista military structure, independent of Edén Pastora, on the southern front.[94] Frustrated in his politi-cal aspirations and disenchanted with Sandinista politics, Pastora had left Nicaragua in 1981 and organized his own armed group (based in Costa Rica) to fight against the Sandinista regime.

Among Francés's key contacts were the aforementioned CIA operative John Hull, MCRL director Bernardo Urbina Pinto, and a Senator Helms aide, Nat Hamrick.[95] Francés disclosed in testi-mony before Sandinista authorities that he discussed with Ham-rick the need to impose economic pressures on the Costa Rican president, Luis Alberto Monge (1982–1986), via the International Monetary Fund (IMF) and the U.S. Agency for International De-velopment (AID). The aim was to guarantee that Monge "would ensure that Costa Rica provide us with the right conditions for the [anti-Sandinista] operations."[96] A month after his inauguration, Monge went to Washington to confirm his country's support for the Reagan administration's strategy in Central America, in exchange for badly needed U.S. economic assistance (Costa Rica was in its worst economic crisis at the time). By the end of 1982, a new $100 million IMF standby agreement was approved, and AID assistance to Costa Rica increased from $13 million in 1981 to $212 million in 1983.[97]

The Moonies and Others

Among the key groups that facilitated the interaction between the Argentine military regime and the anti-Communist network was CAUSA, created in 1980 as the political arm of Sun Myung Moon's Unification Church. Through CAUSA, the Unification Church participated in the Bolivian coup d'état and assisted the military regimes of El Salvador and Guatemala, as well as the Nicaraguan Contras. Reportedly, CAUSA contributed with funds, lobbying efforts on behalf of those governments and the Contras, and propaganda activities. The Moonie organization was also an important bridge between the U.S. New Right and the anti-Communist network, including U.S.-based Religious Right organizations that lobbied for congressional appropriations for the Contras.[98] These groups tried to influence U.S. public opinion by denouncing alleged religious persecution by the Sandinista government.[99]

Another sponsor of the Argentine Central American program was P-2, the Italian Masonic lodge Propaganda Due. This powerful political and business network was interwoven with the transnational anti-Communist movement and involved in the international financial black market and arms-trafficking business.

The lodge's objective in Italy was the development of a parallel state apparatus encompassing the political, financial, and military spheres. An Italian prosecutor defined P-2 as "a secret association that pursued illegal political ends and aimed at modifying the state's structure via crimes that threatened the public order."[100]

The lodge sought to dominate key sectors of Italy's political and social arenas, building its power on control of the intelligence services. By 1977, a majority of high-ranking intelligence officials were P-2 members.[101]

Led by its grand master, a former Fascist official, Licio Gelli, the P-2 lodge built a parallel network in Latin America, centered in Argentina and Uruguay, avowedly aimed at serving as a safety net to prevent Communists from coming to power in the region. An influential member of Juan Domingo Perón's entourage, Gelli was a close associate of Triple A founder José López Rega, Admiral Emilio Massera, and General Suárez Mason. According to Massera, the grand master "helped us in the anti-subversive struggle and in promoting our image abroad."[102] It has been suggested that Gelli supplied Massera with funds to purchase urban counterinsurgency equipment for the Navy Mechanics School's task force 3.3.2.[103]

With the establishment in Buenos Aires of the Banco Ambrosiano, headed by Gelli's partner Roberto Calvi, investments in Argentina linked to P-2 greatly increased in the late 1970s. While fighting against Communism, Gelli and his navy and army partners became involved in highly profitable public construction contracts and purchases of sophisticated military equipment from Italy.[104] The P-2 lodge was reportedly linked to the South American drug-trafficking network and to the kidnapping ring led by Suárez Mason.[105] There is also a report of close ties between Gelli and Argentina's Florida-based task force, particularly with Battalion 601 agent Sánchez Reisse.[106]

Private Finance from Argentina

Argentine financiers and businessmen contributed to fund the secret operations of Battalion 601 in Central America. A prominent entrepreneur in Buenos Aires funded the expenses of fifty

Central American officers who received counterinsurgency instruction in Argentina at the end of 1980.[107]

As disclosed by Sánchez Reisse, Argentine businessman Carlos Pedro Blaquier, whose Ingenio Ledesma in Tucumán Province was one of Argentina's major sugar processing factories, supplied $250,000 for the counterrevolutionary operation in Central America. Blaquier's motive for funding the anti-Sandinista effort, Sánchez Reisse said, was that "one of the members of his family was kidnapped by the Montoneros in Argentina, so he likes to help the people who are on the other side of this."[108] Blaquier's business was linked to the scandal triggered by the fraudulent bankruptcy of Gelli's Banco Ambrosiano.[109]

One of Argentina's most powerful corporations, Bridas, was also linked to the extraterritorial campaign. Possibly it was one of the main private supporters.[110] Bridas, an oil business, was among the groups that benefited immensely from the economic policies of the military regime. During the authoritarian period, from 1976 to 1983, the Bridas group expanded from seven to forty-one companies. Like other major Argentine corporations, it transferred its massive foreign debt to the Argentine state.[111] Bridas tycoon Carlos Alberto Bulgheroni, allegedly a P-2 member, was closely linked to Massera and, particularly, to Suárez Mason, who served on the Bridas board of directors after retiring from active duty in late 1979. As noted earlier, as director of YPF he subsequently engineered an illegal multi-million-dollar business based on the adulteration of gasoline. Bridas was YPF's major contractor at the time.[112]

The Long-Term Domestic Impact on Argentina

One of the most striking features of the complex network of domestic and transnational organizations described in this chapter was its long-term impact on Argentina's constitutional state. That network reflected the existence of an "invisible power" (secret services, religious sects, Masonic lodges, drug trafficking, gunrunning, and kidnapping rings) parallel to the visible state and highly autonomous from the regime in which it developed.

The theme of invisible power, though largely neglected by social scientists, is highly significant in contemporary politics, because it refers to one of the central principles of the constitutional state; namely, that of *publicity*, in its fundamental meaning of "being open to public scrutiny." If secret power maintains its salience in a democratic regime, it conspires against the consolidation of that political system, because it precludes the openness of government and prevails as an influential antistate.[113]

The nontraditional phenomenon of invisible power includes the network of intelligence services and other secret organizations that has been termed by Norberto Bobbio as *cryptogovernment*, meaning "the totality of actions carried out by paramilitary political forces which operate behind the scenes in collaboration with the secret services, or with sections of them, or at least with their connivance."[114] The solidification and professionalization of the secret state in Argentina during the military period resulted in a power, allegedly omniscient, responsible to no one but itself, that remained basically untouched throughout the transition to democracy. The secret state (particularly the military apparatus of espionage) developed to repress the population at home was used for a similar aim abroad and, in turn, improved and deployed in the domestic realm later.[115]

Not only, in the postmilitary period, did intelligence personnel escape indictments, but they continued to operate as part of a powerful domestic network with strong international linkages. The processes described earlier accentuated, for the Argentine intelligence services, a continuing pattern of secrecy and lack of accountability. Their domestic activities have remained, to a large extent, impervious to any effective control by state agencies and evaluation by the legislature, the courts, and private citizens. As a result, the intelligence apparatus, which constitutes a key domain of the state coercive system and therefore one that should be subject to the democratic process, represents an important authoritarian enclave that poses serious limits to the deepening of democracy.[116]

The Argentine secret state also prevailed as the repository of knowledge on urban counterinsurgency. The Argentine knowhow developed during the dirty war and subsequently transferred to neighboring countries, especially Bolivia and countries in Central America, served as a highly valuable commodity into the 1990s. This was illustrated by the presence of Argentine experts on urban counterinsurgency in Chiapas, Mexico, in 1994. The Argentines were advising the Mexican security forces in their operations against the Zapatista National Liberation Army (Ejército Zapatista de Liberación Nacional, EZLN), the peasant guerrilla force that emerged on New Year's Day, 1994, precipitating a national crisis in Mexico. Following the EZLN uprising, a group of Mexican army and police officers traveled to Buenos Aires to receive intelligence training on counterinsurgency. Reportedly, the Mexicans were interested in learning about Argentina's successful guerrilla demobilizing effort in the 1970s.[117] Human rights reports on the Mexican army's full-scale military assault on the Zapatista rebels disclosed numerous cases of arbitrary arrests and detentions, disappearances, summary executions, and torture, including interrogation with the application of electroshock, the primary method used in the Argentine detention centers during the 1970s dirty war.[118]

Conclusion

The purpose of this book has been to examine the internationalization of Argentina's counterinsurgency apparatus in the late
1970s and early 1980s, with attention to that South American
country's involvement in the Central American conflict. Such an
investigation offers new insights into a significant, albeit hardly
studied, dimension of Argentina's repressive state apparatus. The
book also illuminates the role of covert action, whether officially
sanctioned or not, in shaping U.S. foreign policy in the hemisphere. Undoubtedly, this case of Argentina's extraterritorial activity not only provides a novel perspective of the country's repressive
apparatus under military dictatorship and an account of its cooperation with the United States, but it may also offer lessons for
further comparative analysis of counterrevolution, state-sponsored
violence, the dynamics of surrogacy, and transnational coalitions.
The book's main theses can be summarized as follows:

1. *Argentina's extraterritorial operations were carried out by those
elements of the authoritarian regime most directly involved in the
clandestine repressive campaign of the dirty war.*

The clandestine strategy adopted by the military regime contributed to increase the power and organizational autonomy of the
security community. These formal and informal attributes were
vital for the implementation of the extraterritorial program. State
violence resources no longer needed for internal control and the
annihilation of dissidents in Argentina were utilized to support

foreign governmental and nongovernmental actors perceived as ideological allies.

2. *The transfer of repressive technology to military and paramilitary forces engaged in counterrevolutionary efforts elsewhere was a central feature of the Argentine extraterritorial venture.*

For the Argentine security forces, the annihilation of domestic "subversion" represented a problem of logistics that demanded a definite expertise in unconventional warfare. Such expertise was transferred to other security forces as part of Argentina's extraterritorial program. The pattern of human rights violations, corruption, and erosion of institutional mechanisms of control went with the know-how and was thus exported.

3. *Argentina acted alone in becoming involved in the organization and training of a Contra army. Later, when the Reagan administration decided to give full-fledged support to the anti-Sandinista program, Argentina emerged as a U.S. surrogate in Central America.*

Argentina's anti-Communist intervention in the hemisphere was consistent with the military's claim that the nation had faced Soviet-sponsored aggression via Cuba. Based on a perception that the Carter administration's human rights policy was yielding terrain to Communist expansionism, the Argentine military decided to fill in for the United States. This decision was guided by, among other factors, a conviction that Argentina could expand its influence in Central America, Bolivia, and elsewhere in Latin America if it capitalized on its experienced counterinsurgency apparatus. The military high command also sought to increase sales of Argentine arms and know-how to other national security states. Following the inauguration of President Reagan, the United States became involved with the Argentine counterrevolutionary program in Central America. The two administrations shared the view that popular unrest was largely a result of international Communist action intent on deepening indigenous sources of discontent.

4. *The Argentine training and supervision of a U.S.-backed Con-*

tra army aimed to promote counterrevolutionary insurgency by deploying a relatively small number of advisers in the region.

Argentine experts were responsible for the training of instructors, field commanders, and combatants of the anti-Sandinista forces. Training was focused on guerrilla warfare (with emphasis on psychological action) and semiconventional army operations. The participation of veterans of Argentina's dirty war in a CIA covert operation evidenced that the United States could sanction state terrorism if it proved to be effective against a regime perceived as a threat to U.S. values and democracy.

5. *The counterrevolutionary venture in Central America was facilitated by collaboration between states and transnational nonstate organizations. The ideologically-based coalitions involved complex linkages.*

Interactions between ideological bedfellows developed into transnational informal networks that provided a major support structure for military and paramilitary rightists in the hemisphere. Key elements of the structure were (*a*) the multinational apparatus for repression organized by Southern Cone military regimes and (*b*) cooperative ventures between intelligence services and criminal networks engaged in trafficking in drugs and arms. The principle of anti-Communism served as a rationale for these clandestine ventures.

6. *Perceiving the involvement of Argentine advisers in Central America as vital to U.S. policy, the military leadership assumed that the United States would remain neutral in the event of an Argentine occupation of the Malvinas/Falkland Islands. This was a mistake.*

The perceived impact of Argentina's covert intelligence program on U.S.–Argentine relations contributed to shaping the military junta's strategic decision to invade the Malvinas/Falklands. It should be noted, however, that the Argentine involvement in the anti-Sandinista venture was not originally conceived as a quid pro quo for U.S. neutrality or mediation in case of a confrontation between Argentina and Britain over the islands: it was a corollary of Argentina's military encroachment in the region.

7. The intelligence apparatus directly involved in the extraterritorial counterrevolutionary program turned into a threat to Argentina's new democracy.

The clandestine state strengthened during the authoritarian period. Backed by an international network of foreign intelligence services, religious sects, secret lodges, and rings of gunrunners and drug dealers, it emerged an invisible power that conspired against democracy. Argentina's constitutional state was—and is—damaged. Veterans of the Central American operation became involved in terrorist actions, military uprisings, and organized crime in Argentina. The decentralized, autonomous, largely unaccountable security apparatus, having fought a dirty war within and beyond the national borders, persisted—and persists—as an enclave of authoritarianism in the new Argentine democracy.

Acronyms

AAA (Triple A)   Alianza Anticomunista Argentina (Argentine Anti-Communist Alliance)

ADREN   Alianza Democrática Revolucionaria Nicaragüense (Nicaraguan Democratic Revolutionary Alliance)

AID   Agency for International Development

AIFLD   American Institute for Free Labor Development

ANSESAL   Agencia Nacional de Servicios Especiales de El Salvador (National Security Agency of El Salvador)

ARDE   Alianza Revolucionaria Democrática (Democratic Revolutionary Alliance) (Nicaragua)

ARENA   Alianza Republicana Nacionalista (Nationalist Republican Alliance) (El Salvador)

BCRA   Banco Central de la República Argentina (Central Bank of the Republic of Argentina)

CAL   Confederación Anticomunista Latinoamericana (Latin American Anti-Communist Confederation)

CALFA   Centro de Apoyo Logístico de las Fuerzas Armadas (Logistical Support Center for the Armed Forces) (Honduras)

CAUSA   Confederation of Associations for the Unity of the Societies of America

CEA Conferencia de Ejércitos Americanos (Conference of American Armies)

CIA Central Intelligence Agency

CIP Centro de Instrucción Policial (Police Training Center) (Honduras)

COB Central Obrera Boliviana (Bolivian Trade Union Federation)

COE Comando de Operaciones Especiales (Command of Special Operations) (Honduras)

CONADEP Comisión Nacional sobre la Desaparición de Personas (National Commission on the Disappeared) (Argentina)

COPROSA Comisión para la Promoción Social de la Arquidiócesis (Commission for Social Promotion in the Archdiocese) (Nicaragua)

COSEP Consejo Superior de la Empresa Privada (Superior Council of Private Enterprise) (Nicaragua)

CRIM Centro de Reunión de Inteligencia Militar (Center for Military Intelligence) (Argentina)

DCI Director of Central Intelligence

DGFM Dirección General de Fabricaciones Militares (General Directorate of Military Industries) (Argentina)

DGSE Dirección General de Seguridad del Estado (General Directorate for State Security) (Nicaragua)

DIA Defense Intelligence Agency

DIN Departamento de Investigación Nacional (National Directorate of Investigation) (Bolivia)

DINA Dirección de Información Nacional (National Information Directorate) (Chile)

DNI Dirección Nacional de Investigaciones (National Investigations Directorate) (Honduras)

EDESA Empresa de Desarrollos Especiales (Special Developments Enterprise) (Argentina)

EEBI Escuela de Entrenamiento Básico de Infantería (Basic Infantry Training School) (Nicaragua)

EGP Ejército Guerrillero de los Pobres (Guerrilla Army of the Poor) (Guatemala)

ELN Ejército de Liberación Nacional (National Liberation Army) (Nicaragua)

EMGE Estado Mayor General del Ejército (Army General Staff) (Argentina)

EPS Ejército Popular Sandinista (Sandinista Popular Army) (Nicaragua)

ERP Ejército Revolucionario del Pueblo (People's Revolutionary Army) (Argentina)

ESA Ejército Secreto Anticomunista (Secret Anti-Communist Army) (Guatemala)

ESG Escola Superior de Guerra (Brazilian War College)

ESMA Escuela de Mecánica de la Armada (Navy Mechanics School) (Argentina)

EXIMBANK Export-Import Bank

EZLN Ejército Zapatista de Liberación Nacional (Zapatista National Liberation Army) (Mexico)

FAD Fuerzas Armadas Democráticas (Democratic Armed Forces) (Nicaragua)

FAGANIC Federación de Ganaderos de Nicaragua (Nicaraguan Federation of Cattle Ranchers)

FAL-OPAC Fuerzas Anticomunistas de León–Organización Popular Anticomunista (Anti-Communist Forces of León–Popular Anti-Communist Organization)

FALANGE Fuerzas Armadas de Liberación Anticomunista–Guerra de Eliminación (Anti-Communist Armed Forces of Liberation–War of Elimination) (El Salvador)

FARAC Fuerzas Armadas Anticomunistas (Anti-Communist Armed Forces) (Nicaragua)

FDN Fuerza Democrática Nicaragüense (Nicaraguan Democratic Force)

FMLN Frente Farabundo Martí de Liberación Nacional (Farabundo Martí National Liberation Front) (El Salvador)

FRENICA Frente Revolucionario Nicaragüense (Nicaraguan Revolutionary Front)

FSLN Frente Sandinista de Liberación Nacional (Sandinista National Liberation Front) (Nicaragua)

FUR Fuerza Unida Revolucionaria (Revolutionary United Force) (Nicaragua)

FUSEP Fuerza de Seguridad Pública (Public Security Force) (Honduras)

GN Guardia Nacional (National Guard) (Nicaragua)

GT 3.3.2 Grupo de Tareas 3.3.2 (Task Force 3.3.2) (Argentina)

GTE Grupo de Tareas Exterior (Extraterritorial Task Force) (Argentina)

IACHR Inter-American Commission on Human Rights

IDB Inter-American Development Bank

IMF International Monetary Fund

JCR Junta Coordinadora Revolucionaria (Revolutionary Coordinating Junta)

LIC Low-Intensity Conflict

MAP Movimiento de Acción Popular (Popular Action Movement) (Nicaragua)

MCRL Movimiento Costa Rica Libre (Free Costa Rica Movement)

MILPAS Milicias Populares Anti-Sandinistas (Popular Anti-Sandinista Militias) (Nicaragua)

MILPAS Milicias Populares Anti-Somocistas (Popular Anti-Somocista Militias) (Nicaragua)

MINT Ministerio del Interior (Ministry of the Interior) (Nicaragua)

MIR Movimiento de Izquierda Revolucionaria (Leftist Revolutionary Movement) (Bolivia)

MISURA Miskito, Sumu, Rama organization (Nicaragua)

MISURASATA Unity of the Miskitos, Sumus, Ramas, and Sandinistas (Nicaragua)

MLN Movimiento de Liberación Nacional (National Liberation Movement) (Guatemala)

NSD National Security Doctrine

NSDD National Security Decision Directive

OAS L'Organisation de l'Armée Secrète (Secret Army Organization) (France)

OAS Organization of American States

OLAS Organización Latinoamericana de Solidaridad (Organization for Latin American Solidarity)

ORPA   Organización del Pueblo en Armas (Organization of People in Arms) (Guatemala)

OSN   Oficina de Seguridad Nacional (Office of National Security) (Nicaragua)

P-2   Propaganda Due (Italy)

PCD   Partido Conservador Democrático (Democratic Conservative Party) (Nicaragua)

PLO   Palestine Liberation Organization

PRN   Proceso de Reorganización Nacional (Process of National Reorganization) (Argentina)

PRT   Partido Revolucionario de los Trabajadores (Revolutionary Workers' Party) (Argentina)

PSD   Partido Social Demócrata (Social Democratic Party) (Nicaragua)

SES   Servicio Especial de Seguridad (Special Security Service) (Bolivia)

SIDE   Secretaría de Inteligencia de Estado (State Intelligence Agency) (Argentina)

SIE   Servicio de Inteligencia de Ejército (Army Intelligence Service) (Argentina)

SNI   Serviço Nacional de Informações (National Information Service) (Brazil)

TAR   Transporte Aéreo Rioplatense (River Plate Air Transport) (Argentina)

TESON   Tropas Especiales y de Operaciones Nocturnas (Special and Nighttime Operations Troops) (Honduras)

TIAR   Tratado Interamericano de Asistencia Recíproca (Inter-American Treaty of Reciprocal Assistance)

UDN-FARN Unión Democrática Nicaragüense–Fuerzas Armadas Revolucionarias Nicaragüenses (Nicaraguan Democratic Union–Nicaraguan Revolutionary Armed Forces)

UGB Unión Guerrera Blanca (White Warrior's Union) (El Salvador)

UNHCR U.N. High Commission for Refugees

UNO Unión Nacional Opositora (National Opposition Union) (Nicaragua)

WACL World Anti-Communist League

YPF Yacimientos Petrolíferos Fiscales (State-owned Oil Company) (Argentina)

Chronology of Events in Argentina, the United States, and Central America

1967–79	Anastasio Somoza Debayle rules Nicaragua
March 24, 1976	Military coup in Argentina
January 1977	Jimmy Carter takes office, pledges to promote a U.S. foreign policy based on human rights
1977–79	Civil war in Nicaragua
1977	Argentina begins involvement in Somoza's campaign against Sandinista insurgents
1978	The Argentine army establishes bases in the United States to coordinate its operations in Central America
1979	Argentine advisers offer counterinsurgency training in Central America
July 19, 1979	Sandinista revolution triumphs in Nicaragua
January 1980	Argentina refuses to adhere to the U.S. grain embargo against the Soviet Union
Mid-1980	Exiled Nicaraguan guardsmen establish the September 15 Legion
July 1980	"Cocaine coup" in Bolivia receives active Argentine support
August 1980	Gustavo Alvarez Martínez appointed as commander of the FUSEP in Honduras

September 1980	The Latin American Anti-Communist Confederation meets in Buenos Aires
Fall 1980	Carter authorizes a CIA covert action program to support anti-Sandinista organizations in Nicaragua
Late 1980	Argentine advisers organize and train exiled guardsmen in Guatemala
November 1980	Republican triumph in U.S. presidential elections
December 1980	Argentine-trained guardsmen attack a short-wave radio station in Costa Rica
January 1981	Ronald Reagan inaugurated as president, promises to restore U.S. global military preeminence
March 1981	Reagan authorizes the CIA to support counterrevolutionary efforts in Central America
April 1, 1981	Reagan terminates all economic aid to Nicaragua
Spring 1981	Anti-Sandinista rebels receive intelligence and military training in Buenos Aires
Spring 1981	Under Argentine supervision, the September 15 Legion moves its base of operations to Honduras
August 1981	The FDN created at a meeting in Guatemala City
August 1981	The United States, Argentina, and Honduras establish a three-sided accord to run the anti-Sandinista venture
November 23 1981	Reagan approves NSDD 17, empowering the CIA to create a rebel force (the Argentines are already training a Contra army)

December 1, 1981	Reagan signs a finding that authorizes the CIA to work with foreign governments to build an anti-Sandinista paramilitary movement
January 1982	Alvarez Martínez appointed as commander in chief of the Honduran armed forces
March 1982	Argentine-trained Contra commandos blow up two bridges in northern Nicaragua
April 2, 1982	Argentine troops invade the Falkland Islands (Islas Malvinas)
June 14, 1982	Argentine troops surrender to the British forces
Late 1982	As a result of the U.S. decision to cooperate with the British government during the Falklands/Malvinas conflict, Argentina drastically curtails its involvement in the Contra venture
July-December 1983	The United States stages major military exercises with Honduras
December 1983	Elected President Raúl Alfonsín inaugurated in Argentina
Early 1984	The CIA takes full control over the Contra training and logistics
March 1984	Alvarez Martínez ousted by an internal military coup
Late 1984	The last Argentine advisers to the Contras leave Honduras

Notes

AUTHOR'S NOTE: This book is based on a large variety of primary and secondary sources, both in English and Spanish. Some of the following notes have been written utilizing a composite style, i.e., a list of sources separated by semicolons. I have adopted this style in two types of cases throughout the book. First, where an account is based on the amalgamation of several sources, I have arranged the references following the order in which they are introduced in the text. Second, I have used this style where I considered it important to provide the reader with multiple sources to support a particularly relevant statement.

Most of the people involved in the intelligence and military activities described in this book were known by aliases. For some readers, it might be important to have access to this information in order to identify specific individuals. I have listed the names and corresponding aliases, where these are known to me, in the index.

Spanish usage for names in the bibliography may present some difficulties for the English-speaking reader. Please note that Spanish-language authors with two last names are alphabetically listed in the bibliography by their first last name.

FOREWORD

1. James D. Cockcroft, *Latin America: History, Politics, and U.S. Policy*, 2nd. ed. (Chicago: Nelson–Hall Publishers, 1996), pp. 541, 168; and William I. Robinson, *A Faustian Bargain: U.S. Intervention in the Nicaraguan Elections and American Foreign Policy in the Post–Cold War Era* (Boulder: Westview Press, 1992).

2. See Cockcroft, pp. 122–125, 348, and 551–553.

3. See John A. Booth and Thomas W. Walker, *Understanding Central America* (Boulder: Westview Press, 1993), p. 147 and footnote 26, p. 208.

4. Peter Kornbluh, *Nicaragua: The Price of Intervention* (Washington, D.C.: Institute for Policy Studies, 1987), pp. 75–76.

5. See Jonathan Kwitny, "Money, Drugs and the Contras," *Nation,*

August 29, 1987, pp. 145–66; Leslie Cockburn, *Out of Control: The Story of the Reagan Administration's Secret War in Nicaragua, the Illegal Arms Pipeline, and the Contra Drug Connection* (New York: Atlantic Monthly Press, 1987); and *Inside the Shadow Government: Declarations of Plaintiffs' Council Filed by the Christic Institute, U.S. District Court, Miami, Florida, March 31, 1988* (Washington, D.C.: 1988). For a good treatment of the relationship among drugs, organized crime, and the CIA, see Jonathan Kwitny, *The Crimes of Patriots: A True Tale of Dope, Dirty Money, and the CIA* (New York: W. W. Norton, 1987).

6. Note that the U.S. media almost always framed the word "Sandinistas" with the pejorative term "leftist." Curiously, however, the various dictatorships Washington was supporting at the time were rarely if ever framed with "rightist" or, for that matter, any other negative adjective.

7. Booth and Walker, *Understanding Central America*, p. 70.

8. The French used this tactic in both Indochina and Algeria. The CIA practiced it directly in Vietnam in Operation Phoenix in 1969. And U.S.-advised and -equipped Latin American military and police forces used this technique on a large scale throughout the hemisphere from the late 1960s through the early 1990s. For a good discussion of the U.S. involvement with state terror in two countries, see Michael McClintock, *The American Connection: State Terror and Popular Resistance in El Salvador* and *The American Connection: State Terror and Popular Resistance in Guatemala* (London: Zed Books, 1985).

CHAPTER 1

1. Jaime E. Malamud-Goti, *Game Without End: State Terror and the Politics of the Justice* (Norman: University of Oklahoma Press, 1996). Malamud-Goti was a senior adviser on institutional and legal matters to President Raúl Alfonsín (1983–89).

2. Ibid., pp. 80–81, citing Silvia Sigal and Eliseo Verón, *Perón o muerte: los fundamentos discursivos del fenómeno peronista* (Buenos Aires: Legasa, 1986).

3. Alfred Stepan, *Rethinking Military Politics: Brazil and the Southern Cone* (Princeton: Princeton University Press, 1988), pp. 24–25. During the dirty war, factions within the security forces became involved in vio-

lent clandestine conflicts. Terrorism became a device used in resolving intramilitary disputes and the war within the military apparatus resulted in numerous casualties—Carlos H. Acuña and Catalina Smulovitz, "Militares en la transición argentina: del gobierno a la subordinación constitucional," in C. Acuña et al., *Juicios, castigos y memorias: Derechos humanos y justicia en la política argentina* (Buenos Aires: Nueva Visión, 1995), pp. 34–35.

4. Malamud-Goti, *Game Without End*, pp. 74–75.

5. Acuña and Smulovitz, "Militares en la transición argentina," pp. 32–34. See Andrés Fontana, "De la crisis de Malvinas a la subordinación condicionada: conflictos intramilitares y transición política en Argentina," working paper, Kellogg Institute, August 1986, p. 33.

6. Juan E. Corradi, "Toward Societies without Fear," in Juan E. Corradi, Patricia Weiss Fagen, and Manuel A. Garretón, eds., *Fear at the Edge: State Terror and Resistance in Latin America* (Berkeley: University of California Press, 1992), pp. 279–280.

7. Carina Perelli, "From Counterrevolutionary Warfare to Political Awakening: The Uruguayan and Argentine Armed Forces in the 1970s," *Armed Forces and Society* 20, no. 1 (fall 1993): 28–29. For a concise review of the literature on the National Security Doctrine, see Joan Patrice McSherry, "Democratization and the Politics of National Security in Argentina," Ph.D. dissertation, City University of New York, 1994, pp. 111–17.

8. Alain Rouquié, *The Military and the State in Latin America* (Berkeley: University of California Press, 1987), p. 276.

9. Roberto Russell and Juan Tokatlian, *Argentina y la crisis centroamericana, 1976–1985*, Research Report no. 36, Facultad Latinoamericana de Ciencias Sociales (FLACSO), 1986, p. 5. See David Pion-Berlin and George A. Lopez, "Of Victims and Executioners: Argentine State Terror, 1975–1979," *International Studies Quarterly* 35 (1991): 63–86.

10. Quoted in Brian Loveman and Thomas M. Davies, eds., *The Politics of Antipolitics: The Military in Latin America*, 2nd. ed. (Lincoln: University of Nebraska Press, 1989), p. 199.

11. Margaret E. Crahan, "National Security Ideology and Human Rights," in Crahan, ed., *Human Rights and Basic Needs in the Americas* (Washington, D.C.: Georgetown University Press, 1982), p. 104.

12. Quoted in Donald C. Hodges, *Argentina's "Dirty War": An Intellectual Biography* (Austin: University of Texas Press, 1991), p. 124, citing *La Nación*, April 14, 1976. As an analyst noted, "total security becomes like a snowball rolling downhill, continually growing in size with those who are 'infiltrated' by Marxism. . . . In their search for total security regimes end by marginalizing the majority of a society which will never be secure enough for those in power"—Robert Calvo, "The Church and the Doctrine of National Security," *Journal of Interamerican Studies and World Affairs* 21, no. 1 (February 1979): 84.

13. Manuel Antonio Garretón, "Fear in Military Regimes: An Overview," in Corradi et al., eds., *Fear at the Edge*, pp. 15–16.

14. Ibid., p. 23.

15. Corradi, "Toward Societies without Fear," in Corradi et al., *Fear at the Edge*, pp. 279–80.

16. Tulio Halperin Donghi, "Argentina's Unmastered Past," *Latin American Research Review* 23, no. 2 (1988): 13.

17. Corradi, "Toward Societies without Fear," pp. 279–80.

18. Quotes from speeches by two generals—the first from Videla, the second from Galtieri, cited in Loveman and Davies, *Politics of Antipolitics*, pp. 200, 203. A government report read, "On the 24th of March, 1976, the armed forces took over the political power of the Argentine Republic, together with the responsibility of curbing the progressive disintegration of the state, the widespread chaos and conditions of extreme social defenselessness [*sic*] prevailing at that time," Poder Ejecutivo Nacional, *Terrorism in Argentina*, Buenos Aires, January 7, 1980, p. 3.

19. Genaro Arriagada Herrera, "Ideology and Politics in the South American Military (Argentina, Brazil, Chile and Uruguay)," paper presented at the Woodrow Wilson International Center for Scholars, Washington, D.C., March 21, 1979, p. 1. See Osiris G. Villegas, *Tiempo Geopolítico Argentino* (Buenos Aires: Pleamar, 1975), p. 176.

20. Generals Roberto Viola and L. A. Jaúregui, press conference, April 1977, quoted in Hodges, *Argentina's "Dirty War,"* p. 181. On the characterization of subversion, see Poder Ejecutivo Nacional, *Terrorism in Argentina.* "This report," the prologue reads (p. 3), "produces the evidence of the birth, development and dénouement of the terrorist phenomenon in Argentina and of its reappearance, at a later date, far from her frontiers."

21. Centro de Estudios Legales y Sociales (CELS), "The Doctrine of Global Parallelism," MS, Buenos Aires, 1981, in author's files, pp. 1–16. This report is an English version of "El caso argentino: desapariciones forzadas como instrumento básico y generalizado de una política. La doctrina del paralelismo global. Su concepción y aplicación," January 1981. On the conception and impact of the report, see Emilio F. Mignone, *Derechos humanos y sociedad: el caso argentino* (Buenos Aires: CELS/Ediciones del Pensamiento Nacional, 1991), pp. 54–58.

22. Hodges, *Argentina's "Dirty War,"* p. 180. As Jean Franco said, the *desaparecidos* "became fictions without civil existence or history"—J. Franco, "Gender, Death, and Resistance: Facing the Ethical Vacuum," in Corradi et al., *Fear at the Edge*, p. 112. See also Frank Graziano, *Divine Violence: Spectacle, Psychosexuality, and Radical Christianity in the Argentine "Dirty War"* (Boulder: Westview Press, 1992).

23. CELS, "Doctrine," p. 12.

24. I follow Alfred Stepan's use of the concept of security community as "those elements of the regime most directly involved in the planning and execution of repression, intelligence gathering, interrogation, torture, and internal clandestine armed operations"—Stepan, *Rethinking Military Politics*, p. 30.

25. Interview with a retired captain, Carlos H. Raimondi, director of politics at the Argentine Foreign Ministry under the military regime, in Buenos Aires, August 4, 1993. "From the rank of captain upwards, all members of the armed forces had to participate personally in at least one antisubversive operation." This practice was aimed at creating a strong solidarity network among the officer corps—interview with Col. José Luis García, retired, Centro de Militares Democráticos (CEMIDA), in Buenos Aires, August 10, 1993.

26. See Comisión Nacional sobre la Desaparición de Personas (CONADEP), *Nunca Más: The Report of the Argentine National Commission on the Disappeared* (New York: Farrar, Straus and Giroux, 1986). A case study on state terror in Chile argued that "torture is first and foremost a political phenomenon and should not be characterized as the disturbed, aberrant, or out-of-control behavior of the torturers. It is a routine practice employed in a sophisticated and systematic way. Its methods are widely taught and are adapted locally by repressive governments, which use torture to control and destroy individual adversaries and their

organizations"—Sofia Salimovich, Elizabeth Lira, and Eugenia Weinstein, "Victims of Fear: The Social Psychology of Repression," in Corradi et al., *Fear at the Edge*, p. 78. It is important, however, to acknowledge that sometimes torture is an unorganized and unregulated practice.

27. Franco, "Gender, Death, and Resistance," p. 106.

28. Pion-Berlin and Lopez, "Of Victims and Executioners": 63.

29. Hannah Arendt, *Eichmann in Jerusalem: A Report on the Banality of Evil* (New York: Viking Press, 1963), p. 253.

30. U.S. embassy, Buenos Aires, confidential cable, "The Tactic of Disappearance," to Secretary of State, September 26, 1980, p. 3, reproduced in Iain Guest, *Behind the Disappearances: Argentina's Dirty War Against Human Rights and the United Nations* (Philadelphia: University of Pennsylvania Press, 1990), pp. 430–435.

31. Horacio Verbitsky, "La solución final," *Página 12*, March 3, 1995; CELS, "Doctrine," p. 15. See also Horacio Verbitsky, *El vuelo* (Buenos Aires: Planeta, 1995).

32. Sgt. Víctor Ibañez, as quoted in *New York Times*, April 25, 1995.

33. Interview with navy Capt. Adolfo Scilingo, retired, in Verbitsky, *El vuelo*, pp. 26, 38–39, quote from pp. 64–65.

34. See Michel Foucault, *Discipline and Punish: The Birth of the Prison* (New York: Vintage, 1979), pp. 10–13.

35. U.S. embassy cable, "The Tactic of Disappearance," section 2, p. 3.

36. Crahan, "National Security Ideology," p. 101. As Pion-Berlin and Lopez argued, a free-market economics ideology also guided the military's program of state terror, providing a focus for the selection of victims from the membership of certain trade unions. The free-market economic program was strongly opposed by key antiliberal circles within the armed forces—Pion-Berlin and Lopez, "Of Victims and Executioners": 71–74.

37. Crahan, "National Security Ideology," pp. 121–122(n.8).

38. Ramón J. A. Camps, "Apogeo y declinación de la guerrilla en la Argentina," *La Prensa* (Buenos Aires) January 4, 1981; Pion-Berlin and Lopez, "Of Victims and Executioners": 69–71. On the National Security Doctrine, see Genaro Arriagada Herrera, *El pensamiento político de los militares (estudios sobre Chile, Argentina, Brasil y Uruguay)* (Santiago:

Editorial Aconcagua, 1981), esp. pp. 183–207; and José Comblin, *The Church and the National Security State* (Maryknoll: Orbis Books, 1979). On the NSD in Argentina, see David Pion-Berlin, "The National Security Doctrine, Military Threat Perception and the 'Dirty War' in Argentina," *Comparative Political Studies* 21 (1988): 382–407.

39. French National-Catholicism resulted from "the marriage between the strong nationalist values of [French] military officers to the intégriste school of thought provided by such groups as Cité Catholique, the Centre d'Etudes Supérieures de Psychologie Sociale, the Centre d' Etudes Politiques et Civiques, or the group Armée-Nation"—Perelli, "From Counterrevolutionary Warfare To Political Awakening": 40(n.14).

40. Ibid. On the French counterrevolutionary doctrine, see John Steward Ambler, *Soldiers Against the State: The French Army in Politics* (Columbus: Ohio State University Press, 1966).

41. Alfred Stepan, *The State and Society: Peru in Comparative Perspective* (Princeton: Princeton University Press, 1978), pp. 31–32, 37.

42. Perelli, "From Counterrevolutionary Warfare To Political Awakening": 40(n.14).

43. Interviews in Buenos Aires with the following retired army officers: Gen. José Teófilo Goyret, August 5, 1993; Gen. Ernesto Víctor López Meyer, August 4, 1993; and Col. Horacio P. Ballester, July 28, 1993. In the early 1970s, the prestigious military journal *Estrategia* published several articles by Gen. André Beaufre, one of the most important spokesmen of the French current of thought developed during the Algerian war of independence. See André Beaufre, "La violencia," *Estrategia* 5 (January-February 1970): 5–9; Beaufre, "Perspectivas estratégicas en la década del 70," *Estrategia* 9 (January-February 1971): 5–14. See also José T. Goyret, "El pensamiento estratégico del general Beaufre," *Estrategia* 7 (May-June, 1970): 104–110, and *Estrategia* 8 (July-August 1970): 15–26. It is important to point out that the increasing concern with internal security was initially associated with the anti-Peronist demobilization project advanced by the new military government of the *Revolución Libertadora* (which deposed President Juan D. Perón in 1955). On this theme, see David Rock, *Authoritarian Argentina: The Nationalist Movement, Its History and Its Impact* (Berkeley: University of California Press, 1993). On General Rosas's views on "subversion" and the new profes-

sional role of the army, see Martin Edwin Andersen, *Dossier Secreto: Argentina's Desaparecidos and the Myth of the "Dirty War"* (Boulder: Westview Press, 1993), pp. 63–64, 336(n.10); and Malamud-Goti, *Game Without End*, pp. 73–75.

44. Catholic treatise in political philosophy, cited in Stepan, *State and Society*, p. 31.

45. Geopolitics is the scientific study of "the influence of geographic factors in the life and evolution of states, in order to extract conclusions of a political character"—Jorge E. Atencio, *¿Qué es la geopolítica?* (Buenos Aires: Pleamar, 1965), cited in Crahan, "National Security Ideology," pp. 103–104.

46. See Jack Child, *Geopolitics and Conflict in South America* (New York: Praeger, 1985); and Robert Chisholm, "From National Defence to National Security: 'Geopolitical Darwinism' and Military Thought in South America," Master's thesis, Queen's University, Kingston, Ontario, Canada, 1989. A good illustration of geopolitical thought as developed by the South American military is Augusto Pinochet Ugarte, *Geopolítica*, 2nd. ed. (Santiago: Andrés Bello, 1974).

47. Particularly important was the intellectual influence of Cité Catholique (Ciudad Católica).

48. Interview with Col. Mohamed Alí Seineldín, at the military prison, Magdalena, August 21, 1993; the quotation is from Seineldín's speech on behalf of the *Movimiento por la Identidad Nacional e Integración Iberoamericana (MINeII)*, given at the military prison, Magdalena, October 3, 1992. Seineldín led the military insurrections of December 1, 1988 (known as *Operación Virgen del Valle*), and December 3, 1990. Seineldín claimed that the "operational-tactic military success" obtained by the armed forces in the counterinsurgency war of the 1970s had become a "political defeat" under democracy, threatening the very survival of the military institution. On the military insurrections under the Alfonsín and Menem administrations, see, for instance, David Pion-Berlin, "Between Confrontation and Accommodation: Military and Government Policy in Democratic Argentina," *Journal of Latin American Studies* 23 (October 1991): 543–571; and Deborah Norden, "Democratic Consolidation and Military Professionalism: Argentina in the 1980s," *Journal of Interamerican Studies and World Affairs* 32, no. 3 (fall 1990): 151–176.

49. See Sandra McGee Deutsch and Ronald H. Dolkart, eds., *The Argentine Right: Its History and Intellectual Origins, 1910 to the Present* (Wilmington: SR Books, 1993).

50. The U.S. training program in Argentina was centered on military and police counterinsurgency techniques. "The United States did not understand that the subversive warfare was ideological," stressed a retired army officer. "Revolutionary war was not the correct term [for what happened in Argentina]. The correct one was ideological subversion"—interview with Col. Miguel Angel Li Puma, in Buenos Aires, August 18, 1993.

51. On the transformation of the military's role in the region, see Alfred Stepan, "The New Professionalism of Internal Warfare and Military Role Expansion," in A. Stepan, ed., *Authoritarian Brazil: Origins, Policies and Future* (New Haven: Yale University Press, 1973), pp. 47–68; and Frank McCann, "Origins of the 'New Professionalism' of the Brazilian Military," *Journal of Interamerican Studies and World Affairs* 21, no. 4 (November 1979): 507, 520.

52. McSherry, "Democratization and the Politics of National Security," pp. 98–117.

53. Arriagada, "Ideology and Politics in the South American Military," pp. 8–9.

54. Osiris G. Villegas, *Guerra Revolucionaria Comunista* (Buenos Aires: Pleamar, 1963), pp. 122, 124, 192.

55. Hodges, *Argentina's "Dirty War,"* pp. 128–129; Horacio Verbitsky, *La última batalla de la tercera guerra mundial* (Buenos Aires: Legasa, 1984), p. 21; Eduardo Luis Duhalde, *El Estado terrorista argentino* (Barcelona: Argos Vergara, 1983), p. 81. See U.S. Congress, testimony of Leandro Sánchez Reisse before the Subcommittee on Terrorism, Narcotics and International Operations of the Senate Committee on Foreign Relations, July 23, 1987, pp. 15–16.

56. Oscar Cardoso, Ricardo Kirschbaum, and Eduardo van der Kooy, *Malvinas, la trama secreta* (Buenos Aires: Sudamericana-Planeta, 1983), p. 27.

57. Mark Falcoff, *A Tale of Two Policies: U.S. Relations with the Argentine Junta, 1976–1983* (Philadelphia: Foreign Policy Research Institute, 1989), p. 43.

58. Aldo C. Vacs, "A Delicate Balance: Confrontation and Cooperation between Argentina and the United States in the 1980s," *Journal of Interamerican Studies and World Affairs* 31, no. 4 (winter 1989): 27; CONADEP, *Nunca Más*, p. 443. The Onganía administration created the National Security Council (Consejo Nacional de Seguridad, CONASE). This council was exclusively focused on the issue of internal security.

59. Li Puma interview.

60. Duhalde, *El Estado terrorista argentino*, pp. 114–115, 125; "Argentina Redraws the Ideological Map of South America," *Latin America Weekly Report*, September 19, 1980, p. 5.

61. Duhalde, *El Estado terrorista argentino*, pp. 114–115; Verbitsky, *La última batalla*, pp. 21–22.

62. Quoted in Hodges, *Argentina's "Dirty War,"* p. 129.

63. Carlos Guillermo Suárez Mason, head of the First Army Corps, said in 1979: "Faced with the advance of Marxism's total operations, it is imperative to have an integral response. . . . It would be absurd to think that we have won the war against subversion just because we have eliminated its armed threat"—quoted in Hodges, *Argentina's "Dirty War,"* p. 183.

64. "Argentina Redraws the Ideological Map," p. 5.

65. Even though anti-Communism played a central role in shaping Argentina's foreign policy, the military leadership, in an effort independent of ideological constraints, tried to increase commercial sales. For example, the Argentine military regime refused to adhere to the U.S.-European embargo on grain sales to the USSR following the Soviet invasion of Afghanistan in December 1979 (see chapter 2).

66. For instance, Argentina's geopolitical thinkers traditionally stressed the need to create an Argentine sphere of influence in the South Atlantic region. Argentina had a long-standing interest in constituting a South Atlantic Treaty Organization to face possible non-Western threats in the oceanic region.

67. Cf. Pion-Berlin and Lopez, "Of Victims and Executioners": 67.

68. Interview with Gen. Miguel Angel Mallea Gil, retired, former vice chief of staff, Office of the President (under Videla), and military attaché to the United States, in Buenos Aires, August 18, 1993.

69. Mallea Gil interview; Verbitsky, *La última batalla*, p. 127.

70. Acuña and Smulovitz, "Militares en la transición argentina," pp. 28–33.

71. Li Puma interview; a military general staff normally consists of four sections: personnel, logistics, operations, and intelligence. Before the *Proceso* gave preeminence to the intelligence section, organizational power was concentrated in the division of operations.

72. Laura Kalmanowiecki, "Military Power and Policing During the Justo Administration, 1932–1938," paper presented at the Eighteenth International Congress of the Latin American Studies Association, Atlanta, March 10–12, 1994. See Robert A. Potash, *El ejército y la política en Argentina, 1928–1945* (Buenos Aires: Editorial Sudamericana, 1981), pp. 135–136.

73. Stepan, *Rethinking Military Politics*, p. 24. The new intelligence agency lacked prestige among key sectors of the armed forces.

74. Before the emphasis on internal security, the armed forces worked primarily on the basis of the so-called ABC (Argentina, Brazil, Chile) hypothesis of conflict. Accordingly, the military intelligence services were largely focused on collecting information on Brazil and Chile. However, they carried out that task with limited resources and elementary techniques—interview with Gen. Eugenio Alfredo Dalton, retired, in Buenos Aires, August 6, 1993.

75. See Alan Wolfe, *The Limits of Legitimacy: Political Contradictions of Contemporary Capitalism* (New York: The Free Press, 1977), p. 203. Wolfe's analysis of the "dual state" in the United States is highly significant for my discussion.

76. Federico Mittelbach, *Informe sobre desaparecedores* (Buenos Aires: La Urraca, 1986), p. 9.

77. See Duhalde, *El Estado terrorista argentino*, pp. 13, 19, 145, 131.

78. Stepan, *Rethinking Military Politics*, table on p. 70, citing CONADEP, *Nunca Más*, p. 284, *Brasil: Nunca Mais* (Petropólis: Editora Vozes, 1985), pp. 291–293, and Charles Gillespie, "Party Strategies and Redemocratization: Theoretical and Comparative Perspectives on the Uruguayan Case," Ph.D. dissertation, Yale University, 1987, p. 460.

79. Stepan, *Rethinking Military Politics*, pp. 24–25; L. A. Bittencourt Emílio, "The 'Abertura' in Brazil: the Day-After of the Brazilian Intelligence 'Monster,'" working paper, Instituto de Pesquisa Econômica Aplicada (IPEA), November 1992, pp. 7–11.

80. The recourse to comprehensive clandestine repressive operations

by the armies of the French in Algeria and the United States in Vietnam had contributed to the erosion of the military hierarchy and the increase of corruption within the military institution—Acuña and Smulovitz, "Militares en la transición argentina," pp. 32–33.

81. U.S. embassy cable, "The Tactic of Disappearance," section 2, p. 2.

82. This account of the Argentine intelligence apparatus is based on the following interviews conducted in Buenos Aires: Argentine army general, name withheld on request, August 4, 1993; Rogelio García Lupo, July 30, 1993; and Juan José Salinas, July 31, 1993. See Jorge Grecco and Marcela Luza, "Secuestros extorsivos: la historia del horror," *Somos* (Buenos Aires), December 9, 1991, pp. 10–15. It is important to point out that traditionally within the ranks of the Argentine armed forces a career in intelligence was commonly viewed as an occupation for underqualified officers who could not aspire to major military posts.

83. Interviews with Col. Mohamed Alí Seineldín and Maj. Héctor Romero Mundani, July and August 1992, in Malamud-Goti, *Game Without End*, pp. 174–75.

84. On the autonomy and resources of the intelligence apparatus, see Ana Barón, "La conexión Sánchez Reisse-Suárez Mason-Guglielminetti," *Somos*, February 25, 1987, p. 22; "Servicios bien intactos," *Página 12*, July 25, 1993; and Peter Dale Scott and Jonathan Marshall, *Cocaine Politics: Drugs, Armies, and the CIA in Central America* (Berkeley: University of California Press, 1991), p. 43. Cf. Wolfe's analysis of the CIA as part of the semisecret state that carried out U.S. policies in the cold war—Wolfe, *Limits of Legitimacy*, esp. pp. 201–205.

85. A useful definition of counterintelligence was the one given by the Brazilian War College (Escola Superior de Guerra, ESG). The ESG defined counterintelligence as "a group of measures designed to neutralize the effectiveness of hostile Intelligence Services and to safeguard National Security, as well as to identify psychological offensives launched against its citizens"—Escola Superior de Guerra, *Doutrina Básica* (Rio de Janeiro: ESG, 1979), p. 290, quoted in Bittencourt Emílio, "The 'Abertura' in Brazil," p. 9.

86. Comando General del Ejército, EMGE, Jefatura II Inteligencia—hereafter, Cdo. J. Ej. (EMGE-Jef. II)—annex 1 (Intelligence) to the

secret directive of the Army General Commander no. 404/75, "War Against Subversion," signed by Gen. Roberto Eduardo Viola, Buenos Aires, October 28, 1975, p. 10. Army Intelligence Battalion 601 was terminated in the postauthoritarian period. The unit was reorganized as the Centro de Reunión de Inteligencia Militar (CRIM), assigned to gather and analyze information for the army commander in chief.

87. General Suárez Mason was part of the army's "hard" sector, which included, among others, Gen. Ibérico M. Saint Jean (governor of the Buenos Aires Province), then-Col. Ramón J. Camps (police chief of the Buenos Aires Province), Gen. Luciano Benjamín Menéndez (commander of the Third Army Corps, Córdoba), Gen. René O. Azpitarte (commander of the Fifth Army Corps, Bahía Blanca), and Col. Roberto L. Roualdés (intelligence chief, First Army Corps). Early on, this faction advocated a strong dictatorial regime and the violent suppression of all forms of opposition. In the first year of the *Proceso*, Suárez Mason's First Army Corps already showed clear signs of operational autonomy with respect to the military government and the armed forces—Claudio Uriarte, *Almirante Cero: biografía no autorizada de Emilio Eduardo Massera* (Buenos Aires: Planeta, 1991), pp. 123–125, 128, 141–142. On the role of Suárez Mason, Roualdés, Col. Raúl Alberto Gatica, and Intelligence Battalion 601 in the so-called war against economic subversion, see Grecco and Luza, "Secuestros extorsivos," esp. pp. 10, 12.

88. Poder Ejecutivo Nacional, *Terrorism in Argentina*, pp. 5–6.

89. Ibid.

90. Cdo. J. Ej. (EMGE-Jef. II), "War Against Subversion," pp. 1–9. According to military intelligence, Montoneros operated simultaneously via their clandestine militias, semicovert political-vindicatory apparatus, and legal-political structure. Reportedly, one of their major goals was to assume the leadership of the labor union movement. The intelligence report noted that the ERP was trying to open an urban front in Buenos Aires city to supplement its rural front in the Tucumán Province.

91. Cdo. J. Ej. (EMGE-Jef. II), annex 1 to secret directive no. 504/77, "Continuation of the Offensive Against Subversion During the Period 1977/1978," signed by Gen. Roberto Eduardo Viola, Buenos Aires, April 20, 1977, pp. 1–15. By mid-1977, the military obtained a conclusive victory over the Montoneros and the ERP. According to Viola (*La Nación*,

September 30, 1977), seven or eight thousand guerrillas had been "killed or detained" by September of that year. "By late 1978," General Díaz Bessone said, "the military victory over the revolutionaries in Argentina was a fact. But the war would continue in the political arena"—Ramón Genaro Díaz Bessone, *Guerra Revolucionaria en la Argentina (1959–1978)* (Buenos Aires: Fraterna, 1986), p. 359.

92. Cdo. J. Ej. (EMGE-Jef. II), secret directive no. 504/77, "Continuation," pp. 11–14.

93. U.S. embassy cable, "The Tactic of Disappearance," section 2, p. 2.

94. See Ramón J. A. Camps, "Cómo se planificó la campaña terrorista latinoamericana," *La Prensa*, December 28, 1980.

95. Cdo. J. Ej. (EMGE-Jef. II), annex 1 to secret directive no. 404/75, "Summary of the Origins, Evolution, and Doctrine of the PRT-ERP and JCR," signed by Col. Carlos Alberto Martínez, army intelligence vice chief, Buenos Aires, October 28, 1975, p. 7.

96. Ibid., pp. 7–9.

97. See U.S. Congress, Sánchez Reisse testimony, pp. 37–38, 81–82, 106–108.

98. Cdo. J. Ej. (EMGE-Jef. II), annex 1 to secret directive no. 604/79, "Continuation of the Offensive Against Subversion," signed by Gen. Alberto Alfredo Valín, army intelligence chief, Buenos Aires, December 24, 1981, pp. 1–21. See Guest, *Behind the Disappearances*. On the Argentine human rights movement, see Alison Brysk, *The Politics of Human Rights in Argentina: Protest, Change, and Democratization* (Stanford: Stanford University Press, 1994).

99. Cdo. J. Ej. (EMGE-Jef. II), secret directive no. 604/79, "Continuation," p. 5.

100. Interview with Emilio Echaverry Mejía, a former major in the Nicaraguan national guard and FDN chief of operations, April 1991, in Guillermo Alberto Monkman, "The Institutionalization of the Doctrine of National Security in Argentina: The Military and Foreign Policy," Ph.D. dissertation, University of South Carolina, 1992, p. 275. See Christopher Dickey, *With the Contras: A Reporter in the Wilds of Nicaragua* (New York: Simon and Schuster, 1987), pp. 90–92; and Peter Kornbluh, *Nicaragua: The Price of Intervention* (Washington, D.C.: Institute for Policy Studies, 1987), p. 27.

101. U.S. Congress, Sánchez Reisse testimony, pp. 14–17, 26–27, 36–37, 111.

102. Verbitsky, *La última batalla*, p. 65; Duhalde, *El Estado terrorista argentino*, p. 114. The Argentine military intelligence services developed a closer cooperation with Uruguay and Paraguay than with Brazil (and possibly Chile). In spite of serious differences in terms of their national interests, anti-Communism provided a common ground for collaboration among the countries of the Southern Cone.

103. Scott Anderson and Jon Lee Anderson, *Inside the League* (New York: Dodd, Mead, 1986), p. 142. According to the U.S. Senate Foreign Relations Committee, Operation Condor carried out attacks against its enemies following a pattern in which one "team [was] charged with drawing up the Condor 'hit list' in a particular country. Then a second team [was] dispatched to locate the targeted victims and conduct surveillance on them. Finally, a third team, drawn from one or more member police agencies, [was] sent to carry out the 'sanction' decided upon" —Anderson and Anderson, *Inside the League*, p. 143.

104. CONADEP, *Nunca Más*, p. 255.

105. Scott and Marshall, *Cocaine Politics*, p. 42; Alipio Paoletti, *Como los Nazis, como en Vietnam* (Buenos Aires: Contrapunto, 1987), pp. 419–438. Secret documents on Gen. Alfredo Stroessner's political repression in Paraguay, found in December 1992 at police headquarters in Asunción, provided important evidence of the collaboration among Southern Cone security forces in the 1970s and 1980s. Those files contained information on some five hundred Argentine citizens who had been kidnapped, tortured, and murdered by security forces. There was also a June 1978 letter from Gen. Manuel Contreras, director of the Chilean secret police (DINA), to Paraguay's police chief, Gen. Francisco Britez Borges proposing an exchange of information and prisoners between the two countries. In addition, the secret archive contained reports from the Brazilian intelligence services regarding Argentine exiled political dissenters intensely sought after by their country's security forces— Luis Bruschtein, "Archivos del infierno," *Página 12*, February 7, 1993; *Página 12*, February 11, 1993, and January 26, 1996. See also Centro de Estudios Legales y Sociales, *Uruguay/Argentina: coordinación represiva* (Buenos Aires: CELS, 1982).

106. Immediately after the kidnapping of Gutiérrez Ruiz, the head of one of Argentina's most prestigious military academies (an army general) sought to give protection to the former Uruguayan congressman. Evidence of the close cooperation between the Argentine and the Uruguayan security forces was the fact that Gutiérrez Ruiz was rapidly assassinated to prevent his release—García interview.

107. Transcript of Héctor Francés videotaped testimony before Sandinista authorities, December 6, 1982, in author's files, p. 62.

108. Horacio Verbitsky, "El vuelo del cóndor," *Página 12*, January 28, 1996; affidavit of Rodolfo Peregrino Fernández, CADHU, Madrid, April 26, 1983, in author's files, p. 8. See Horacio Verbitsky, *La posguerra sucia: un análisis de la transición* (Buenos Aires: Legasa, 1984), pp. 127–130, 132–140. Former DINA agent Michael Townley was the key link in the Prats, Letelier, and Leighton operations. He was extradited to the United States in 1978. In 1995, a Chilean tribunal sentenced former DINA head General Contreras to seven years in prison for his involvement in the 1976 assassination of Letelier. In January 1996, former DINA operative Arancibia Clavel was detained in Argentina and charged with the assassination of Prats—*Página 12*, January 24, 26, and 27, 1996. Seineldín served as Argentine military attaché to Panama (1984–1986) and as adviser to General Noriega's armed forces (1986–1988). He exerted a strong influence on the Panamanian military. In 1994, Panama's foreign minister accused Seineldín of playing the role of adviser to the Panamanian Task Force E2, the country's most ruthless intelligence unit, dedicated to political repression—Li Puma interview; *Clarín*, June 18, 1994.

109. Scott and Marshall, *Cocaine Politics*, pp. 30, 42–43, 204, 259. See Anderson and Anderson, *Inside the League*, pp. 142–143.

110. Statement by Amalia Larralde, quoted in CONADEP, *Nunca Más*, p. 134.

111. On these extraterritorial operations conducted by paramilitary groups, see Verbitsky, *La última batalla*, pp. 65–74; Juan Gasparini, *La pista suiza* (Buenos Aires: Legasa, 1986), p. 75; and Duhalde, *El Estado terrorista argentino*, pp. 113–114. See testimony of Néstor Norberto Cendón before CONADEP, in Paoletti, *Como los Nazis, como en Vietnam*, pp. 425–426.

112. Juan J. Salinas, "Mercenarios argentinos en Centroamérica (III),"

El Porteño, February 1989: 18–19. Colonels Roberto Roualdés, Jorge Muzzio, and Alejandro Arias Duval (known as Arizmendi) were probably the officers in charge of the Intelligence Battalion 601 extraterritorial network. See José Luis D'Andrea Mohr, "La línea y la memoria," *Pregón*, January 11, 1989.

113. On the 1980 military coup in Bolivia, see Gregorio Selser, *Bolivia: El cuartelazo de los cocadólares* (México, D.F.: Mex-Sur, 1982).

114. Videla quoted in Sergio Joselovsky, "El ejército del 'Proceso' y su intervención en Centroamérica," *Humor* (Buenos Aires), author's copy undated, circa fall 1984: 63.

115. Interview with Adm. Alberto R. Varela, retired, in Buenos Aires, August 17, 1993. See Roberto Russell, "Las relaciones Argentina-Estados Unidos: del alineamiento heterodoxo a la recomposición madura," in Mónica Hirst, ed., *Continuidad y cambio en las relaciones América Latina-Estados Unidos* (Buenos Aires: Grupo Editor Latinoamericano, 1987), p. 24.

116. Americas Watch, *Almost Nine Years and Still No Verdict In the "Trial of Responsibilities,"* New York, December 1992, pp. 2–3.

117. U.S. Congress, Sánchez Reisse testimony, p. 154. With the fall of the military regime, Suárez Mason fled from Argentina and expanded his illegal activities abroad. By 1985, when he set his headquarters in the United States, he was considered "one of Latin America's chief drug traffickers"—Scott and Marshall, *Cocaine Politics*, p. 47, citing *Panorama* (Milan), November 10, 1985. On the connection between the international anti-Communist movement and drug trafficking, see Scott and Marshall, *Cocaine Politics*, chapter 5.

118. Americas Watch, *Almost Nine Years*, p. 3; Americas Watch, *The Trial of Responsibilities: The García Meza Tejada Trial*, New York, September 10, 1993, p. 4; Michael Levine, *The Big White Lie: The CIA and the Cocaine/Crack Epidemic* (New York: Thunder's Mouth Press, 1993), p. 57.

119. Telephone conversation with a former U.S. ambassador (appointed to Latin America in the 1980s), June 23, 1993.

120. Scott and Marshall, *Cocaine Politics*, pp. 43, 45–47, 205. See Levine, *The Big White Lie*, pp. 55–60.

121. Telephone conversation, former U.S. ambassador.

122. Americas Watch, *Almost Nine Years*, p. 3.

123. Americas Watch, *The Trial of Responsibilities*, pp. 2, 4, 7–8; Levine, *The Big White Lie*, p. 58. An official document "accrediting an Argentine army major to the Bolivian army" (presented at the trial of García Meza and his collaborators) provided further evidence of the participation of Argentine advisers in the Bolivian repressive apparatus. On April 21, 1993, the Bolivian supreme court convicted General García Meza, Colonel Arce Gómez, and several of their collaborators for crimes that included sedition, armed insurrection, genocide, and fraud. Arce Gómez had been previously convicted of drug trafficking in the United States—Americas Watch, *The Trial of Responsibilities*, pp. 1–3, 5–6, 9–11.

1. 4. Jack Blum, former special counsel to Senator John Kerry, quoted in Scott and Marshall, *Cocaine Politics*, p. 44.

125. U.S. Congress, Sánchez Reisse testimony, pp. 10, 44; Scott and Marshall, *Cocaine Politics*, p. 42.

126. Osiris G. Villegas, *Testimonio de un alegato* (Buenos Aires: Compañía Impresora Argentina, 1990), p. 49.

127. Juan Corradi, "The Mode of Destruction: Terror in Argentina," *Telos* 54 (1982–1983): 70.

128. Cdo. J. Ej. (EMGE-Jef. II), secret directive no. 504/77, "Continuation." Cf. Acuña and Smulovitz, "Militares en la transición argentina," pp. 31, 39–40.

129. Seineldín interview.

130. It is important to remember that ultrarightist groups responsible for the upsurge of political violence in 1974–1975 nurtured the staff of the security forces directly engaged in repression. See Ignacio González Janzen, *La Triple-A* (Buenos Aires: Contrapunto, 1986).

131. Gen. Santiago Omar Riveros, quoted in Verbitsky, *La última batalla*, p. 21.

132. Gen. Ramón Camps, quoted in Duhalde, *El Estado terrorista argentino*, p. 81.

133. See Robert Wesson, ed., *The Latin American Military Institution* (New York: Praeger, 1986), p. 150.

CHAPTER 2

Some documents were consulted through the following microfiche collections: Declassified Documents Reference System (Woodbridge: Research Publications, various years) (hereafter, DDRS); National Security Archive, ed., *Nicaragua: The Making of U.S. Policy, 1978–1990* (Alexandria: Chadwyck-Healey, 1991) (hereafter, NSA, *Nicaragua*).

1. See, for instance, Margaret E. Crahan, "Religion, Revolution, and Counterrevolution: The Role of the Religious Right in Central America," in Douglas A. Chalmers, Maria do Carmo Campello de Souza, and Atilio A. Boron, eds., *The Right and Democracy in Latin America* (New York: Praeger, 1992), pp. 163–165, 177.

2. See Ariel C. Armony, "Argentina and the Origins of Nicaragua's Contras," *Low Intensity Conflict and Law Enforcement* 2, no. 3 (winter 1993): 434–459.

3. Address by President Carter at commencement exercises at Notre Dame University, May 22, 1977, *American Foreign Policy Current Documents 1977–80* (hereafter *AFP Documents*) (Washington, D.C.: U.S. Department of State, 1984), pp. 6–7.

4. For an analysis of Latin America as a gray area, see Lars Schoultz, *National Security and United States Policy Toward Latin America* (Princeton: Princeton University Press, 1987), pp. 268–307. See also Schoultz, *Human Rights and United States Policy Toward Latin America* (Princeton: Princeton University Press, 1981).

5. Robert A. Pastor, "The Carter Administration and Latin America: A Test of Principle," in John D. Martz, ed., *United States Policy in Latin America: A Quarter Century of Crisis and Challenge, 1961–1986* (Lincoln: University of Nebraska Press, 1988), pp. 81–90.

6. Address to the nation by President Carter, October 1, 1979, *AFP Documents*, p. 1348.

7. Pastor, "Carter Administration," p. 87.

8. Carter address, October 1, 1979, p. 1350.

9. Daniel Yankelovich and Larry Kaagan, "Assertive America," *Foreign Affairs* 60 (1980): 696.

10. Cynthia J. Arnson, *Crossroads: Congress, the President, and Central America 1976–1993*, 2nd. ed. (University Park: Pennsylvania State University Press, 1993), pp. 2–3, 24.

11. Roy Gutman, *Banana Diplomacy: The Making of American Policy in Nicaragua 1981–1987* (New York: Simon and Schuster, 1988), p. 35.

12. U.S. Department of State cable, Secretary of State to U.S. am-

bassador to Nicaragua Lawrence Pezzullo, June 29, 1979, cited in Morris Morley and James Petras, *The Reagan Administration and Nicaragua: How Washington Constructs Its Case for Counterrevolution in Central America* (New York: Institute for Media Analysis, 1987), p. 39.

13. U.S. embassy, Managua, secret cable, Ambassador Lawrence Pezzullo to assistant secretary of state, Viron Vaky, "Nicaraguan Scenario," June 30, 1979, pp. 1–2.

14. Morley and Petras, *Reagan Administration and Nicaragua*, p. 40.

15. Arnson, *Crossroads*, p. 35.

16. Viron P. Vaky, "Hemispheric Relations: 'Everything Is Part of Everything Else,'" *Foreign Affairs* 60 (1980): 662.

17. Schoultz, *National Security*, pp. 46–47.

18. U.S. Congress, House Committee on Foreign Affairs, Subcommittee on Inter-American Affairs, *Review of the Presidential Certification of Nicaragua's Connection to Terrorism*, Hearings, September 30, 1980, p. 1.

19. Arnson, *Crossroads*, pp. 37, 49.

20. See National Security Archive, ed., *The Iran-Contra Affair: The Making of a Scandal, 1983–1988* (Alexandria: Chadwyck-Healey, 1990), p. 30; John Brecher et al., "A Secret War for Nicaragua," *Newsweek*, November 8, 1982: 44; Robert C. Toth and Doyle McManus, "Contras and CIA: A Plan Gone Awry," *Los Angeles Times*, March 3, 1985. A number of Nicaraguans who worked for the CIA under Carter's program of covert operations, e.g., Orlando Bolaños, would later be important players in the anti-Sandinista movement.

21. Quoted in Toth and McManus, "Contras and CIA."

22. The 1974 Hughes-Ryan amendment to the Foreign Assistance Act forbade the CIA from engaging in covert activities unless the president "finds that each such operation is important to the national security of the United States and reports, in a timely fashion, a description and scope of such operation to the appropriate committees of the Congress" —Arnson, *Crossroads*, p. 13.

23. Toth and McManus, "Contras and CIA."

24. Address to the nation by President Carter, January 14, 1981, *AFP Documents 1981* (Washington, D.C.: U.S. Department of State, 1984), pp. 22–23. See Robert A. Pastor, *Condemned to Repetition: The United States and Nicaragua* (Princeton: Princeton University Press, 1987), pp.

227–228; and Harold Molineu *U.S. Policy Toward Latin America: From Regionalism to Globalism* (Boulder: Westview Press, 1990), pp. 144–155.

25. Aldo C. Vacs, "A Delicate Balance: Confrontation and Cooperation Between Argentina and the United States in the 1980s," *Journal of Interamerican Studies and World Affairs* 31, no. 4 (winter 1989): 28–33. See Carlos Escudé, *La Argentina vs. las grandes potencias (el precio del desafío)* (Buenos Aires: Editorial de Belgrano, 1986); and Escudé, *La Argentina: ¿paria internacional?* (Buenos Aires: Editorial de Belgrano, 1984). Also see Joseph Tulchin, *Argentina and the United States* (Boston: Twayne, 1990).

26. Interview with Capt. (retired) Carlos H. Raimondi, in Buenos Aires, August 4, 1993.

27. Guillermo Alberto Monkman, "The Institutionalization of the Doctrine of National Security in Argentina: The Military and Foreign Policy," Ph.D. dissertation, University of South Carolina, 1992, pp. 216–217.

28. Mark Falcoff, *A Tale of Two Policies: U.S. Relations with the Argentine Junta, 1976–1983* (Philadelphia: Foreign Policy Research Institute, 1989), p. 21; Molineu, *U.S. Policy Toward Latin America*, pp. 147–148. The Ford administration had opposed a proposed cut in military aid to Argentina for human rights abuses. The rationale for that decision was that military assistance enabled the U.S. government "to influence the course of events by maintaining this contact with Argentina rather than by not doing it"—U.S. Congress, House Committee on Appropriations, Subcommittee on Foreign Operations and Related Agencies, *Foreign Assistance and Related Agencies Appropriations for 1976*, pt. 4, 1975, p. 272, cited in Schoultz, *Human Rights*, p. 221.

29. Arnson, *Crossroads*, p. 11.

30. See Vacs, "A Delicate Balance": 23–33; Wolf Grabendorff, "¿De país aislado a aliado preferido? Las relaciones entre la Argentina y los Estados Unidos: 1976–1981," in Peter Waldmann and Ernesto Garzón Valdez, eds., *El poder militar en la Argentina, 1976–1981* (Buenos Aires: Galerna, 1983), pp. 155–159.

31. Interview with Gen. (retired) Miguel Angel Mallea Gil, in Buenos Aires, August 18, 1993. Compare the figures given by Mallea Gil with the number of *desaparecidos* in the dirty war. According to Amnesty International, there were more than 15,000 victims of state repression. Argentine

human rights organizations—such as *Madres de Plaza de Mayo* and *Servicio de Paz y Justicia*—estimated the number of people disappeared as nearly 30,000. The National Commission on the Disappeared (CONADEP) calculated that there were more than 9,000 victims of state repression—Carlos H. Acuña and Catalina Smulovitz, "Militares en la transición argentina: del gobierno a la subordinación constitucional," in C. Acuña et al., *Juicios, castigos y memorias: Derechos humanos y justicia en la política argentina* (Buenos Aires: Nueva Visión, 1995), p. 27. See Alison Brysk, "The Politics of Measurement: The Contested Count of the Disappeared in Argentina," *Human Rights Quarterly* 16, no. 4 (November 1994): 676–692. The claim by the armed forces that they fought a war against a powerful enemy from 1976 onward was persuasively challenged by Daniel Frontalini and María Cristina Caiati, *El mito de la guerra sucia* (Buenos Aires: Centro de Estudios Legales y Sociales [CELS], 1984). These authors argued that the guerrilla movements had been militarily defeated prior to the March 1976 coup d'état.

32. Kathryn Sikkink, "The Effectiveness of U.S. Human Rights Policy: The Case of Argentina and Guatemala," paper presented at the Sixteenth International Congress of the Latin American Studies Association, Washington, D.C., April 4–6, 1991. See also Lisa L. Martin and Kathryn Sikkink, "U.S. Policy and Human Rights in Argentina and Guatemala, 1973–1980," in Peter B. Evans, Harold K. Jacobson, and Robert D. Putnam, eds., *Double-Edged Diplomacy: International Bargaining and Domestic Politics* (Berkeley: University of California Press, 1993).

33. Sikkink, "Effectiveness," p. 1.

34. The account of competing agendas within the military leadership is based on Sikkink, "Effectiveness," pp. 17–18, 30; and interview with a former high-ranking official of the Videla administration, name withheld on request, in Buenos Aires, August 18, 1993.

35. Mallea Gil interview.

36. Ibid.

37. The following account of U.S.-Argentine relations under Carter is based on Juan de Onís, "Four Years After the Coup," *New York Times*, March 26, 1980; Grabendorff, "¿De país aislado a aliado preferido?," p. 159; and Vacs, "A Delicate Balance": 33. See Aldo C. Vacs, "The 1980

Grain Embargo Negotiations: The United States, Argentina, and the Soviet Union," rev. ed., Pew Case Studies in International Affairs, Washington, D.C., 1992.

38. Quoted in Ann Crittenden, "Assistant Secretary of State Patricia M. Derian," *New York Times*, May 30, 1980.

39. Patricia Derian, memorandum, cited in Martin Edwin Andersen, *Dossier Secreto: Argentina's Desaparecidos and the Myth of the "Dirty War"* (Boulder: Westview Press, 1993), p. 260.

40. Raimondi interview.

41. U.S. Congress, testimony of Leandro Sánchez Reisse before the Subcommittee on Terrorism, Narcotics and International Operations of the Senate Committee on Foreign Relations, July 23, 1987.

42. John Ranelagh, *The Agency: The Rise and Decline of the CIA* (New York: Simon and Schuster, 1986), p. 706.

43. U.S. Congress, Sánchez Reisse testimony, pp. 8–9, 14, 27, 111.

44. Ibid., pp. 14–17, 26–27, 36–37, 111. The Florida-based task force was headed by a civilian agent of army intelligence, Raúl Antonio Guglielminetti, known as Maj. Rogelio Guastavino (see chapter 5). Under the command of the head of the First Army Corps, Gen. Carlos Guillermo Suárez Mason, Guglielminetti participated in the kidnapping of businessmen and bankers during the dirty war. See Juan Gasparini, *La pista suiza* (Buenos Aires: Legasa, 1986), pp. 275–276; and Juan J. Salinas, "Los Mercenarios Argentinos (I)," *El Porteño*, July 1988: 7.

45. Subsequent to the inauguration of elected President Raúl Alfonsín in December 1983, Battalion 601 became the center of a vast network of old hands of the dirty war involved in criminal activities and terrorist acts that threatened the new democratic government.

46. U.S. Congress, Sánchez Reisse testimony, pp. 18–19, 56. See David Corn, "The CIA and the Cocaine Coup," *Nation*, October 7, 1991: 405.

47. Edgar Chamorro, *Packaging the Contras: A Case of CIA Disinformation* (New York: Institute for Media Analysis, 1987), pp. 5–6. According to Chamorro, "Aguirre was well-known to the CIA and the State Department, having been involved with them over the years in vetting Nicaraguan personalities, arms trafficking, and relations with conservative political groups in the Caribbean." See also Oscar Cardoso, Ricardo

Kirschbaum, and Eduardo van der Kooy, *Malvinas, la trama secreta* (Buenos Aires: Sudamericana-Planeta, 1983), pp. 22–23, 26–30. Reportedly, the CIA covertly funded Contra leader Col. Enrique Bermúdez under the Carter administration—Sam Dillon, *Comandos: The CIA and Nicaragua's Contra Rebels* (New York: Henry Holt, 1991), p. 341.

48. Schoultz, *National Security*, pp. 13–14.

49. Address by Reagan before the Foreign Policy Association, New York City, June 9, 1977, in Ronald Reagan, *A Time for Choosing: The Speeches of Ronald Reagan, 1961–1982* (Chicago: Regnery Gateway in cooperation with Americans for the Reagan Agenda, 1983), pp. 206–207, 210.

50. Arnson, *Crossroads*, p. 55.

51. Ranelagh, *The Agency*, p. 704.

52. Committee of Santa Fe, *A New Inter-American Policy for the Eighties* (Washington, D.C.: Council for Inter-American Security, 1980).

53. U.S. Congress, House Committee on Appropriations, Subcommittee on Foreign Operations and Related Agencies, *Foreign Assistance and Related Programs Appropriations for 1981*, pt. 1, 1980, p. 282.

54. Platform hearings of the 1980 Republican National Convention, Detroit, July 8 and 10, quoted in Gutman, *Banana Diplomacy*, p. 20.

55. Quoted in "No Easy Options in Latin America," *Latin America Weekly Report*, November 14, 1980: 9.

56. Gutman, *Banana Diplomacy*, p. 21.

57. Committee of Santa Fe, *A New Inter-American Policy*, pp. 1, 4–5, 9, 13–14, 45–46, 53.

58. Statement by the secretary of state-designate, Alexander Haig Jr., before the Senate Foreign Relations Committee, January 9, 1981, *AFP Documents 1981*, pp. 1–2.

59. Commencement address by Haig at Fairfield University, May 24, 1981, *AFP Documents 1981*, p. 43.

60. Statement by Haig before the Senate Armed Services Committee, July 30, 1981, *AFP Documents 1981*, p. 50.

61. Jeane Kirkpatrick, "U.S. Security and Latin America," in Howard J. Wiarda, ed., *Rift and Revolution: The Central American Imbroglio* (Washington, D.C.: American Enterprise Institute for Public Policy Research, 1984), p. 333.

62. Jeane Kirkpatrick, "Dictatorships and Double Standards," *Com-*

mentary 68 (November 1979): 37. See Thomas Carothers, *In the Name of Democracy: U.S. Policy Toward Latin America in the Reagan Years* (Berkeley: University of California Press, 1991): 109.

63. Prepared statement by Lt. Gen. Ernest Graves, director, Security Assistance Agency, Department of Defense, before the Senate Foreign Relations Committee, May 4, 1981, *AFP Documents 1981*, pp. 1186–1187.

64. Quote from Schoultz, *National Security*, p. 325. On the United States, Latin America, and the global balance of power, ibid., pp. 268–307.

65. Quote from *Weekly Compilation of Presidential Documents: Reagan*, no. 19 (May 2, 1983), p. 614.

66. Schoultz, *National Security*, p. 259.

67. Testimony of former National Security adviser Robert McFarlane, in Joel Brinkley and Stephen Engelberg, eds., *Report of the Congressional Committees Investigating the Iran-Contra Affair* (New York: Random House, 1988), p. 411.

68. Address by Thomas Enders, assistant secretary of state for inter-American affairs, before the Council of the Americas, June 3, 1981, *AFP Documents 1981*, pp. 1191–1193.

69. Prepared statement by Enders before the Subcommittee on Western Hemisphere Affairs of the Senate Foreign Relations Committee, December 14, 1981, *AFP Documents 1981*, pp. 1366–1367.

70. U.S. Department of State report, "Communist Interference in El Salvador" (known as the White Paper), February 23, 1981, *AFP Documents 1981*, p. 1236.

71. Enders, prepared statement before the Subcommittee on Western Hemisphere Affairs, p. 1368.

72. U.S. Department of State report, "Cuba's Renewed Support for Violence in Latin America," December 14, 1981, *AFP Documents 1981*, pp. 1207, 1210.

73. Press briefing by Haig, February 27, 1981, *AFP Documents 1981*, p. 1275.

74. U.S. Department of State, secret memorandum, "Taking the War to Nicaragua," McFarlane to Haig, quoted in Toth and McManus, "Contras and CIA."

75. Gutman, *Banana Diplomacy*, p. 29. See Schoultz, *National Security*, pp. 272–273.

76. CIA secret policy paper to Department of State, February 26, 1981 (NSA, *Nicaragua*).

77. State Department secret memorandum, "Covert Action Proposal for Central America," McFarlane to Haig, February 27, 1981 (NSA, *Nicaragua*).

78. State Department secret memorandum, "Talking Points," McFarlane to Haig, February 27, 1981 (NSA, *Nicaragua*).

79. CIA secret presidential finding (draft), February 27, 1981 (NSA, *Nicaragua*).

80. Executive Office of the President, secret presidential finding from Ronald Reagan, March 9, 1981, in U.S. Congress, Senate Select Committee on Secret Military Assistance to Iran and the Nicaraguan Opposition and House Select Committee to Investigate Covert Arms Transactions with Iran, *Report of the Congressional Committees Investigating the Iran-Contra Affair*, Appendix A, Source Documents, 1988, p. 1156.

81. Statement issued by the State Department, April 1, 1981, *AFP Documents 1981*, p. 1298.

82. Interview with Lawrence Pezzullo, March 1986, in Gutman, *Banana Diplomacy*, p. 37.

83. State Department, Bureau of Public Affairs, *Nicaraguan Biographies: A Resource Book*, special report no. 174 (Washington, D.C.: Bureau of Public Affairs, 1988), pp. 3–5.

84. Ibid., p. 4. See Morley and Petras, *Reagan Administration and Nicaragua*, pp. 82–84.

85. Arnson, *Crossroads*, p. 50. A former high-ranking Sandinista official interviewed by the author in Nicaragua (July 10, 1993) corroborated this account.

86. Carothers, *In the Name of Democracy*, pp. 78–80.

87. Quoted in Christopher Dickey, *With the Contras: A Reporter in the Wilds of Nicaragua* (New York: Simon and Schuster, 1987), p. 111.

88. Ranelagh, *The Agency*, pp. 658–659, 673–675.

89. R. Jeffrey Smith, "CIA Chief Fires 2 Over Scandal In Guatemala," *Washington Post*, September 30, 1995.

90. The CIA violated the law when it failed to instruct Congress appropriately about the Iran-Contra operation in 1987. This legacy of misrepresentation resurfaced in the early 1990s when officials in the

Operations Directorate's Latin America division "knowingly misled" Congress regarding CIA secret payments to a Guatemalan military officer linked to two political murders in that country. A report by President Bill Clinton's Intelligence Oversight Board attributed the wrongdoing to "CIA mismanagement, the absence of a systematic congressional notification process, and a routine desire by lower-echelon officials to protect the identities of all CIA sources." However, it can be argued that the 1990s Guatemala affair evidenced that the CIA continued to operate as a covert, omniscient face of the state with exclusive jurisdiction to deploy its intelligence apparatus based on its own, indisputable weltanschauung—Smith, "CIA Chief Fires 2." See Alan Wolfe, *The Limits of Legitimacy: Political Contradictions of Contemporary Capitalism* (New York: The Free Press, 1977), pp. 201–205.

91. Ranelagh, *The Agency*, pp. 674, 680–681; Arnson, *Crossroads*, pp. 64–65, 74.

92. Arnson, *Crossroads*, p. 79.

93. Don Oberdorfer and Patrick E. Tyler, "U.S.-Backed Nicaraguan Rebel Army Swells to 7,000 Men," *Washington Post*, May 8, 1983.

94. Quoted in Leslie H. Gelb, "Argentina Linked to Rise in Covert U.S. Actions Against Sandinists," *New York Times*, April 8, 1983.

95. As former intelligence operative Sánchez Reisse stated in his deposition before Congress, "people from the Government of Argentina, together with people from the Government of the United States, decided that it was better and it was much [safer] that Argentine troops and Argentine advisers were, for instance, in El Salvador or Costa Rica and Honduras, [than] directly involving troops from [the] United States at that time in certain situations in Central America"—U.S. Congress, Sánchez Reisse testimony, p. 16.

96. Quoted in John M. Goshko, "Haig Won't Rule Out anti-Nicaragua Action," *Washington Post*, November 13, 1981. See also Holly Sklar, *Washington's War on Nicaragua* (Boston: South End Press, 1988), p. 95.

97. Peter Kornbluh, *Nicaragua: The Price of Intervention* (Washington, D.C.: Institute for Policy Studies, 1987), pp. 22–23. For more information about NSDD 17 and accompanying documents, see Oberdorfer and Tyler, "U.S.-Backed Nicaraguan Rebel Army"; Sklar, *Washington's War*, pp. 98–100; and Dickey, *With the Contras*, pp. 111–112.

98. Joanne Omang, "Rebel Fund Diversion Rooted in Early Policy," *Washington Post*, January 1, 1987; Daniel Hadad, "Comandante 3-80: jefe militar de la 'Contra,'" *Somos* (Buenos Aires), January 14, 1987: 6.

99. Quoted in Joseph E. Persico, *Casey: From the OSS to the CIA* (New York: Viking, 1990), p. 273.

100. Ibid.

101. Executive Office of the President, secret presidential finding from Ronald Reagan, December 1, 1981 (NSA, *Nicaragua*).

102. CIA secret memorandum, "Scope of CIA Activities under the Central America Finding," n.d. (DDRS).

103. Quoted in Oberdorfer and Tyler, "U.S.-Backed Nicaraguan Rebel Army."

104. In early August 1981, Clarridge had replaced Néstor Sánchez as head of the CIA Latin America Division. Sánchez was transferred to the Defense Department.

105. Report by the Institute for Policy Studies, Washington, D.C., March 5, 1982. See *Barricada*, November 4, 1982. Subsequent press reports revealed that U.S. and Argentine advisers had outlined a plan to organize the resistance forces into a more conventional army with capacity for major military actions.

106. Bob Woodward, *Veil: The Secret Wars of the CIA, 1981–1987* (New York: Simon and Schuster, 1987), pp. 172, 176, 187–188. As disaffected anti-Sandinista leader Edgar Chamorro said, "we got contras because [the United States] put together Somocistas, Argentineans and the CIA. You cannot expect too much democracy from that"—interview with Chamorro, November 1986, quoted in Sklar, *Washington's War*, p. 75.

107. Nicaragua's military support to the Farabundo Martí National Liberation Front (FMLN) had apparently ceased for the most part in February 1981. According to former CIA agent David McMichael, the agency undoubtedly knew that the arms pipeline had been largely cut off. "The decision to start the Contra war," McMichael stated, "was taken at the same time as the flow of arms stopped"—quoted in Vegard Bye, *La paz prohibida: El laberinto centroamericano en la década de los ochenta* (San José, Costa Rica: Departamento Ecuménico de Investigaciones, 1991), p. 96.

108. Persico, *Casey*, pp. 274–275.

109. I am indebted to former U.S. Ambassador Edwin Corr for his key insight on this issue. Key players in this informal process were John Carbaugh, a staffer to Senator Helms; Nat Hamrick, a North Carolina businessman who had been a partner of Somoza's family; and Francisco Aguirre, a Washington, D.C.–based former national guard colonel linked to the CIA and close friend of Walters, its former deputy director. Hamrick and Aguirre met with the deputy chief of army intelligence, Col. Mario Davico, in March 1981 (following the visit of President-designate Viola to the United States). At that meeting in Buenos Aires, they arranged the specifics of the U.S.-Argentine cooperation in the anti-Sandinista venture. Hamrick was a friend of Carbaugh and Gerardo Schamis, an Argentine diplomat closely linked to the Argentine army leadership. Prior to Reagan's victory in the 1980 elections, Hamrick had given Schamis access to the Republican candidate's inner circle. Consequently, Schamis served as a main link between the Reagan administration and the Argentine military government. In turn, Carbaugh had a vast network of contacts within powerful Latin American right-wing factions. One of his key associates was Salvadoran death-squad leader Roberto D'Aubuisson. Carbaugh strongly supported Col. José Osvaldo Ribeiro, political head of operations of the Argentine general staff in Honduras. Ribeiro had been involved in the transnational Condor network and commanded a clandestine detention center (El campito) in Campo de Mayo (Buenos Aires Province) during the dirty war. This account is based on an interview with Juan José Salinas, in Buenos Aires, July 31, 1993; Gutman, *Banana Diplomacy*, pp. 22, 49–57, 104; and Chamorro, *Packaging the Contras*, pp. 5–6.

110. Interview with a former Argentinean ambassador who held a key position in the Foreign Ministry's division of Central America, the Caribbean, and Mexico (1981–1982), name withheld on request, in Buenos Aires, August 11, 1993.

111. Quote from affidavit of Edgar Chamorro, Washington, D.C., September 5, 1985, for the International Court of Justice, "Case Concerning Military and Paramilitary Activities In and Against Nicaragua," in author's files, pp. 4–5. See John Brecher et al., "A Secret War for Nicaragua," *Newsweek*, November 8, 1982.

112. It has been suggested that General Mallea Gil, a graduate from the

U.S. military academy at West Point, was the main Argentine connection to Vernon Walters. Presumably, he was also the Argentine officer most trusted by the Pentagon (Mallea Gil was designated Argentine military attaché to the United States in early 1981)—interview with Col. (retired) Horacio P. Ballester, in Buenos Aires, July 28, 1993; Raimondi interview.

113. Jesús Iglesias Rouco, "Conversaciones estratégicas," *La Prensa* (Buenos Aires), March 6, 1981.

114. General Viola and Ambassador Aja Espil quoted in Falcoff, *A Tale of Two Policies*, p. 45.

115. Horacio Verbitsky, *La última batalla de la tercera guerra mundial* (Buenos Aires: Legasa, 1984), p. 97, citing *La Prensa*, March 19, 1981, and *Clarín*, March 21–22, 1981.

116. Cardoso et al., *Malvinas*, pp. 29–30.

117. Raimondi interview.

118. U.S. Congress, House Foreign Affairs Committee, Subcommittees on Human Rights and International Organizations and on Inter-American Affairs, *Review of United States Policy on Military Assistance to Argentina*, Hearings, April 1, 1981, quote from p. 2.

119. Mallea Gil interview.

120. Raimondi interview.

121. Report by ABC Television, February 3, 1982; *Excelsior* (Mexico City), February 12, 1982.

122. Quoted in Persico, *Casey*, p. 273.

123. Persico, *Casey*, pp. 272–273; Falcoff, *A Tale of Two Policies*, p. 47. On the decision-making logic of the military leadership in the early 1980s, see Andrés Fontana, "Fuerzas armadas, partidos políticos y transición a la democracia en Argentina," Centro de Estudios de Estado y Sociedad (CEDES), Buenos Aires, 1984; and Fontana, "De la crisis de Malvinas a la subordinación condicionada: conflictos intramilitares y transición política en Argentina," working paper, Kellogg Institute, August 1986.

124. Raimondi interview.

125. See Ignacio González Janzen, *La Triple-A* (Buenos Aires: Contrapunto, 1986).

126. Interview with Col. Mohamed Alí Seineldín, at the military prison, Magdalena, August 21, 1993; Raimondi interview. See Roberto Russell and Juan Tokatlian, "Argentina y la crisis Centroamericana

(1976–1985)," in Boris Yopo, R. Russell, and J. Tokatlian, *La Unión Soviética y Argentina frente a la crisis Centroamericana* (San José, Costa Rica: Facultad Latinoamericana de Ciencias Sociales [FLACSO], 1987), p. 38. Argentina's long-standing aim of recovering the Malvinas was perceived by the military junta as an issue that could unite the people behind the Galtieri government, which was confronted with a serious economic and social crisis at home—Vacs, "A Delicate Balance": 35.

127. Interviews in Buenos Aires with Gen. (retired) José Teófilo Goyret, August 5, 1993; Col. (retired) Miguel Angel Li Puma, August 18, 1993; and Raimondi. A key source to understanding the military's perception of the Argentine role in Central America is the testimony given to the Rattenbach Commission by Adm. Jorge Isaac Anaya, member of the Argentine junta and navy commander, in Comisión de Análisis y Evaluación de las Responsabilidades Políticas y Estratégico-Militares en el Conflicto del Atlántico Sur (CAERCAS), *Informe Rattenbach* (Buenos Aires: Ediciones Espartaco, 1988), p. 42.

128. This account of the assumptions held by the Argentine military leadership is based on the following sources: Mallea Gil interview; Frontalini and Caiati, *El mito de la guerra sucia*, p. 18; CAERCAS, *Informe Rattenbach*, p. 44. The decision to invade the Malvinas was taken by a small group of high-ranking officers at the level of the general staff of the armed forces. The heads of the army corps had not been officially briefed about the operation before its launching—interview with Gen. (retired) Eugenio Alfredo Dalton, in Buenos Aires, August 6, 1993. There is a vast body of literature on the Malvinas/Falklands war. See, for instance, Lawrence Freedman and Virginia Gamba-Stonehouse, *Signals of War: The Falklands Conflict of 1982* (Princeton: Princeton University Press, 1991); and David Lewis Feldman, "The United States Role in the Malvinas Crisis, 1982: Misguidance and Misperception in Argentina's Decision to Go to War," *Journal of Interamerican Studies and World Affairs* 27, no. 2 (summer 1985): 1–24.

129. Cardoso et al., *Malvinas*, pp. 59–63. Raimondi was the informant.

130. Mallea Gil interview.

131. Alexander M. Haig Jr., *Caveat: Realism, Reagan, and Foreign Policy* (New York: Macmillan, 1984), pp. 263, 266.

132. Juan José Salinas, "Los mercenarios argentinos (II)," *El Porteño*, August 1988: 33; Raimondi interview. The rest of my informants in Argentina corroborated this account.

133. See U.S. Department of State, Bureau of Public Affairs, *Documents on the Nicaraguan Resistance: Leaders, Military Personnel, and Program*, special report no. 142 (Washington, D.C.: Bureau of Public Affairs, 1986), p. 3; Jaime Morales Carazo, *La Contra* (México, D.F.: Planeta, 1989), p. 57.

134. Gutman, *Banana Diplomacy*, pp. 104, 107. See International Court of Justice (ICJ), Case Concerning Military and Paramilitary Activities In and Against Nicaragua (*Nicaragua v. United States of America*), Merits, Judgment, ICJ Reports, 1986, p. 523.

CHAPTER 3

Some documents were consulted through the following microfiche collections: Declassified Documents Reference System (Woodbridge: Research Publications, various years) (hereafter, DDRS); National Security Archive, ed., *Nicaragua: The Making of U.S. Policy, 1978–1990* (Alexandria: Chadwyck-Healey, 1991) (hereafter, NSA, *Nicaragua*); National Security Archive, ed., *El Salvador: The Making of U.S. Policy, 1977–1984* (Alexandria: Chadwyck-Healey, 1989) (hereafter, NSA, *El Salvador*).

1. On the state-sponsored violence, see Andrew R. Morrison and Rachel A. May, "Escape from Terror: Violence and Migration in Post-Revolutionary Guatemala," *Latin American Research Review* 29, no. 2 (1994): 114.

2. Michael McClintock, *The American Connection: State Terror and Popular Resistance in Guatemala* (London: Zed Books, 1985), pp. 271–272.

3. The figures are from the United Nations High Commissioner for Refugees, limited official-use cable to Department of State from Gerald B. Helman, December 18, 1979 (NSA, *Nicaragua*).

4. The Argentine network in Costa Rica is examined briefly in chapter 5.

5. "Adiestramiento militar," *Acción Cívica* (Managua), March 1976, p. 12. See Richard Millett, *Guardians of the Dynasty: A History of the U.S.*

Created Guardia Nacional de Nicaragua and the Somoza Family (Maryknoll: Orbis Books, 1977), pp. 251–252.

6. CIA, "Hired Guns for Nicaragua," memo, classification unknown, my copy undated, circa 1975 (DDRS).

7. See testimony of Amalia Larralde before the National Commission on the Disappeared (Sábato Commission), Comisión Nacional sobre la Desaparición de Personas (CONADEP), *Nunca Más* (Buenos Aires: EUDEBA, 1984), p. 143.

8. Interview with a former national guard lieutenant, Rodolfo Ampié Quiróz, in Managua, July 2 and 5, 1993. Following directives from the government of María Estela (Isabel) Martínez de Perón (1974–1976), Seineldín trained ultraright Triple A commandos in the Campo de Mayo military base, Buenos Aires Province, in 1975. He was later identified as the visible link between the army and the Triple A. According to Seineldín's neighbors in Paraná, Entre Ríos, he made several trips to Central America in 1977–1978—affidavit of Rodolfo Peregrino Fernández, Madrid, April 26, 1983, p. 8; Juan Salinas and Julio Villalonga, *Gorriarán, la Tablada y las "guerras de inteligencia" en América Latina* (Buenos Aires: Mangin, 1993), p. 94. Seineldín did not agree to discuss his alleged involvement in the Central American counterrevolutionary effort when I interviewed him at the military penitentiary, Magdalena, Buenos Aires Province, August 21, 1993, although he did discuss related matters.

9. The officer mentioned in note 8, Ampié Quiróz, interviewed in July 1993. Ampié Quiróz, an EEBI instructor trained in Argentina (1972–1973 and 1978), was sentenced by a Sandinista special tribunal to 30 years in prison for the crimes of "*asesinato atroz, asociación para delinquir y contra el orden internacional*"—Court documents, Eighth Special Tribunal, case against Rodolfo Ernesto Ampié Quiróz, in author's files. In October 1983, Ampié fled from the Tipitapa jail and soon joined the FDN.

10. Ampié Quiróz interview. In Córdoba his group was addressed by Gen. Luciano Benjamín Menéndez, commander of the Third Army Corps.

11. Ampié Quiróz interview.

12. See Acdel Edgardo Vilas, *Tucumán: el hecho histórico*—"El plan táctico que posibilitó la victoria contra el Ejército Revolucionario del Pueblo (ERP) en 1975," undated pamphlet, in author's files.

13. Eduardo Luis Duhalde, *El Estado terrorista argentino* (Barcelona: Argos Vergara, 1983), p. 118; Roberto Bardini, *Monjes, mercenarios y mercaderes: la red secreta de apoyo a los Contras* (México, D.F.: Alpa Corral, 1988), pp. 103–105.

14. Oscar Cardoso, Ricardo Kirschbaum, and Eduardo van der Kooy, *Malvinas, la trama secreta* (Buenos Aires: Sudamericana-Planeta, 1983), p. 27; Sergio Joselovsky, "El ejército del 'Proceso' y su intervención en Centroamérica," *Humor* (Buenos Aires), my copy undated, circa fall 1984: 63.

15. Ampié Quiróz interview; Ernesto Tenembaum, "Me dedicaba al ablande," *Página 12*, November 29, 1982. Within hours of the revolutionary triumph, several EEBI officers were evacuated to Miami in CIA planes disguised with Red Cross markings—interview with Lizzeth Chávez, former member of EEBI's female police, in Managua, July 6, 1993.

16. Argentine operative Carlos Dürich confirmed the role played by the navy and the army's faction under the leadership of General Díaz Bessone—interview with Juan José Salinas, in Buenos Aires, July 31, 1993.

17. Leonardo Frei, "Nicaragua bajo fuego argentino," *Caras y Caretas* (Buenos Aires), March 1984.

18. Quote from *Foreign Broadcast Information Service–Latin America* (hereafter, *FBIS-LAT*), July 27, 1979.

19. I have the following documents by EDESA in my files: "Reforma de Estatutos: 'Empresa de Desarrollos Especiales S.A.,'" January 5, 1977; "Memoria y Balance: EDESA S.A.," April 30, 1978.

20. Graffigna speeches, August 10, September 24, and November 16, 1979, quoted in Horacio Verbitsky, *La última batalla de la tercera guerra mundial* (Buenos Aires: Legasa, 1984), p. 83. Quote from September speech.

21. Interview with Luis Bruschtein, in Buenos Aires, July 30, 1993; quote from Donald C. Hodges, *Argentina's "Dirty War": An Intellectual Biography* (Austin: University of Texas Press, 1991), p. 223. See Jorge Sigal, "Gorriarán Merlo, fantasma y realidad," *Somos* (Buenos Aires), July 20, 1992: 8; and Salinas and Villalonga, *Gorriarán*, p. 45.

22. Conversation with Tomás Borge aide Margarita Suzán, in Managua, June 25, 1993. On the role of the Argentines in the southern front, see Christopher Dickey, *With the Contras: A Reporter in the Wilds of Nicaragua* (New York: Simon and Schuster, 1987), p. 30; Henri Weber,

"The Struggle for Power," in Peter Rosset and John Vandermeer, eds., *Nicaragua: Unfinished Revolution* (New York: Grove Press, 1986), p. 202; and Claribel Alegría and D. J. Flakoll, *Somoza: expediente cerrado* (Managua: El Gato Negro–Latino Editores, 1993), p. 21. Some of the Argentine combatants in the southern front were Juan Manuel Murúa, Hugo Alfredo Irurzún, Roberto Sánchez (who would become Managua's vice chief of police), and José Luis Caldú. The last two died in the assault on La Tablada army barracks outside Buenos Aires launched by the Everyone for the Fatherland Movement (Movimiento Todos por la Patria, MTP) on January 23, 1989—Salinas and Villalonga, *Gorriarán*, pp. 46–47, 49, 79–80; Alipio Paoletti, *Como los Nazis, como en Vietnam* (Buenos Aires: Contrapunto, 1987), pp. 427, 442–443(n.6).

23. Interview with a former Argentine guerrilla cadre who worked at Nicaragua's Ministry of the Interior, name withheld on request, in Managua, June 28, 1993.

24. Martha Honey, *Hostile Acts: U.S. Policy in Costa Rica in the 1980s* (Gainesville: University Press of Florida, 1994), pp. 376–377.

25. See U.S. embassy, Paraguay, updates on Somoza's assassination, confidential cables to Department of State from Lyle F. Lane, September 18, 19, 20, 22, 24 and October 7, 1980 (NSA, *Nicaragua*).

26. *Barricada* (Managua), September 18, 1980.

27. Martin Edwin Andersen, *Dossier Secreto: Argentina's Desaparecidos and the Myth of the "Dirty War"* (Boulder: Westview Press, 1993), pp. 292–293. For a detailed account of the operation, see Alegría and Flakoll, *Somoza: expediente cerrado*; and "Así maté a Somoza," *Siete Días* (Buenos Aires), July 27, 1983.

28. Conversation with Tomás Borge, minister of the interior under the Sandinista government, in Managua, July 8, 1993; Honey, *Hostile Acts*, p. 378. Some sources held that Francés actually defected from Battalion 601. In my conversation with Borge, he stressed, "We kidnapped him in San José, Costa Rica."

29. Jorge G. Castañeda, *Utopia Unarmed: The Latin American Left After the Cold War* (New York: Alfred A. Knopf, 1993), p. 268. In January 1989, Gorriarán Merlo led the attack on La Tablada military base. Several of those involved in the assault were former ERP members. In 1995, Gorriarán was detained in Mexico as a result of a cooperative effort of Ar-

gentine and Mexican intelligence agencies. He was extradited to Argentina under several criminal charges dating back to the 1970s. As of August 1996, he was awaiting trial.

30. A former Montonero interviewed by the author in Buenos Aires (August 18, 1993) said there were approximately thirty-five Montonero guerrillas in the Simón Bolívar Brigade. See Dickey, *With the Contras*, p. 30.

31. Richard Gillespie, *Soldiers of Perón: Argentina's Montoneros* (New York: Oxford University Press, 1982), p. 311; interview with Mario Firmenich, in Hodges, *Argentina's "Dirty War,"* p. 292. The account of the Montonero-Sandinista meeting in Cuba is from Castañeda, *Utopia Unarmed*, pp. 13–14.

32. Quotes from *FBIS-LAT*, July 23, 1979. See Andersen, *Dossier Secreto*, p. 287.

33. Quote from *FBIS-LAT*, July 23, 1979. See Juan Gasparini, *La pista suiza* (Buenos Aires: Legasa, 1986), pp. 184–185.

34. Gasparini, *La pista suiza*, p. 185.

35. Andersen, *Dossier Secreto*, p. 287.

36. Andersen, *Dossier Secreto*, pp. 117–118, 319–320. See Martin Edwin Andersen, "Dirty Secrets of the 'Dirty War,' " *Nation*, March 13, 1989.

37. Andersen, *Dossier Secreto*, p. 319.

38. Dickey, *With the Contras*, pp. 54–55.

39. Interview with Carlos Alberto Lobo in *Siete Días*, March 13, 1983: 74–76. See also *Buenos Aires Herald*, January 19, 1985. As disclosed by Rogelio García Lupo, Chile had a counterinsurgency squad in Nicaragua, too—García Lupo, *Paraguay de Stroessner* (Buenos Aires: Grupo Editorial Zeta, 1989), pp. 179–180.

40. Dickey, *With the Contras*, p. 54; Juan José Salinas, "De Perón a Somoza, via Massera," *El Porteño* (Buenos Aires), December 1987: 18–21. Another member of the Argentine hit team was Alfredo Zarattini, an intelligence operative linked to Mario Sandoval Alarcón and Lionel Sisniega Otero, leaders of Guatemala's National Liberation Movement (Movimiento de Liberación Nacional, MLN), and the Salvadoran national guard—Salinas and Villalonga, *Gorriarán*, pp. 165, 168–169.

41. This account of Echaverry Mejía is based on the following sources: interview with a former captain, José Luis D'Andrea Mohr, in

Buenos Aires, August 14, 1991; interview with a former national guard lieutenant colonel, Abel Céspedes, July 7, 1993, in Managua; CIA, "Emilio Echaverry Mejía," memo, classification unknown, December 19, 1983 (DDRS).

42. Salinas and Villalonga, *Gorriarán*, p. 167.

43. Ibid., p. 46.

44. U.S. Congress, testimony of a defector from the Salvadoran army, Capt. Ricardo Alejandro Fiallos, before the Subcommittee on Foreign Operations of the House Appropriations Committee, April 29, 1981; testimony of Néstor Norberto Cendón, a former member of Army Intelligence Battalion 601, before the Sábato Commission, in Alipio Paoletti, *Como los Nazis, como en Vietnam*, pp. 425–426. See Department of State, "Dissent paper on El Salvador and Central America," to Dissent Channel from ESCATF/D, re.: DM-ESCA no. 80-3, November 6, 1980, in Michael McClintock, *The American Connection: State Terror and Popular Resistance in El Salvador* (London: Zed Books, 1985), pp. 343–344 (it must noted that there has been much debate about the authenticity of this document).

45. U.S. Congress, testimony of Leandro Sánchez Reisse before the Subcommittee on Terrorism, Narcotics and International Operations of the Senate Committee on Foreign Relations, July 23, 1987, pp. 26–27, 36–37, III.

46. Prior to Reagan's inauguration, Israel transferred intelligence information computing and communications equipment to El Salvador for antiguerrilla operations—interview with Ambassador Thomas Pickering, in Max G. Manwaring and Court E. Prisk, eds., *El Salvador at War: An Oral History* (Washington, D.C.: National Defense University, 1988), p. 309.

47. Laurie Becklund, "Death Squad Members: 'Over the Edge,'" *Los Angeles Times*, December 19, 1983; Duhalde, *El Estado terrorista argentino*, pp. 120–121, 128. The UGB and FALANGE were reported to have close links to Salvadoran upper-class networks—Cynthia Arnson, "Background Information on the Security Forces in El Salvador and U.S. Military Assistance," Institute for Policy Studies, Washington, D.C., March 1980, p. 6. Throughout 1980, the Salvadoran government denied any links between anti-Communist death squads and the security forces.

However, a defector from the Salvadoran army, Fiallos, stated that the death squads were "made up of members of the security forces and acts of terrorism credited to these squads such as political assassinations, kidnappings, and indiscriminate murder [were], in fact, planned by high-ranking military officers and carried out by members of the security forces." Fiallos accused the high command of the armed forces (specifically, Col. José Guillermo García and Col. Jaime Abdul Gutiérrez) of having direct control over state repression. See Christopher Dickey, "Behind the Death Squads," *New Republic*, December 26, 1983.

48. Former U.S. ambassador to El Salvador, Robert E. White, personal communication with author, February 29, 1996.

49. U.S. Congress, testimony of Amnesty International before the Subcommittee on Inter-American Affairs of the House Committee on Foreign Affairs, March 1981.

50. McClintock, *The American Connection: El Salvador*, pp. 299–300.

51. Becklund, "Death Squad Members"; Craig Pyes, "'The Doctor' Prescribes Torture for the Hesitant," *Albuquerque Journal*, December 20, 1983.

52. Duhalde, *El Estado terrorista argentino*, p. 146. In the Argentine case, military sources estimated the margin of error of the operations at about 25 percent, which added up to some 7,500 victims of "mistakes."

53. "Dissent paper on El Salvador," in McClintock, *The American Connection: El Salvador*, p. 331.

54. Quoted in Becklund, "Death Squad Members."

55. Americas Watch, *U.S. Reporting on Human Rights in El Salvador: Methodology at Odds with Knowledge*, New York, June 1982, p. 33.

56. Interview with an American expert assigned to El Salvador, November 1989, in Benjamin C. Schwarz, *American Counterinsurgency Doctrine and El Salvador: The Frustrations of Reform and the Illusions of Nation Building* (Santa Monica: RAND, 1991), p. 80(n.27). On the nature of the counterinsurgency war waged by the Salvadoran army, see Mark Danner's account of the El Mozote massacre by the American-trained Atlacatl Battalion, *The Massacre at El Mozote: A Parable of the Cold War* (New York: Vintage, 1994).

57. Timothy P. Wickham-Crowley, *Guerrillas and Revolution in Latin America: A Comparative Study of Insurgents and Regimes Since 1956*

(Princeton: Princeton University Press, 1992), pp. 282–291. The Salvadoran military's *tanda* system, the promotion of an academic graduating-class cohort through the ranks together, contributed not only to the collective nature of the Salvadoran armed forces but also to their unprofessional and ruthless behavior—Schwarz, *American Counterinsurgency Doctrine*, p. vi.

58. See Wickham-Crowley, *Guerrillas and Revolution in Latin America*, p. 285.

59. Quoted in Becklund, "Death Squad Members."

60. This account of D'Aubuisson is based on the following sources: interview with Roberto D'Aubuisson, in *Pensamiento Propio* (Managua), May/June 1984: 36–37; Laurie Becklund, "Death Squads: Deadly 'Other War,'" *Los Angeles Times*, December 18, 1983; Allan Nairn, "Behind the Death Squads," *Progressive*, May 1984: 25, 28; Craig Pyes, "Two Dinner Parties Meet, And Two Americans Die," *Albuquerque Journal*, December 19, 1983. Two of the principal conspirators of the 1981 murders (the "Sheraton murders") linked to D'Aubuisson were a national guard captain, Eduardo Avila, and a national guard lieutenant, Rodolfo López Sibran.

61. Former Triple A member Luis Guazzaroni acted as liaison between Army Intelligence Battalion 601 and D'Aubuisson. Capt. Roberto Alfieri, adviser to the Salvadoran national guard, was another Argentine identified in El Salvador. After the Falklands/Malvinas war, he remained in Central America as part of a drug-trafficking and extortion/kidnapping ring reportedly commanded by General Suárez Mason—Juan José Salinas, "Los mercenarios argentinos (II)," *El Porteño*, August 1988: 35–36.

62. Becklund, "Death Squad Members"; Salinas, "De Perón a Somoza": 18–21. Jorge Flores Allende and Carlos Noria, members of the Argentine ultraright organization *Falange de Fe*, reportedly served as advisers to the Salvadoran military—Salinas, "Mercenarios argentinos (III)": 21.

63. General Directorate of Military Industries (Dirección General de Fabricaciones Militares, DGFM), "Financiación de venta de material bélico a la República de El Salvador," secret memo to army commander in chief, Gen. Leopoldo F. Galtieri, from Gen. Augusto J. B. Alemanzor, January 18, 1982.

64. Central Bank of the Republic of Argentina (Banco Central de la República Argentina, BCRA), Directorate's "Secret Session," "Acta Nº 'S' 2," February 11, 1982.

65. General Directorate of Military Industries, memo no. 624/33, ref.: E.02940/82, February 1, 1982.

66. Sánchez Reisse testimony, p. 44.

67. Mark Falcoff, *A Tale of Two Policies: U.S. Relations with the Argentine Junta, 1976–1983* (Philadelphia: Foreign Policy Research Institute, 1989), p. 43. Secretary of State Alexander Haig, speaking to a congressional committee, stated, "It is clear that if we terminate military assistance to El Salvador—which receives limited assistance from Argentina, Venezuela, and other Central American countries—it would be a fatal blow"—quoted in U.S. embassy, Argentina, "Parties Question Argentina Involvement in Central America," confidential cable to Department of State from Harry Shlaudeman, March 12, 1982 (NSA, *El Salvador*).

68. Horacio Verbitsky, *La última batalla de la tercera guerra mundial* (Buenos Aires: Legasa, 1984), pp. 96, 98; Duhalde, *El Estado terrorista argentino*, p. 121.

69. "Military Diplomacy Tilts Argentine Foreign Policy Towards Washington," *Latin America Weekly Report* (hereafter, *LAWR*), September 11, 1981: 1.

70. Quoted in "The Walters Friendship Formula," *LAWR*, October 2, 1981: 8.

71. "'Che' Galtieri Plans His Own Vietnam," *LAWR*, October 9, 1981; "Viola's Health Wanes and Galtieri Gets the U.S. Seal of Approval," *LAWR*, November 13, 1981: 1.

72. U.S. embassy, Argentina, "More on Argentina, El Salvador and Central America," confidential cable to Department of State from Harry Shlaudeman, February 26, 1982 (NSA, *El Salvador*). Colonel Flores Lima was one of the army commanders strongly endorsed by the U.S. embassy in El Salvador.

73. Quoted in Scott Anderson and Jon Lee Anderson, *Inside the League* (New York: Dodd, Mead, 1986), p. 303, citing *Noticias Argentinas* (Buenos Aires), February 24, 1982.

74. Quoted in *El Día* (Mexico), March 19, 1981. See also Guillermo Almeyra, "El gendarme del sur," *Uno Más Uno* (Mexico), March 25, 1981.

75. On state terror in Guatemala, see McClintock, *The American Connection: Guatemala*; Carlos Figueroa Ibarra, *El recurso del miedo: ensayo sobre el Estado y el terror en Guatemala* (San José, Costa Rica: Editorial Universitaria Centroamericana, 1991); Susanne Jonas, *The Battle for Guatemala: Rebels, Death Squads, and U.S. Power* (Boulder: Westview Press, 1991); Ricardo Falla, *Massacres in the Jungle: Ixcán, Guatemala, 1975–1982* (Boulder: Westview Press, 1994).

76. The third wave began in May 1978 with the massacre at Panzós, Alta Verapaz, in which army troops killed more than one hundred peasants.

77. The main guerrilla groups were the Guerrilla Army of the Poor (Ejército Guerrillero de los Pobres, EGP) and the Organization of People in Arms (Organización del Pueblo en Armas, ORPA).

78. Falla, *Massacres in the Jungle*, p. 183; Figueroa Ibarra, *El recurso del miedo*, p. 25. See also Jim Handy, *Gift of the Devil: A History of Guatemala* (Boston: South End Press, 1984), p. 180. For the extent of human rights violations in Guatemala, see the reports of Human Rights Watch/Americas (formerly Americas Watch), Amnesty International, and those of the Inter-American Commission on Human Rights of the Organization of American States.

79. McClintock, *The American Connection: Guatemala*, pp. 187–188, 191–194; Jonas, *The Battle for Guatemala*, pp. 120, 195. A far-rightist group of Guatemalan businessmen (reportedly linked to death-squad activity), Association of Friends of the Nation (Asociación de Amigos del País), actively sought resumption of U.S. military assistance to Guatemala. "The U.S. has refused to lend technical, financial and even moral support to a country struggling to gain stability and prosperity," noted the group's English-language newsletter, prepared by the public relations firm Deaver and Hannaford. Michael Deaver and Peter Hannaford, aides to Ronald Reagan, also served as foreign agents for the Argentine military junta and the government of Taiwan. Following a 1981 visit to Guatemala by Vernon Walters and Reagan's decision to give the State Department the green light for the sale of military equipment to Guatemala, the conservative publication welcomed the new U.S. foreign policy: "Rather than applying the narrow criterion of human rights policy to a government whose survival is threatened daily by the growing

left-wing guerrilla movement, President Reagan has taken the broader view and the more far-sighted position, both for the sake of the U.S. economy and the welfare of Guatemala"—quotes from *Guatemala Newsletter* (Guatemala City), September 1980: 1; ibid., August 1981: 4. See Vegard Bye, *La paz prohibida: el laberinto centroamericano en la década de los ochenta* (San José, Costa Rica: Departamento Ecuménico de Investigaciones, 1991), pp. 44–45. On Deaver and Hannaford, see Ronald Brownstein and Nina Easton, *Reagan's Ruling Class: Portraits of the President's Top One Hundred Officials* (New York: Pantheon Books, 1983), p. 652.

80. On this aspect of Argentina's assistance to Guatemala, see the following sources: "Argentina Redraws the Ideological Map of South America," *LAWR*, September 19, 1980: 6; Duhalde, *El Estado terrorista argentino*, pp. 122–23; Alejandro Dabat and Luis Lorenzano, *Argentina: The Malvinas and the End of Military Rule* (London: Verso, 1984), pp. 80–81.

81. "Odisea en el Caribe de un avión argentino," *La Semana* (Buenos Aires), July 6, 1977; interview with Rogelio García Lupo, in Buenos Aires, July 30, 1993.

82. Central Bank of the Republic of Argentina, Directorate's "Secret Session," "Acta Nº 'S' 1," January 14, 1982; General Directorate of Military Factories, secret contract, May 19, 1983, signed by Gen. Horacio Varela Ortiz, DGFM director, and Gen. Oscar Mejía Víctores, Guatemala's defense minister—who would replace Ríos Montt as head of state in the August 1983 military coup.

83. *Guardian* (London), December 29, 1981; Duhalde, *El Estado terrorista argentino*, p. 122.

84. Anderson and Anderson, *Inside the League*, p. 177; McClintock, *The American Connection: Guatemala*, pp. 142, 169–171, 193, 219.

85. "Testing Time for Military Solutions in Guatemala and El Salvador," *LAWR*, November 6, 1981.

86. Ibid.

87. Jonas, *The Battle for Guatemala*, pp. 95, 149.

88. McClintock, *The American Connection: Guatemala*, pp. 245, 263.

89. Enrique Yeves, *La Contra, una guerra sucia* (Buenos Aires: Grupo Editorial Zeta, 1990), p. 42. While in Guatemala, Lau was allegedly hired

by D'Aubuisson to conduct the assassination of the Archbishop of San Salvador, Oscar A. Romero. In March 1981, Lau, the legion's G-2 (intelligence) chief, traveled to Buenos Aires with a group of Nicaraguan guardsmen for a counterinsurgency course in the Campo de Mayo military base. See Dickey, *With the Contras*, pp. 83–84, 88, 114, 286; and Craig Pyes, "Who killed Archbishop Romero?" *Nation*, October 13, 1984.

90. Interview with José Efrel Martínez Mondragón, in Elisabeth Reimann, *Confesiones de un Contra, historia de "Moisés" en Nicaragua* (Buenos Aires: Legasa, 1986), pp. 76–77.

91. Shirley Christian, *Nicaragua, Revolution in the Family* (New York: Vintage Books, 1986), pp. 176, 204.

92. Interview with Francisco Martínez Zelaya, in Managua, July 1, 1993. Since the Sandinistas lost the elections of 1990, most of the GN rank and file who had participated in the Contra war became a marginal group in Nicaraguan society. While some former GN officers made a living out of development projects financed by foreign sources, most of the men at the lower ranks stayed unemployed.

93. Argentine advisers might have become involved in training anti-Sandinista rebels in the fall of 1979 since they were already operating in Central America by this time. Recent evidence confirms that the Argentines were providing counterinsurgency training to the region's security forces by 1979. In November 1996, soon after I corrected the edited copy of this book, Leo Valladares, the Human Rights Ombudsman of Honduras, sent me a document in which a former Argentine intelligence agent disclosed his participation in the counterrevolutionary program in Central America. In his deposition before a federal criminal court in Buenos Aires, Rafael López Fader stated that, in mid-1979, he was commissioned by the Argentine army intelligence command to serve as adviser to special troops in Honduras. He stayed in Central America until November 1983. López Fader submitted various documents to the court that verified his testimony, in particular, photographs, a bank statement from Tegucigalpa, and an identification card that identified him as civilian personnel belonging to army intelligence. This agent's deposition reconfirms important aspects of my account of the Argentine military role in Central America—Juzgado Nacional en lo Criminal y Correccional Federal no. 5 (Dr. Norberto M. Oyarbide), case no. 10,000, "Sivak, Os-

valdo Fabio víctima de secuestro extorsivo," deposition of Rafael López Fader, Buenos Aires, August 20, 1996, in author's files.

94. Ministry of the Interior, General Directorate for State Security, Nicaragua, secret memo re participation of the Argentine armed forces and their intelligence services in the aggression against Nicaragua, my copy undated, circa 1984.

95. This account of the Argentine group's liaisons is based on these sources: *Soberanía*, April 1982; conversation with Alvaro Argüello Hurtado, S.J., in Managua, July 6, 1993; Salinas and Villalonga, *Gorriarán*, p. 177. Villagra participated in the legion's first military action under Argentine supervision.

96. Conversation with Tomás Borge, in Managua, July 8, 1993. See transcript of Héctor Francés videotaped testimony before Sandinista authorities, December 6, 1982, in author's files. A shortened version of the testimony of Francés was published in Edgar Chamorro, *Packaging the Contras: A Case of CIA Disinformation* (New York: Institute for Media Analysis, 1987).

97. Ministry of the Interior, General Directorate for State Security, Nicaragua, secret memo, circa 1984.

98. Salinas and Villalonga, *Gorriarán*, pp. 184–185. Carlos Vivas was one of the members of the new team.

99. Martínez Zelaya interview. Other sources on this early Contra activity are the following: Dickey, *With the Contras*, p. 82; U.S. embassy, Nicaragua, confidential cable to Department of State from Harry E. Bergold Jr., May 20, 1985 (NSA, *Nicaragua*); Reimann, *Confesiones de un Contra*, p. 25.

100. Dickey, *With the Contras*, pp. 90–92; Peter Kornbluh, *Nicaragua: The Price of Intervention* (Washington, D.C.: Institute for Policy Studies, 1987), p. 27.

101. Dickey, *With the Contras*, p. 117.

102. Roy Gutman, *Banana Diplomacy: The Making of American Policy in Nicaragua 1981–1987* (New York: Simon and Schuster, 1988), p. 49.

103. In addition to his training in the Honduran and Argentine military academies, Alvarez Martínez attended "the infantry officer advanced course at Fort Benning, Georgia, and the counterinsurgency operations course at Fort Bragg, North Carolina; the Peruvian command

and general staff course; and the combined operations course at Fort Gulick in the Panama Canal Zone"—CIA, "Gustavo Alvarez Martínez," memo, classification unknown, August 25, 1983 (DDRS).

104. See Americas Watch, *Human Rights in Honduras: Signs of "The Argentine Method,"* New York, December 1982, pp. 2–19.

105. Interview with Víctor Meza, in Anderson and Anderson, *Inside the League*, p. 224. Evidence of death-squad activity was found in 1979 and early 1980. When Alvarez was commander of the Second Military Zone, bodies of executed criminals appeared in the area of San Pedro Sula. With his appointment as chief of FUSEP, those irregular practices began to be focused against political dissidents—Americas Watch, *Human Rights in Honduras*, p. 9.

106. See Leticia Salomón, "The National Security Doctrine in Honduras: Analysis of the Fall of General Gustavo Alvarez Martínez," in Nancy Peckenham and Annie Street, eds., *Honduras: Portrait of a Captive Nation* (New York: Praeger, 1985), pp. 197–207; and Leticia Salomón, *Política y militares en Honduras* (Tegucigalpa: Centro de Documentación de Honduras, 1992), particularly pp. 1–94.

107. General Alvarez Martínez, quoted in Roberto Bardini, "Asesores argentinos en Honduras," *Humor*, January 1984: 43, and in Anderson and Anderson, *Inside the League*, p. xiv. As head of the Fourth Infantry Battalion in La Ceiba, Alvarez had been responsible for the assault on the banana-workers' cooperative at Las Isletas in 1977.

108. Alvarez was ousted by an internal military coup led by the air force commander, Gen. Walter López, in March 1984. Alvarez was assassinated on January 25, 1989. The Cinchonero Popular Liberation Movement claimed responsibility for the action, but some sources attributed the killing to a rival faction within the armed forces—*La Tribuna* (Tegucigalpa), January 26, 1989; Tom Barry and Kent Norsworthy, *Honduras: A Country Guide* (Albuquerque: Inter-Hemispheric Education Resource Center, 1990), p. 45.

109. Quoted in Lars Schoultz, *National Security and United States Policy Toward Latin America* (Princeton: Princeton University Press, 1987), p. 173.

110. Philip E. Wheaton, *Inside Honduras: Regional Counterinsurgency Base* (Washington, D.C.: EPICA, 1982), p. 31. See Richard Lapper and

James Painter, *Honduras: State for Sale* (London: Latin American Bureau, 1985). Honduras became involved in the Salvadoran civil war in early 1980, when Honduran troops collaborated with the Salvadorans in a massacre of civilians in northern Chalatenango. In 1981, Honduras entered a U.S.-sponsored counterrevolutionary alliance with El Salvador and Guatemala. See American Civil Liberties Union and Americas Watch, *Report on Human Rights in El Salvador*, New York, January 1982, pp. 177–178.

111. Originally known as the Department of Special Investigations (Departamento de Investigaciones Especiales, DIES), Battalion 3-16 was the highest ranking unit in the army.

112. Affidavit of José Barrera Martínez, México, D.F., July 2, 1987, in National Commissioner for the Protection of Human Rights in Honduras, *Honduras: The Facts Speak for Themselves* (New York: Human Rights Watch/Americas, 1994), p. 189.

113. The Cobras unit was an urban counterinsurgency force created under the aegis of Alvarez. TESON was the acronym for Special and Nighttime Operations Troops (Tropas Especiales y de Operaciones Nocturnas).

114. Inter-American Court of Human Rights, testimony of Florencio Caballero, October 6, 1987, and Barrera Martínez affidavit, in National Commissioner for the Protection of Human Rights in Honduras, *Honduras: The Facts*, pp. 160–199; Anderson and Anderson, *Inside The League*, pp. 224–225.

115. The account of Ciga Correa that follows is based on these sources: *Uno Más Uno*, August 19, 1980; Francés transcript, p. 5; Barrera Martínez affidavit, pp. 189, 191; Andersen, *Dossier Secreto*, pp. 119, 284; Paoletti, *Como los Nazis, como en Vietnam*, p. 405. See also Horacio Verbitsky, *La posguerra sucia: un análisis de la transición* (Buenos Aires: Legasa, 1984), pp. 127–130, 132–140. One of the first victims of the Group of Fourteen was Gerardo Salinas, an attorney who defended political prisoners, killed in Tegucigalpa in June 1980. It is possible that Ciga Correa was one of the instructors who trained a commando group of former Nicaraguan guardsmen in Buenos Aires in early 1981—*Barricada*, August 24, 1983.

Another Argentine adviser was Roberto Alfieri González. A member

of the ESMA Task Force 3.3.2, he had been implicated in the torture of
political prisoners and the kidnapping of several businessmen in Buenos
Aires. As explained in chapter 1, intelligence operatives participated in a
kidnapping ring during the Argentine dirty war while ostensibly fighting
against "economic subversion." Alfieri González, a police officer, served
as intelligence adviser to the Salvadoran national guard in 1980 and subsequently operated in Guatemala and Honduras. In 1988, he was detained by Honduran authorities accused of extortion and
assassination—press cable (IPS), February 3, 1984; Centro de Estudios
Legales y Sociales (CELS) archives; *Tiempo* (San Pedro Sula), March 19,
1988; *El Heraldo* (Tegucigalpa), March 22 and April 5, 1988; *La Tribuna*,
April 5, 1988.

The Argentine military mission in Honduras also included Col. Jorge
Eugenio O'Higgins (Argentine military attaché in Tegucigalpa, who
trained Honduran and Contra forces and was allegedly involved in the
kidnapping and murder of labor and student leaders), Col. Rafael de la
Vega (adviser to the Honduran army), Col. Roberto Carmelo Gigante (an
adviser to paramilitary groups who in 1983 was awarded a military deco-
ration by the Honduran army commander in chief), Maj. César Garro
(adviser to FUSEP), Alfredo Mario Mingolla (Israeli-trained intelligence
officer who collaborated with the Honduran and Guatemalan security
forces and was also involved in the 1980 cocaine coup in Bolivia), Col.
Emilio Jasón, Lt. Colonel Cabrera, Maj. García Cano, Julio Jorge Ianan-
tuone, Horacio Capelo, Antonio Rauch, Julio César Casanova Ferro,
Gustavo Guasti, Félix Brenes, Jorge Flores Allende, Carlos Noria, Víctor
Gard, Juan Carlos Galessio, D'Espeche, Báez, and Chacamé (first names
not available). Some of the Argentine advisers assigned to Honduras had
previously operated in Mexico and Costa Rica, tracking down Argentine
exiles—Roberto Bardini, "Los militares argentinos exportan su guerra
sucia a América Central," *El Día*, February 8, 1983; Bardini, "La red mer-
cenaria del Proceso," *Caras y Caretas*, June 1984; Bardini, "Asesores argentinos," *Humor*, January 1984. See also Bardini, *Monjes, mercenarios y
mercaderes*, p. 124; *Tiempo*, December 5, 1983; Salinas, "Mercenarios argentinos (I), (II), (III)"; Joselovsky, "El ejército del 'Proceso'"; Ministerio
de Relaciones Exteriores y Culto (Argentina), "Memoria Año 1981," p. 41;
Peter Dale Scott and Jonathan Marshall, *Cocaine Politics: Drugs, Armies,*

and the CIA in Central America (Berkeley: University of California Press, 1991), pp. 44–45; and *Barricada*, March 30, 1983.

116. Americas Watch, *Human Rights in Honduras*, p. 14.

117. See the following sources: National Commissioner for the Protection of Human Rights, *Honduras: The Facts*, pp. 123, 227; Caballero testimony, pp. 164–165; Americas Watch, *Human Rights in Honduras*, pp. 5–6, 11–12; Anderson and Anderson, *Inside the League*, p. 226. As of December 1993, sixteen clandestine cemeteries had been found in Honduras—*La Prensa* (New York), December 29, 1993.

118. This account of Hernández is based on the following sources: Caballero testimony, pp. 166–167; Barrera Martínez affidavit, p. 188; *Tiempo*, June 13, 1981, and September 6, 1982; Donald E. Schulz and Deborah Sundloff Schulz, *The United States, Honduras, and the Crisis in Central America* (Boulder: Westview Press, 1994), pp. 80, 84; and Dickey, *With the Contras*, pp. 116, 153, 261.

119. Even though it is a fact that the CIA approved Argentine operations in Central America under the Carter administration, there is no evidence of presidential endorsement of such activities. The incoming Reagan administration, of course, had a policy of full-fledged support for the counterrevolutionary program.

120. Interview with Argentine Foreign Service official assigned to Central America in 1981–1982, name withheld on request, in Buenos Aires, August 11, 1993. This source confirmed the official relationship between the Argentine military junta and the Honduran, Salvadoran, and Guatemalan governments regarding covert paramilitary programs in those countries. Col. Jorge Eugenio O'Higgins was the military attaché in Honduras (1981–1984). By 1988, he was head of the army intelligence division (EMGE-Jef. II). Col. Humberto Pompilio Ferruci served as military attaché in Guatemala and El Salvador from 1981 onward.

121. U.S. embassy, Nicaragua, confidential cable to Department of State from Thomas J. O'Donnell, March 1, 1980 (NSA, *Nicaragua*).

122. Caballero testimony, pp. 180–182; Sánchez Reisse testimony, pp. 14–17, 26–27, 36–37, 111.

123. U.S. Department of State, secret cable to U.S. embassy, Honduras, from Haig, February 5, 1981 (NSA, *Nicaragua*).

124. Ministerio de Relaciones Exteriores y Culto, Argentina, "Memo-

ria Año 1981," pp. 137–138; Salinas and Villalonga, *Gorriarán*, pp. 151–152. In mid-1982, Argentina sold additional war supplies to Honduras for $8 million—General Directorate of Military Industries (DGFM), secret letter to the president of the Central Bank, Argentina, from Gen. Horacio Varela Ortiz, July 26, 1982.

125. DGFM secret letter to the president, Central Bank, Argentina, from Varela Ortiz, December 29, 1981.

126. Falcoff, *A Tale of Two Policies*, citing U.S. embassy sources (November 1981), p. 43.

127. *El Día*, March 19, 1986. A few Argentine officers made huge profits from the transactions with Honduras—interview with D'Andrea Mohr; Duhalde, *El Estado terrorista argentino*, pp. 123–24.

128. U.S. Army Maj. Gen. Robert Laurence Schweitzer (a National Security Council adviser under President Reagan) sought to promote Alvarez Martínez's plan after the two met in the summer of 1980—Gutman, *Banana Diplomacy*, pp. 46–49.

129. Interview with a former Contra combatant, Camilo Dormoz, in Bluefields, Nicaragua, June 29, 1993.

130. On these activities of former guardsmen in Honduras, see the following documents: U.S. embassy, Honduras, secret cable to State Department from Mari-Luci Jaramillo, July 30, 1979; U.S. embassy, Nicaragua, confidential cables to State Department from Lawrence A. Pezzullo, November 9, 1979; U.S. embassy, Nicaragua, confidential cables to State Department from Thomas J. O'Donnell, February 7, 1980, March 1, 1980, July 31, 1980, and September 12 and 17, 1980; State Department, confidential memo to deputy secretary from Thomas O. Enders, May 6, 1981 (NSA, *Nicaragua*).

131. Interviews with Chávez and Martínez Zelaya.

132. This account of Contra involvement in domestic repression is based on the following sources: Sam Dillon, *Comandos: The CIA and Nicaragua's Contra Rebels* (New York: Henry Holt, 1991), pp. 99–101; Linda Drucker, "A Contra's Story," *Progressive*, August 1986, pp. 25–26; CIA secret cable and Caballero testimony, quoted in National Commissioner, *Honduras: The Facts*, pp. 133–134. See Martínez Mondragón interview, in Reimann, *Confesiones de un Contra*, p. 90. See also Schulz and Schulz, *The United States, Honduras, and the Crisis*, pp. 85–86.

133. See, for example, the testimony of José Gregorio Najera Andrade in *Barricada*, March 30, 1983. An Argentine-trained Guatemalan military intelligence operative, Najera worked for the CIA and the Honduran army intelligence service. He was responsible, in coordination with the Honduras Logistical Support Center for the Armed Forces (Centro de Apoyo Logístico de las Fuerzas Armadas, CALFA), for resupply operations at the Contra base of Las Trojes. See also Gregorio Selser, *Honduras, república alquilada* (México, D.F.: Mex-Sur, 1983), pp. 88–92, 124–129, 260–263, 338–341.

134. See Schoultz, *National Security*, pp. 13–14.

135. Walter Goobar, "Escuela de dictadores," *Página 12*, August 8, 1993.

136. D'Andrea Mohr interview.

CHAPTER 4

Some documents were consulted through the following microfiche collection: National Security Archive, ed., *Nicaragua: The Making of U.S. Policy, 1978–1990* (Alexandria: Chadwyck-Healey, 1991) (hereafter, NSA, *Nicaragua*).

1. I owe the expression "the dirty war in Central America" to Wayne Smith.

2. Interview with Abel Céspedes, in Managua, July 6, 1993.

3. See James M. Malloy, *Bolivia: The Uncompleted Revolution* (Pittsburgh: University of Pittsburgh Press, 1970) for a brief definition of revolutionary situations and revolutions.

4. This section reproduces some material from Ariel C. Armony and Robert Chisholm, "Is Social Revolution Possible in a Liberal Era? Revolution and Compromise in Nicaragua 1979–1990," paper delivered at the annual meeting of the American Political Science Association, New York, September 1994.

5. See Jack A. Goldstone, "Revolution," in Mary Hawkesworth and Maurice Kogan, eds., *Encyclopedia of Government and Politics* (London: Routledge, 1992), pp. 1055–1056.

6. Orlando Núñez, ed., *La guerra en Nicaragua* (Managua: Centro

para la Investigación, la Promoción y el Desarrollo Rural y Social [CIPRES], 1991), p. 26.

7. It is important to stress that the insurrectionary coalition was glued together by its opposition to the Somoza regime: it was not a consolidated revolutionary movement that sought the structural transformation of society and citizenry. On the anti-Somoza nature of the insurrection, see, for instance, Henri Weber, *The Sandinist Revolution* (London: Verso, 1981), or Dennis Gilbert, *Sandinistas* (Oxford: Basil Blackwell, 1988).

8. Núñez, *La guerra en Nicaragua*, pp. 18–19; Thomas W. Walker, *Nicaragua: The Land of Sandino* (Boulder: Westview Press, 1991), pp. 15–19.

9. U.S. Deputy Representative at the United Nations, statement before the U.N. General Assembly, October 8, 1981, in U.S. Department of State, *American Foreign Policy Current Documents 1981* (Washington, D.C.: U.S. Department of State, 1984), p. 1350.

10. See John A. Booth and Thomas W. Walker, *Understanding Central America*, 2nd. ed. (Boulder: Westview Press, 1989), pp. 129–130.

11. Evidence of the bourgeoisie's antipathy toward the revolution can be seen in the decline of the private sector's share in investment from two-thirds to less than one-fifth of the total between 1979 and 1984, evidence of a capital strike in the earliest stages of the revolution—Bill Gibson, "Overview of the Nicaraguan Economy," in Rose J. Spalding, ed., *The Political Economy of Revolutionary Nicaragua* (Boston: Allen and Unwin, 1987), p. 37. On the attitude of the bourgeoisie and the divisions over their relation to the Sandinistas' revolutionary goals, see Gilbert, *Sandinistas*.

12. Real income for agricultural workers decreased by 46.9 percent from 1978/79 to 1981/82—Forrest D. Colburn, *Post-Revolutionary Nicaragua: State, Class, and the Dilemmas of Agrarian Policy* (Berkeley: University of California Press, 1986), p. 114 (table). Colburn notes the impoverishment of rural workers and the perception among basic grain producers of their own impoverishment by Sandinista agricultural policies—Colburn, "Foot Dragging and Other Peasant Responses to the Nicaraguan Revolution," in Colburn, ed., *Everyday Forms of Peasant Resistance* (Armonk: M. E. Sharpe, 1989), pp. 183–187.

13. See Forrest D. Colburn, *Managing the Commanding Heights: Nicaragua's State Enterprises* (Berkeley: University of California Press, 1990). It can be argued that the Sandinista regime was unable to provide "the relevant benefits with . . . sensitivity to the specific features of local political and social arrangements" —Theda Skocpol, "What Makes Peasants Revolutionary?" *Comparative Politics* 14 (April 1982): 366.

14. Vera Gianotten, Ton de Wit, and Rodrigo Montoya, *Nicaragua: cuestión agraria y participación campesina* (Lima: DESCO, 1987), pp. 43–46. See Alejandro Bendaña, ed., *Una tragedia campesina: testimonios de la resistencia* (Managua: Edit-Arte/CEI, 1991). As the Contra war escalated, the agrarian reform program changed in 1985 from an emphasis on the creation of a state-owned agricultural sector and the promotion of production cooperatives to the distribution of individual land titles in the hope of winning back peasant support. Alejandro Martínez Cuenca argues that the desire to win back peasant support was an important part of the reasoning for the change in land distribution after 1985—Cuenca, *Sandinista Economics in Practice* (Boston: South End Press, 1992), p. 58.

15. Núñez, *La guerra en Nicaragua*, pp. 30–39.

16. Margaret E. Crahan, "Religion, Revolution, and Counterrevolution: The Role of the Religious Right in Central America," in Douglas A. Chalmers, Maria do Carmo Campello de Souza, and Atilio A. Boron, eds., *The Right and Democracy in Latin America* (New York: Praeger, 1992), p. 174.

17. Walker, *Nicaragua: The Land of Sandino*, pp. 98–99. See John A. Booth, *The End and the Beginning: The Nicaraguan Revolution*, 2nd. ed. (Boulder: Westview Press, 1985), pp. 208–215.

18. Laura Enríquez, *Harvesting Change: Labor and Agrarian Reform in Nicaragua, 1979–1990* (Chapel Hill: University of North Carolina Press, 1991), pp. 7–8.

19. See Eric Wolf, *Peasant Wars of the Twentieth Century* (New York: Harper and Row, 1969), pp. 289–290. Bendaña, among others, argues that the Marxist mind-set of the Sandinista leadership was critical in their failure to understand the diversity and fragmentation of Nicaragua's agrarian social structure—Bendaña, *Una tragedia campesina*, p. 41.

20. Centro de Investigación y Estudios de la Reforma Agraria (CIERA), *La reforma agraria en Nicaragua, 1979–1989*, vol. 4 (Managua: CIERA, 1989), pp. 312–313.

21. Núñez, *La guerra en Nicaragua*, pp. 32, 44. On the relationship between dissatisfaction with the political system and mobilized political participation, see Mitchell A. Seligson, "Trust, Efficacy and Modes of Political Participation: A Study of Costa Rican Peasants," *British Journal of Political Science* 10 (January 1980): 75–99.

22. See Barrington Moore Jr., *Social Origins of Dictatorship and Democracy: Lord and Peasant in the Making of the Modern World* (Boston: Beacon Press, 1966), p. 460; Wolf, *Peasant Wars*, p. 295; and Joel S. Migdal, *Peasants, Politics and Revolution: Pressures Toward Political and Social Change in the Third World* (Princeton: Princeton University Press, 1974), pp. 229–230.

23. Jeffrey L. Gould, *To Lead as Equals: Rural Protest and Political Consciousness in Chinandega, Nicaragua, 1912–1990* (Chapel Hill: University of North Carolina Press, 1990), pp. 292–305; Crahan, "Religion, Revolution, and Counterrevolution," p. 177.

24. Colburn, *Post-Revolutionary Nicaragua*, p. 22.

25. Philip J. Williams, "Dual Transitions from Authoritarian Rule: Popular and Electoral Democracy in Nicaragua," *Comparative Politics* 26 (January 1994): 180–182.

26. Angel Saldomando and Elvira Cuadra, "Los problemas de la pacificación en Nicaragua: recomposición de grupos armados y conflictos sociales," Coordinadora Regional de Investigaciones Económicas y Sociales (CRIES), February 1994.

27. See Ariel C. Armony, "The Former Contras," in Thomas W. Walker, ed., *Nicaragua Without Illusions: Regime Transition and Other Changes in the 1990s* (Wilmington: SR Books, 1997).

28. Núñez, *La guerra en Nicaragua*, pp. 271–287, citing several documents from Nicaragua's Ministry of the Interior.

29. Michael T. Klare, "The Interventionist Impulse: U.S. Military Doctrine for Low-Intensity Warfare," in Michael Klare and Peter Kornbluh, eds., *Low-Intensity Warfare: Counterinsurgency, Proinsurgency, and Antiterrorism in the Eighties* (New York: Pantheon, 1988), pp. 65–66.

30. Saldomando and Cuadra, "Los problemas de la pacificación en Nicaragua," pp. 21, 37; CIERA, *La reforma agraria*, vol. 4, pp. 63, 280–281.

31. E. V. K. Fitzgerald, "Estado y economía en Nicaragua," in Raúl Rubén and Jan de Gorot, eds., *El debate sobre la reforma agraria en Nicaragua* (Managua: Editorial Ciencias Sociales, 1988), p. 40.

32. Booth and Walker, *Understanding*, p. 150. See Núñez, *La guerra en Nicaragua*, p. 258.

33. Testimony of Max Rodríguez Martínez, in Bendaña, *Una tragedia campesina*, p. 97.

34. The MILPAS were also known as Chilotes.

35. U.S. Department of State, *Nicaraguan Biographies: A Resource Book* (Washington, D.C.: Bureau of Public Affairs, Office of Public Communication, 1988), p. 5. See testimonies of Rodríguez Martínez, Fausto Sáenz Soza, Isidro García Díaz, Diógenes Membreño Hernández, and José Boanerges Matus, in Bendaña, *Una tragedia campesina*, pp. 68–69, 82, 95–96, 203.

36. Centro de Investigación y Estudios de la Reforma Agraria (CIERA), "Caracterización de las primeras bandas contrarrevolucionarias: el caso de la banda de Dimas," November 1980, in CIERA, *La reforma agraria*, vol. 6, pp. 231–261. The quote is from the interview with Oscar Sobalvarro García, in Managua, July 7, 1993.

37. U.S. Department of State, *Nicaraguan Biographies*, p. 5.

38. Jaime Morales Carazo, *La Contra* (México, D.F.: Planeta, 1989), pp. 31–32. Sobalvarro told me, "My father was a *finquero* [small to medium-scale producer] and *juez de mesta* [rural judge] in Santa Teresa, northern Jinotega, before the revolution. He had earned the respect and trust of our community. In spite of that, the Sandinistas claimed that he was a Somocista. They ravaged our farm and ill-treated my entire family"—Sobalvarro interview.

39. See Knut Walter, *The Regime of Anastasio Somoza, 1936–1956* (Chapel Hill: University of North Carolina Press, 1993), p. 113.

40. Núñez, *La guerra en Nicaragua*, p. 390; Fernando Peñalba, "Brigada 'Omar Torrijos' desarticula bandas revolucionarias," *Patria Libre*, no. 18 (November 1981): 14–18.

41. Interview with Francisco Martínez Zelaya, in Managua, July 6, 1993; García Díaz testimony, p. 86.

42. CIERA, "Caracterización," pp. 249–255.

43. Juan Angel Rivera, whose family's farm was confiscated in 1980, mentioned as key motives for his incorporation into the MILPAS the Sandinistas' disrespect for private property, democracy, human rights, and religious beliefs—Rivera interview, in Managua, July 7, 1993. See Gould, *To Lead as Equals*, pp. 299–305.

44. Núñez, *La guerra en Nicaragua*, pp. 323–331, 368, 382, 385, 392–398; CIERA, "Caracterización," pp. 254–255.

45. Sobalvarro interview; CIERA, "Caracterización," pp. 238, 244–247.

46. Sobalvarro interview. See Morales Carazo, *La Contra*, pp. 31, 33.

47. Sobalvarro interview.

48. "At first," said Rivera, "there were serious disputes with the guardsmen during the training: it was very difficult for us civilians to adjust to military practices. Subsequently, the guardsmen were mainly involved in the administrative tasks of our movement. There were few guardsmen acting as field commanders. The civilian leaders were much more popular with the troops than the military officers"—Rivera interview.

49. See CIERA, "Caracterización," p. 259.

50. Interview with Rodolfo Ampié Quiróz, in Managua, July 2 and 5, 1993.

51. Martínez Zelaya interview. See Christopher Dickey, *With the Contras: A Reporter in the Wilds of Nicaragua* (New York: Simon and Schuster, 1987), pp. 67–68.

52. Núñez, *La guerra en Nicaragua*, p. 272, citing Nicaragua's Ministerio del Interior, Dirección General de Seguridad del Estado, *Cronología de la guerra no declarada* (Managua: Departamento de Relaciones Públicas, MINT, 1984). See also p. 387.

53. The account that follows of anti-Sandinista organizations is based on the following sources: Morales Carazo, *La Contra*, p. 44; Sam Dillon, *Comandos: The CIA and Nicaragua's Contra Rebels* (New York: Henry Holt, 1991), pp. 102–103; Roy Gutman, *Banana Diplomacy: The Making of American Policy in Nicaragua 1981–1987* (New York: Simon and Schuster, 1988), pp. 43–44; Roberto Bardini, *Conexión en Tegucigalpa (El somocismo en Honduras)* (Puebla: Universidad Autónoma de Puebla, 1982), pp. 46–47.

54. Committee of Santa Fe, *A New Inter-American Policy for the Eighties* (Washington, D.C.: Council for Inter-American Security, 1980), p. 53. See Gutman, *Banana Diplomacy*, p. 44. Gordon Sumner served as special adviser to the assistant secretary of state for inter-American affairs during the Reagan administration.

55. This account of counterrevolutionary groups is based on the following sources: CIERA, "Caracterización," pp. 233–234; "Fuerzas ar-

madas asestan nuevos golpes a la contrarrevolución," *Patria Libre*, no. 6 (August 1980): 56–57; "Las fuerzas armadas golpean a la contrarrevolución," *Patria Libre*, no. 7 (September 1980): 44; "Siniestra conspiración contrarrevolucionaria," *Patria Libre*, no. 8 (October-November 1980): 51–57; "Las fronteras serán la tumba de la contrarrevolución," *Patria Libre*, no. 9 (December 1980): 48–49.

56. U.S. embassy, Managua, "GRN State Security Presents Confessed Counterrevolutionaries," confidential cable to secretary of state from Charles H. Brayshaw, July 29, 1981.

57. Núñez, *La guerra en Nicaragua*, pp. 272–274; Sobalvarro interview.

58. Sobalvarro interview; Morales Carazo, *La Contra*, pp. 44–45.

59. Dillon, *Comandos*, pp. 70, 117–120, 200.

60. Raúl Vergara, Deborah Barry, and Rodolfo Castro, *Nicaragua: país sitiado* (Managua: CRIES, 1986), p. 160.

61. Interview with Gen. (retired) Miguel Angel Mallea Gil, in Buenos Aires, August 18, 1993.

62. Betsy Cohn and Patricia Hynds, "The Manipulation of the Religion Issue," in Thomas W. Walker, ed., *Reagan versus the Sandinistas: The Undeclared War on Nicaragua* (Boulder: Westview Press, 1987), p. 115.

63. Interview with a former Nicaraguan national guard sergeant, Mariano Morales, in Managua, July 7, 1993.

64. Gutman, *Banana Diplomacy*, p. 53; *Excelsior* (Mexico), June 20, 1988.

65. Peter Kornbluh, *Nicaragua: The Price of Intervention* (Washington, D.C.: Institute for Policy Studies, 1987), pp. 22–23.

66. Interview with José Efrel Martínez Mondragón, in Elisabeth Reimann, *Confesiones de un Contra: Historia de "Moisés" en Nicaragua* (Buenos Aires: Legasa, 1986), p. 35; Céspedes interview.

67. Morales interview. See Dickey, *With the Contras*, pp. 113–115.

68. Interview with Contra officer Pedro Núñez Cabezas, in Dieter Eich and Carlos Rincón, *The Contras: Interviews with Anti-Sandinistas* (San Francisco: Synthesis Publications, 1985), pp. 46–47; Morales interview.

69. Martínez Mondragón interview, in Reimann, *Confesiones de un Contra*, pp. 29, 35–36.

70. Reportedly, two of the Argentine instructors were Javier Mora

and Osvaldo Saravia Amievas. Mora had served in the Automotores Or-
letti detention camp during the dirty war in Argentina. He was linked to
Raúl Guglielminetti, head of the Florida-based Extraterritorial Task
Force and served as adviser to the Salvadoran armed forces and later as
coordinator of a Contra unit. Saravia, who had trained the Halcones
commando team of the Triple A, was allegedly involved in setting up the
training facilities at the Sagitario Contra base in Honduras—Juan José
Salinas, "Los mercenarios argentinos (II)," *El Porteño*, August 1988:
35–36.

71. Dillon, *Comandos*, pp. 146, 296, 357.

72. Morales interview.

73. Ampié Quiróz interview.

74. Martínez Mondragón interview, in Reimann, *Confesiones de un
Contra*, p. 29.

75. Edgar Chamorro, *Packaging the Contras: A Case of CIA Disinformation* (New York: Institute for Media Analysis, 1987), pp. 6–7.

76. Martínez Mondragón interview, in Reimann, *Confesiones de un
Contra*, p. 31.

77. Ramón J. A. Camps, "Cómo se planificó la campaña terrorista
Latinoamericana," *La Prensa* (Buenos Aires), December 28, 1980.

78. As LIC theorist Sam C. Sarkesian acknowledged, "Revolution
and counterrevolution develop their own morality and ethics that justify
any means to achieve success. Survival is the ultimate morality"—S. C.
Sarkesian, "Low-Intensity Conflict: Concepts, Principles, and Policy
Guidelines," *Air University Review* 6, no. 2 (1985): 11, quoted in Michael
T. Klare and Peter Kornbluh, "The New Interventionism: Low-Intensity
Warfare in the 1980s and Beyond," in Klare and Kornbluh, *Low-Intensity
Warfare*, p. 15. See also p. 53.

79. Benjamin C. Schwarz, *American Counterinsurgency Doctrine and
El Salvador: The Frustrations of Reform and the Illusions of Nation Building* (Santa Monica: RAND, 1991), esp. pp. 81–84.

80. Transcript of Héctor Francés videotaped testimony before Sandinista authorities, December 6, 1982, p. 4.

81. Interview with a former captain, José Luis D'Andrea Mohr, in
Buenos Aires, August 14, 1991. See testimony of Francisco García Rivera,
in Bendaña, *Una tragedia campesina*, p. 173.

82. Morales and Sobalvarro interviews.

83. Morales interview.

84. U.S. embassy, Nicaragua, "Ex-FDN Mondragón Tells His Story," unclassified cable to State Department from Bergold, May 20, 1985 (NSA, *Nicaragua*). See Reimann, *Confesiones de un Contra*.

85. D'Andrea Mohr interview. According to D'Andrea Mohr, former national guardsman Emilio Echaverry, a member of his cohort (1961) at the Argentine Colegio Militar, tried to recruit him for the anti-Sandinista operation. Echaverry told him that the monthly salary for a captain was approximately $5,000 and that the Argentine advisers could not assume governmental positions in case of a military victory over the Sandinistas. After consulting with the Argentine Army General Staff, Echaverry rejected D'Andrea Mohr because his ideas about social justice "resembled those of the Sandinistas."

86. See Juan E. Guglialmelli, "Las FF.AA. en América Latina (FF.AA. y Revolución Nacional)," *Estrategia* 17 (July-August 1972): 9–19; "Fuerzas Armadas para la Liberación Nacional," *Estrategia* 23 (July-August 1973): 7–30; "Geopolítica en la Argentina," *Estrategia* 46–47 (May-August 1977): 5–14; "Economía, Poder Militar y Seguridad Nacional," *Estrategia* 51 (March-April 1978): 7–29.

87. "Fundamentos estratégicos," *El Legionario: Revista oficial de la Legión 15 de Septiembre* 1, no. 3 (June 1981): 9–18.

88. "La mentalidad militar del exilio," ibid.: 8.

89. "Organizaciones terroristas en Latinoamérica," ibid.: 28–29.

90. Ampié Quiróz interview.

91. This account of the connections between anti-Sandinista actors is based on Gutman, *Banana Diplomacy*, pp. 49–53, and on the following cables: U.S. embassy, Managua, confidential cable, "GNR Arrests Counterrevolutionary Plotters," from L. Pfeifle to secretary of state, January 9, 1982; U.S. embassy, Managua, limited official-use cables, "GRN Charges Officials from Venezuela, Argentina, Honduras and El Salvador with Assassination and Sabotage Plot: CIA Charged as Mastermind," and "Foreign Officials Implicated in Counterrevolutionary Plot," both to secretary of state, January 13, 1982; U.S. embassy, Buenos Aires, cable, "Goa Denial of GRN Charges of Involvement with Anti-Sandinistas," from Shlaudeman to secretary of state, January 15, 1982. (See chapter 2, "Argentina as a U.S. Ally.")

92. Enrique Yeves, *La Contra: una guerra sucia* (Buenos Aires: Ediciones B, 1990), p. 67; *Latin America Weekly Report*, February 12, 1982. Valín declined to be interviewed for this book. It has been suggested that the Argentine high command recommended the Reagan administration make dissident guerrilla commander Edén Pastora leader of the anti-Sandinista armed movement. Responding to U.S. doubts about the unpredictability of such project, the Argentines suggested eliminating Pastora once the counterrevolutionary project had been accomplished—interview with former Argentine military attaché in Latin America, in Oscar R. Cardoso, "El último secreto del Proceso: apéndice sobre la experiencia argentina," in Christopher Dickey, *Con los Contras* (Buenos Aires: Sudamericana/Planeta, 1987), p. 310.

93. Interview with Enrique Bermúdez, Associated Press, June 19, 1988, in Morales Carazo, *La Contra*, p. 53.

94. William Baltodano Herrera testified before the Nicaraguan media after being captured by the Sandinistas, accused of mounting a sabotage campaign in the nation's capital, "Interior Minister Borge Holds News Conference," *Foreign Broadcast Information Service–Latin America*, January 15, 1982, pp. P5–P9.

95. Interview with Enrique Bermúdez, in Gutman, *Banana Diplomacy*, p. 56. The UDN experienced internal conflicts between its military and civilian members. Some civilians were accused by the former guardsmen of being Sandinistas. Part of the UDN membership abandoned the counterrevolutionary venture and sought exile in Miami—Sobalvarro interview.

96. Affidavit of Edgar Chamorro, Washington, D.C., September 5, 1985, for the International Court of Justice, "Case Concerning Military and Paramilitary Activities In and Against Nicaragua," p. 5.

97. Morales Carazo, *La Contra*, p. 45.

98. Sobalvarro interview.

99. Interview with Miguel Angel Sosa, in Managua, July 5, 1993. "Bermúdez gave me the task to unify the Matagalpa-based Chilotes. They undertook training in Honduras for three months and then I led them back into Nicaragua," Sosa told me.

100. The delegates were Col. Mario Davico, vice chief of Argentine Army Intelligence, Duane "Dewey" Clarridge, head of the Latin America

Division of the CIA's operations directorate, Col. Gustavo Alvarez Martínez, head of the Honduras Public Security Force, Col. Leónides Torres Arias, chief of Honduran military intelligence, and Gen. Policarpo Paz García, president of Honduras—Gutman, *Banana Diplomacy*, p. 57.

101. Gutman, *Banana Diplomacy*, p. 57. See Morales Carazo, *La Contra*, p. 51; Dickey, *With the Contras*, p. 119; and Holly Sklar, *Washington's War on Nicaragua* (Boston: South End Press, 1988), p. 87.

102. Quoted in Gutman, *Banana Diplomacy*, p. 53. Bermúdez graduated from the Nicaraguan military academy in 1952. He participated in the national guard unit sent by Luis Somoza to the Dominican Republic in 1965 as part of the inter-American peace force constituted under U.S. auspices. During the Nicaraguan insurrection, Bermúdez served as Anastasio Somoza's military attaché in Washington, D.C. After his extended leadership of the Contra forces, Bermúdez was expelled from his post as FDN commander shortly before the February 1990 elections in Nicaragua. Under the Bush administration, the State Department pressured for Bermúdez's dismissal in an effort to purge the Contra leadership of corruption. Bermúdez moved to the United States and returned to Nicaragua after the inauguration of President Violeta Chamorro. On February 16, 1991, Bermúdez was shot dead in the parking lot of the Inter-Continental Hotel in Managua. According to some sources, his assassination was the result of a feud between Contra factions linked to drug trafficking; others claimed he was killed by Sandinista loyalists— Gutman, *Banana Diplomacy*, p. 42; *New York Times*, February 18, 1991 and March 7, 1991. See Donald E. Schulz and Deborah Sundloff Schulz, *The United States, Honduras, and the Crisis in Central America* (Boulder: Westview Press, 1994), pp. 259–260.

103. Interview with Enrique Bermúdez in *Resistencia* (Costa Rica), no. 2 (September-October 1987).

104. General Directorate of Military Factories (Dirección General de Fabricaciones Militares, DGFM), "Financiación de venta de material bélico a la República de Honduras," secret memorandum from Gen. Horacio Varela Ortiz to the president of Argentina's Central Bank, December 29, 1981.

105. Chamorro affidavit, pp. 5–6. Martínez Zelaya (who underwent

training with the Argentines at the Lepaterique base in Honduras and later trained MISURA forces in Puerto Lempira) claimed that the commando team was made up of twelve men, mostly former guardsmen, and that an Argentine operative known as El Diablo played a vital role in the actions—Martínez Zelaya interview.

106. Francés transcript, p. 19.

107. Hoya graduated from the Argentine military college in 1946 and later received advanced training in military intelligence. He retired from active service in 1970. Along with Ribeiro, Hoya organized the army's infiltration into the People's Revolutionary Army (ERP) in 1975—interview with Col. (retired) Horacio Ballester, in Buenos Aires, August 5, 1991; interview with Juan José Salinas, in Buenos Aires, July 31, 1993.

108. *Wall Street Journal*, March 5, 1985.

109. John Carbaugh, quoted in Gutman, *Banana Diplomacy*, p. 104; Salinas interview. See Chamorro, *Packaging the Contras*, p. 6.

110. Letter from unidentified source, ref.: Coronel Osvaldo Ribeiro, Centro de Estudios Legales y Sociales (CELS) archives, in author's files. The information contained in this communication was reliably confirmed by other sources.

111. Francés transcript.

112. Céspedes interview. On the infrastructure under Hoya's command, see Francés transcript as published in *Barricada* (Managua), December 2, 1982.

113. Dickey, *With the Contras*, p. 119.

114. Dickey, *With the Contras*, pp. 127–129, 153. In September 1982, Hoya and Ribeiro became part of a new Contra general staff. It was headed by the CIA station chief in Tegucigalpa and the officer in charge of special U.S. training and paramilitary operations. General Alvarez Martínez and Colonel Calderini represented the Hondurans and Bermúdez and Echaverry represented the Nicaraguan rebels.

115. Gutman, *Banana Diplomacy*, p. 104.

116. Céspedes interview.

117. Ampié Quiróz interview. Sosa and other Contra leaders expressed similar views about the Argentine military personnel working with the FDN.

118. Chamorro affidavit, pp. 3–5.

119. Francés transcript, p. 4; Chamorro affidavit, p. 5; interview with Edgar Chamorro, in Sklar, *Washington's War*, p. 220.

120. Peter Dale Scott and Jonathan Marshall, *Cocaine Politics: Drugs, Armies, and the CIA in Central America* (Berkeley: University of California Press, 1991), pp. 104–109.

121. Dickey, *With the Contras*, pp. 294–295.

122. Gutman, *Banana Diplomacy*, pp. 42, 53.

123. "Comandante 3–80: Jefe militar de la 'Contra,'" *Somos* (Buenos Aires), January 14, 1987: 6.

124. Ampié Quiróz interview.

125. Céspedes interview.

126. Interview with César Arana, in Miami, July 9, 1993.

127. Arms Control and Foreign Policy Caucus, "Who are the Contras? An Analysis of the Makeup of the Military Leadership of the Rebel Forces, and of the Nature of the Private American Groups Providing Them Financial and Material Support," research report, Washington, D.C., April 18, 1985, p. 8.

128. Carlos M. Vilas, *Del colonialismo a la autonomía: modernización capitalista y revolución social en la Costa Atlántica* (Managua: Nueva Nicaragua, 1990), pp. 266, 278–280.

129. Vilas, *Del colonialismo a la autonomía*, pp. 280–282. See Bardini, *Conexión en Tegucigalpa*, pp. 14–24.

130. Cardoso, "El último secreto del Proceso," pp. 309–310; Americas Watch, *Human Rights in Honduras: Signs of "The Argentine Method,"* New York, December 1982, pp. 27, 33. Rivera established his headquarters in Costa Rica, where he organized his own anti-Sandinista group.

131. Vilas, *Del colonialismo a la autonomía*, pp. 280–282; Cardoso, "El último secreto del Proceso," p. 309.

132. *Wall Street Journal*, March 5, 1985.

133. Acdel Edgardo Vilas, *Tucumán: el hecho histórico* ("El plan táctico que posibilitó la victoria contra el Ejército Revolucionario del Pueblo (ERP) en 1975"), undated pamphlet, in author's files, p. 5.

134. Judy Butler, "A Nation Divided: A Chronicle of Nicaragua's Atlantic Coast," unpublished manuscript, in author's files, pp. 102–103.

135. See U.S. embassy, Managua, confidential cable, "Operation Red

Christmas: A Counterrevolutionary Plot," from Linda Pfeifle to secretary of state, February 4, 1982.

136. Butler, "A Nation Divided," p. 104.

137. Manlio Tirado, "Falló una conjura antisandinista," *Excelsior*, February 4, 1982; *Barricada*, February 4, 1982; "Los EEUU dirigen la contrarrevolución," *Soberanía*, no. 3 (February 1982): 52–54.

138. Vilas, *Del colonialismo a la autonomía*, pp. 282–284, 287, 309.

139. "Amenazan con invasión contrarrevolucionaria a Nicaragua," *Patria Libre*, no. 20 (March 1982): 52–55; William I. Robinson, "La Contra: corrupción y grietas," *Pensamiento Propio* 3, no. 25 (August 1985): 63.

140. Interview with Camilo Dormoz, in Bluefields, Nicaragua, June 29, 1993.

141. Sobalvarro interview.

142. Sobalvarro interview. One of the most devastating attacks against the Argentine security forces, which had direct repercussions on the escalation of urban repression, had been the July 1976 bombing of the federal police intelligence headquarters in Buenos Aires, a Montonero operation that killed more than twenty people and injured some sixty others—Martin Edwin Andersen, *Dossier Secreto: Argentina's Desaparecidos and the Myth of the "Dirty War"* (Boulder: Westview Press, 1993), p. 231.

143. This assessment of the Argentine impact on the Contra armed movement is based primarily on my interviews with Martínez Zelaya, Sobalvarro, Ampié Quiróz, and Morales.

144. Sobalvarro interview.

145. Rodríguez Martínez testimony, p. 97.

146. Rivera interview.

147. Rodríguez Martínez testimony, p. 99.

148. Sobalvarro interview.

149. Ibid.

150. Sosa interview.

151. Sobalvarro interview.

152. See Bendaña, *Una tragedia campesina*, p. 232.

153. I conducted twenty interviews with former Contra leaders in Nicaragua in June and July 1993. My assessment of the impact of Argentine training on the Contra military leadership is based on the data collected at that time.

154. John Goshko, "Argentina Ends 'Contra' Aid," *Washington Post*, January 19, 1984.

CHAPTER 5

Some documents were consulted through the following microfiche collection: Declassified Documents Reference System (Woodbridge: Research Publications, various years) (hereafter, DDRS).

1. The first section of this chapter draws on Peter Willetts, ed., *Pressure Groups in the Global System* (New York: St. Martin's, 1982), pp. 1–27, 179–200.

2. The definitions of the types of pressure groups are drawn from Willetts, *Pressure Groups in the Global System*, pp. 2–8.

3. See Scott Anderson and Jon Lee Anderson, *Inside the League* (New York: Dodd, Mead, 1986); and Bruce Hoffman, *The PLO and Israel in Central America: The Geopolitical Dimension* (Santa Monica: RAND, 1988).

4. Interview with Gen. (retired) Miguel Angel Mallea Gil, in Buenos Aires, August 18, 1993.

5. Two prominent cases were Lt. Col. Emilio Echaverry Mejía of the Nicaraguan national guard and Honduran Gen. Gustavo Alvarez Martínez. See CIA memo "Biographical sketch of Emilio Echaverry Mejía," December 19, 1983 (DDRS); CIA memo "Biographical sketch of Gen. Gustavo Alvarez Martínez," August 25, 1983 (DDRS).

6. Affidavit of Rodolfo Peregrino Fernándcz, Madrid, April 26, 1983, in author's files, p. 48; Walter Goobar, "Escuela de dictadores," *Página 12*, August 8, 1993.

7. U.S. Congress, testimony of Leandro Sánchez Reisse before the Subcommittee on Terrorism, Narcotics and International Operations of the Senate Committee on Foreign Relations, July 23, 1987, pp. 14–17, 26–27, 111.

8. Sánchez Reisse testimony, pp. 17, 37.

9. Sánchez Reisse testimony, pp. 34–37.

10. See John A. Booth and Thomas W. Walker, *Understanding Central America*, 2nd. ed. (Boulder: Westview Press, 1989), p. 130.

11. Sánchez Reisse testimony, pp. 9–10, 80; José Luis D'Andrea Mohr,

"La línea y la memoria," *Pregón* (Lanús, Argentina), January 11, 1989.

12. Sánchez Reisse testimony, p. 10.

13. In Neuquén, Guglielminetti operated in the clandestine detention center known as La Escuelita. In Buenos Aires he served in El Banco, Olimpo, Superintendencia de Seguridad Federal, and Garage Azopardo. Under the command of the head of the First Army Corps, Suárez Mason, Guglielminetti conducted intelligence operations in Buenos Aires, handled sales of belongings of disappeared individuals, and participated in the extortion-kidnapping of businessmen and bankers during the dirty war—Centro de Estudios Legales y Sociales (CELS), *Culpables para la sociedad, impunes por la ley* (Buenos Aires: CELS, 1988), p. 24; Juan Gasparini, *La pista suiza* (Buenos Aires: Legasa, 1986), pp. 275–276. Two veterans of the dirty war who worked for the Extraterritorial Task Force were Jorge Rivero, a former Triple A member and SIDE agent, and Jorge Franco, an army officer who served as aide to Sánchez Reisse in the Florida headquarters—Juan José Salinas, "Los mercenarios argentinos (I)," *El Porteño*, July 1988: 7, and "Los mercenarios argentinos (II)," *El Porteño*, August 1988: 33.

14. Scott and Marshall, *Cocaine Politics*, p. 50.

15. Sánchez Reisse testimony, pp. 8–9, 106.

16. For example, Battalion 601 operatives were responsible for the extortion-kidnappings of Carlos Koldobsky (January and July 1979), Jaime Prisant (March 1979), Fernando Combal (May 1979 and March 1981), and Osvaldo Sivak (May 1979 and July 1985). Ostensibly, Battalion 601 was fighting against so-called economic subversion in Argentina—Alberto Riobó, "Sánchez Reisse y el secuestro de banqueros," *La Razón* (Buenos Aires), my copy undated, circa 1987; Jesús Iglesias Rouco, "Testimonios (I): declaraciones de un Subcomisario sobre el caso Sivak" and "Testimonios (II): otras dos declaraciones del Subcomisario Moreschi sobre el caso Sivak," *La Prensa* (Buenos Aires), my copies undated, circa 1986.

17. Sánchez Reisse testimony, pp. 18–19, 56. See David Corn, "The CIA and the Cocaine Coup," *Nation*, October 7, 1991: 405.

18. Sánchez Reisse testimony, pp. 52–54, 140; Scott and Marshall, *Cocaine Politics*, p. 49.

19. Sánchez Reisse testimony, pp. 14, 22–23, 54–55, 133–135. Panama played a major role in the Argentine enterprise. Most of the funds and

weapons for the operations in Central America were transferred via Panama and Manuel Noriega was a close collaborator of Argentine military intelligence.

20. See U.S. Congress, Senate Committee on Foreign Relations, Subcommittee on Terrorism, Narcotics, and International Operations, *Drugs, Law Enforcement and Foreign Policy: A Report* (Washington, D.C.: Government Printing Office, 1989), pp. 53–54, 56–57.

21. Martha Honey, *Hostile Acts: U.S. Policy in Costa Rica in the 1980s* (Gainesville: University Press of Florida, 1994), pp. 267–268, 272–273.

22. Sánchez Reisse testimony, pp. 60–63.

23. On Sánchez Reisse's front company, see the following sources: Sánchez Reisse testimony, pp. 13–18, 96–97, 132–133; Corn, "The CIA and the Cocaine Coup": 404; Ana Barón, "La conexión Sánchez Reisse-Suárez Mason-Guglielminetti," *Somos* (Buenos Aires), February 25, 1987: 20. Before being incorporated in New York, Argenshow had been an Argentine corporation, owned by Sánchez Reisse in partnership with Fernando Combal, an Argentine businessman kidnapped by Battalion 601 operatives in 1979 and 1981. The individual who introduced Sánchez Reisse to Norman Faber was Mike Gould, a U.S. businessman who developed commercial links with Argentina's military regime for the World Soccer Cup in 1978. In the mid-1980s, Sánchez Reisse and Faber set up Integrity Capital Corporation, a U.S.-based money laundering company that employed Argentine army and police officers and had close links with the Cuban exile terrorist organization Omega 7 and CIA agents— Sánchez Reisse testimony, pp. 93–98.

24. Sánchez Reisse testimony, pp. 53–54, 113–115.

25. R. T. Naylor, *Hot Money and the Politics of Debt* (New York: Linden/Simon and Schuster, 1987), p. 292.

26. For additional information on this particular network, see the following sources: Sánchez Reisse testimony, pp. 109–110; U.S. Congress, hearings before the Subcommittee on Terrorism, Narcotics, and International Operations and the Subcommittee on International Economic Policy, Trade, Oceans, and Environment of the Senate Committee on Foreign Relations, May 27, July 15, and October 30, 1987, pp. 244–245; and Scott and Marshall, *Cocaine Politics*, p. 223. Ramón Milián Rodríguez had been trained by a Cuban exile, terrorist Manuel Artime, political officer of the failed Bay of Pigs operation.

27. National Security Archive, ed., *The Iran-Contra Affair: The Making of a Scandal, 1983–1988* (Alexandria: Chadwyck-Healey, 1990), p. 113.

28. National Security Archive, *The Iran-Contra Affair*, pp. 89–90, 113. North's Enterprise was "the group of companies and dummy corporations which handled the flow of funds on the U.S. side for the arms sales to Iran and much of the Contra resupply operations," p. 90.

29. Sánchez Reisse testimony, p. 140.

30. Comisión Nacional sobre la Desaparición de Personas (CONADEP), *Nunca Más: The Report of the Argentine National Commission on the Disappeared* (New York: Farrar, Straus and Giroux, 1986), pp. 133–134. Navy Lt. Alfredo Astiz, responsible for the disappearance of several human rights activists in Argentina, operated out of the Paris Pilot Center.

31. On this issue applied to a different context, see Alan Wolfe, *The Limits of Legitimacy: Political Contradictions of Contemporary Capitalism* (New York: The Free Press, 1977), p. 201.

32. Juan Salinas and Julio Villalonga, *Gorriarán: La Tablada y las "guerras de inteligencia" en América Latina* (Buenos Aires: Mangin, 1993), pp. 200–201.

33. Martin Edwin Andersen, *Dossier Secreto: Argentina's Desaparecidos and the Myth of the "Dirty War"* (Boulder: Westview Press, 1993), p. 258. See Juan Gasparini, *El crimen de Graiver* (Buenos Aires: Grupo Editorial Zeta, 1990).

34. Jorge Grecco y Marcela Luza, "La historia del horror," *Somos*, December 9, 1991: 10–15.

35. The account of Israeli aid to Argentina is based on the following sources: Stockholm International Peace Research Institute (SIPRI), *World Armaments and Disarmament Yearbook 1979* (London: Taylor and Francis, 1979), pp. 204–205; SIPRI, *Yearbook 1982* (London: Taylor and Francis, 1982), p. 207; Edward Schumaker, "Argentina Buying New Arms," *New York Times*, June 6, 1982; *Washington Post*, December 7, 12, 16, 1982; *Latin America Weekly Report* (hereafter, *LAWR*), December 24, 1982, p. 10; Ignacio Klich, "Israel et l'Amérique Latine: Le Pari d'un engagement accru aux côtés de Washington," *Le Monde Diplomatique*, February 1983, p. 17. See Bishara Bahbah, *Israel and Latin America: The Military Connection* (New York: St. Martin's, 1986), pp. 72–73, 123–134.

36. Salinas and Villalonga, *Gorriarán*, p. 181. See "Israel y la dictadura militar: retorno a la tierra prometida," *Página 12*, June 8, 1991.

37. Peregrino Fernández affidavit, p. 37. General Harguindeguy had served as chief of federal police from December 1975 until the March 1976 coup.

38. Peregrino Fernández affidavit, pp. 17–18; Andersen, *Dossier Secreto*, p. 246.

39. See, for instance, Bahbah, *Israel and Latin America*, pp. 123–134; and *LAWR*, February 17, 1984, p. 15.

40. Transcript of Héctor Francés's videotaped testimony before Sandinista authorities, December 6, 1982, pp. 7, 10; Gasparini, *Pista Suiza*, p. 253.

41. See, for instance, *LAWR*, September 11, 1981, pp. 1, 5; Salinas and Villalonga, *Gorriarán*, pp. 142–143; Scott and Marshall, *Cocaine Politics*, pp. 77, 217(n.79).

42. Andersen, *Dossier Secreto*, p. 253. On anti-Jewish violence during the authoritarian regime, see Andersen, *Dossier Secreto*, pp. 242–243; and Jacobo Timerman, *Preso sin nombre, Celda sin número* (Buenos Aires: El Cid Editor, 1982).

43. Contract signed by José María Patetta, Transporte Aéreo Rioplatense (TAR), and Stuart J. McCafferty, Miami, July 7, 1981, in author's files.

44. Scott Armstrong et al., *The Chronology: The Documented Day-by-Day Account of the Secret Military Assistance to Iran and the Contras* (New York: Warner Books, 1987), pp. 7–8. See *La Razón*, August 8, 1981.

45. Contract between TAR and McCafferty.

46. Interview with Rogelio García Lupo, in Buenos Aires, July 30, 1993. Brigadier Guerra was involved in the urban repressive campaign as head of Area 162 (*Partido de Moreno*)—CELS, *Culpables para la sociedad*, p. 43. Some evidence indicates that TAR aircraft might have been used by the military in the dumping of political prisoners, alive, into the Atlantic Ocean (see chapter 1, The Military's Repressive Methodology)— Peregrino Fernández affidavit, p. 47; *Buenos Aires Herald*, March 7, 1995.

47. On the operations of the Argentine TAR freighter company, see the following sources: "El caso del avión caido en Rusia," *La Semana* (Buenos Aires), July 29, 1981; Mario Diament, "La asombrosa historia del avión argentino que cayó en la Unión Soviética," *Siete Días* (Buenos Aires), October 28, 1981; Oscar Raúl Cardoso, "Un favor clandestino a

EE.UU.," *Clarín*, December 20, 1991; Transporte Aéreo Rioplatense S.A., brochure, n.d., in author's files.

48. Armstrong et al., *The Chronology*, pp. 7–8. The incident received ample coverage in the Argentine press. See *Clarín*, July 23 to 31, 1981, August 1 to 6, 1981, *La Razón*, July 25, August 8, 1981, *La Nación*, July 27, 28, 1981, *Buenos Aires Herald*, July 29, 1981, *Convicción*, July 29, 1981, *La Prensa*, August 2, 6, 1981.

49. "Odisea en el Caribe de un avión argentino," *La Semana*, July 7, 1977.

50. Hoffman, *The PLO and Israel in Central America*, p. vii, passim.

51. Cheryl A. Rubenberg, "Israel and Guatemala: Arms, Advice and Counterinsurgency," *Middle East Report* (May-June 1986): 21, quoted in Hoffman, *The PLO and Israel in Central America*, p. 29.

52. Hoffman, *The PLO and Israel in Central America*, pp. 8–13.

53. "Israel Adds Itself to the War Against Nicaragua," *Soberanía*, no. 8 (January 1983): 37.

54. See, for instance, *Guardian* (London), December 10, 1982; *Washington Post*, November 14, 1984; Andrew and Leslie Cockburn, *Dangerous Liaison: The Inside Story of the U.S.-Israeli Covert Relationship* (New York: HarperCollins, 1991), p. 223.

55. Scott and Marshall, *Cocaine Politics*, p. 108.

56. Sánchez Reisse testimony, pp. 50, 187–188.

57. Sánchez Reisse testimony, p. 50.

58. Interview with César Arana, in Miami, July 9, 1993.

59. Edgar Chamorro, *Packaging the Contras: A Case of CIA Disinformation* (New York: Institute for Media Analysis, 1987), p. 5. Some Cuban exiles sought to create a permanent paramilitary infrastructure for an anti-Communist brigade in Latin America—Holly Sklar, *Washington's War on Nicaragua* (Boston: South End Press, 1988), pp. 75–76, 239; Anderson and Anderson, *Inside the League*, pp. 248–249.

60. Scott and Marshall, *Cocaine Politics*, pp. 43–44.

61. García Lupo interview. Rodríguez had worked as an interpreter and guide to Gen. Tomás Sánchez de Bustamante, head of Argentina's First Army Corps, during Sánchez de Bustamante's visit to Vietnam—Felix I. Rodriguez and John Weisman, *Shadow Warrior: The CIA Hero of a Hundred Unknown Battles* (New York: Simon and Schuster, 1989), pp.

203–206. Rodríguez's CIA mentor was Donald Gregg, former CIA region 3 station chief in Vietnam and, from April 1982, national security adviser to Vice President George Bush. In 1985, Gregg recommended Rodríguez for the liaison post at Ilopango air base in El Salvador—National Security Archive, *The Iran-Contra Affair*, pp. 90, 104.

62. Christopher Dickey, *With the Contras: A Reporter in the Wilds of Nicaragua* (New York: Simon and Schuster, 1987), pp. 54, 61; Sklar, *Washington's War*, p. 22.

63. Sánchez Reisse testimony, pp. 50, 187–188; Baltodano Herrera testimony, in *FBIS–LAT*, January 15, 1982, pp. P5–P9. See Anderson and Anderson, *Inside the League*, p. 248; and Scott and Marshall, *Cocaine Politics*, p. 49.

64. Sánchez Reisse testimony, pp. 187–188.

65. Peter Kihss, "Two Castro Foes Are Sought in Bombing," *New York Times*, March 27, 1979.

66. Kihss, "Two Castro Foes"; Robert D. McFadden, "Cuban Refugee Leader Slain in Union City," *New York Times*, November 26, 1979.

67. Peter Maas, *Manhunt* (New York: Random House, 1986), p. 202. See National Security Archive, *The Iran-Contra Affair*, p. 101. The former CIA agent was Rafael "Chi Chi" Quintero, a key operative in the clandestine Contra resupply operation.

68. For example, in January 1981 the FBI arrested seven Alpha 66 operatives in the Florida Keys. They were on a boat carrying "explosive devices, including pipe bombs and hand grenades, as well as a machine gun, several semiautomatic rifles, pistols, ammunition and smokeless gun powder"—Robert Pear, "Seven Exiles Seized in Florida Linked to Raids on Cuba," *New York Times*, January 17, 1981.

69. The Alpha 66 president, Andrés Nazario Sargen, was a WACL member—Anderson and Anderson, *Inside the League*, p. 248; Scott and Marshall, *Cocaine Politics*, p. 49. In the early 1970s, two members of Alpha 66 had worked as advisers to the Costa Rican Security Ministry's Office of Narcotics. They were reportedly involved in drug trafficking, torture, and assassination—Honey, *Hostile Acts*, p. 294.

70. Telephone conversation with a former U.S. Army officer assigned to Latin America in the early 1980s, name withheld on request, June 19, 1995.

71. Sam Dillon, *Comandos: The CIA and Nicaragua's Contra Rebels*

(New York: Henry Holt, 1991), pp. 175–176, 324, 328; Scott and Marshall, *Cocaine Politics*, pp. 59–60.

72. Sklar, *Washington's War*, p. 76; Chamorro, *Packaging the Contras*, p. 5.

73. Interview with José Luis D'Andrea Mohr, in Buenos Aires, August 14, 1991.

74. Sklar, *Washington's War*, p. 76.

75. Sánchez Reisse testimony, p. 139; Juan Gasparini, "La CIA no abandona a sus hombres," *El Periodista de Buenos Aires*, December 11, 1987: 3.

76. García Lupo interview; interview with Juan José Salinas, in Buenos Aires, July 31, 1993.

77. Anderson and Anderson, *Inside the League*, pp. 11, 107, 264.

78. García Lupo interview.

79. Interview with Leandro Sánchez Reisse published in *Somos*, February 25, 1987. See Scott and Marshall, *Cocaine Politics*, pp. 43–49.

80. García Lupo and Salinas interviews.

81. García Lupo interview. See Claudio Uriarte, *Almirante Cero* (Buenos Aires: Planeta, 1992), pp. 123, 141–142.

82. Horacio Verbitsky, *La última batalla de la tercera guerra mundial* (Buenos Aires: Legasa, 1985), pp. 110–115; Horacio Verbitsky, *La posguerra sucia: un análisis de la transición* (Buenos Aires: Legasa, 1985), p. 130.

83. *Ambito Financiero* (Buenos Aires), February 8, 1982.

84. García Lupo interview; Verbitsky, *La posguerra sucia*, pp. 130–131. It was found later that Miori Pereyra had been pocketing 20 percent of the Argentine advisers' salaries during his tenure as administrator of the operation.

85. CAL resolution, quoted in Anderson and Anderson, *Inside the League*, p. 204.

86. "Argentina Redraws the Ideological Map of South America," *LAWR*, September 19, 1980, p. 5.

87. García Lupo interview. According to García Lupo, Suárez Mason obtained $10 million from WACL for the anti-Communist congress.

88. On the 1980 CAL Congress held in Buenos Aires, see Verbitsky, *La última batalla*, pp. 91–92; Anderson and Anderson, *Inside the League*, pp. 75, 147, 204; Scott and Marshall, *Cocaine Politics*, pp. 43, 46.

89. "Argentina Redraws the Ideological Map," *LAWR*, p. 5. The conference's resolutions called Carter's human rights policy "the instrument of a neocolonial project against Latin America." They also condemned both liberation theology and the Jesuits, labeling them as Marxist neocolonizers who organized rural guerrillas "under the pretext of evangelizing"—Anderson and Anderson, *Inside the League*, p. 204, citing *Proceso* (San Salvador), no. 13, September 1–7, 1980: 13–14. See also *Clarín*, September 2, 1980; *La Nación*, September 4, 1980; *La Prensa*, September 9, 1980.

90. A team of Argentine military intelligence officers participated in the kidnapping of three Montonero exiles in Lima in early 1980, allegedly with the connivance of the Peruvian high command—"Argentina Redraws the Ideological Map," *LAWR*, p. 5.

91. Craig Pyes, "The New American Right Cooks Up a Hot Potato," *Albuquerque Journal*, December 22, 1983; Anderson and Anderson, *Inside the League*, pp. 206–207. Endorsement by right-wing sectors of the United States was essential for the creation of ARENA. In early 1980, D'Aubuisson had met with U.S. right-wing groups that promised him support if the Republicans returned to office. "We have spoken with various senators in the Capitol," D'Aubuisson informed his followers in May 1980, "and they asked us that we hold fast until November, that with the new government that the Reagan Republicans will win, our luck will change." Among the anti-Communist groups that supported D'Aubuisson were the Council on Inter-American Security (with its influential Committee of Santa Fe), the Heritage Foundation, and the American Security Council. D'Aubuisson's most important contact in Washington was Senator Helms.

92. Bob Woodward, *Veil: The Secret Wars of the CIA, 1981–1987* (New York: Simon and Schuster, 1987), pp. 187–188.

93. U.S. embassy, Nicaragua, cable from Ambassador McNeil to secretary of state, July 1981, quoted in Honey, *Hostile Acts*, pp. 245, 559(n.19), see also p. 203.

94. Francés transcript, pp. 3, 6–14.

95. Anderson and Anderson, *Inside the League*, pp. 244–246. Other MCRL members working with the Argentines were Carlos Feders and Manuel Oliveira Pinto.

96. Francés transcript, p. 14.

97. Honey, *Hostile Acts*, pp. 59–62.

98. On CAUSA's anti-Communist activities, see Kai Herrmann, "Klaus Barbie: A Killer's Career," *Covert Action* (winter 1986): 18–19; Salinas, "Mercenarios argentinos (I)": 5; Anderson and Anderson, *Inside the League*, p. 129. The visible liaison between CAUSA and the Argentine high command was Gen. Ramón Genaro Díaz Bessone. Two key operatives in the Argentine intelligence venture in Central America, Miori Pereyra and Sánchez Reisse, had ties with the Moon church. Gen. Gustavo Alvarez Martínez of Honduras, a leading actor in the anti-Sandinista operation, was also linked to CAUSA.

99. Margaret E. Crahan, "Religion, Revolution, and Counterrevolution: The Role of the Religious Right in Central America," in Douglas A. Chalmers, Maria do Carmo Campello de Souza, and Atilio A. Boron, eds., *The Right and Democracy in Latin America* (New York: Praeger, 1992), pp. 164, 166, 170, 172–173.

100. Prosecutor Elisabetta Cesqui, quoted in *Página 12*, March 5, 1994.

101. *Página 12*, March 5, 1994.

102. Quote from *La Voz* (Buenos Aires), August 11, 1983, in Andersen, *Dossier Secreto*, p. 372(n.23), see also p. 298.

103. Uriarte, *Almirante Cero*, pp. 108, 145.

104. Andersen, *Dossier Secreto*, pp. 87–88, 144–145, 254, 226, 280–281, 302–303.

105. Penny Lernoux, *In Banks We Trust* (Garden City: Anchor Press, 1984), p. 189; Salinas interview.

106. *El Periodista de Buenos Aires*, December 25, 1987.

107. Verbitsky, *La última batalla*, p. 93.

108. Sánchez Reisse testimony, p. 75.

109. Ibid.

110. Ministry of the Interior, General Directorate for State Security, Nicaragua, secret memo in re participation of the Argentine armed forces and their intelligence services in the aggression against Nicaragua, my copy undated, circa 1984.

111. Luis Majul, *Los dueños de la Argentina* (Buenos Aires: Sudamericana, 1992), p. 86. The foreign debt transferred by Bridas to the Argentine state was $619 million.

112. Majul, *Los dueños de la Argentina*, pp. 88–89.

113. Norberto Bobbio, *The Future of Democracy: A Defence of the Rules of the Game* (Minneapolis: University of Minnesota Press, 1987), pp. 33, 81, 91–92, 94–95.

114. Bobbio, *The Future of Democracy*, p. 95.

115. This analysis is based on Wolfe, *The Limits of Legitimacy*, pp. 200–203.

116. See Manuel Antonio Garretón, *La posibilidad democrática en Chile* (Santiago: FLACSO, 1988); and Alfred Stepan, *Rethinking Military Politics: Brazil and the Southern Cone* (Princeton: Princeton University Press, 1988).

117. Jorge Grecco, "Expertos argentinos asesoran a México en lucha antiguerrillera," *Clarín*, November 30, 1994; Walter Curia, "Denuncian en México malestar militar por asesores argentinos," *Clarín*, December 4, 1994.

118. Human Rights Watch/Americas, *The New Year's Rebellion: Violations of Human Rights and Humanitarian Law During the Armed Revolt in Chiapas, Mexico*, New York, March 1, 1994, pp. 10–23. On the methods used in the Argentine detention centers, see Comisión Nacional sobre la Desaparición de Personas (CONADEP), *Nunca Más*. See also Frank Graziano, *Divine Violence: Spectacle, Psychosexuality, and Radical Christianity in the Argentine "Dirty War"* (Boulder: Westview Press, 1992), pp. 38, 89. The Mexican military police have a long-standing history of brutality against peasants and indigenous peoples. Also, antidrug forces in Mexico have long used "unconventional" intelligence tactics in their regular operations.

Bibliography

Acuña, Carlos H., and Catalina Smulovitz. "Militares en la transición argentina: del gobierno a la subordinación constitucional," in Carlos Acuña et al., *Juicios, castigos y memorias: Derechos humanos y justicia en la política argentina*. Buenos Aires: Nueva Visión, 1995.

Alegría, Claribel, and D. J. Flakoll. *Somoza: expediente cerrado*. Managua: El Gato Negro-Latino Editores, 1993.

Ambler, John Steward. *Soldiers Against the State: The French Army in Politics*. Columbus: Ohio State University Press, 1966.

American Civil Liberties Union and Americas Watch. *Report on Human Rights in El Salvador*. New York, January 1982.

Americas Watch (now Human Rights Watch/Americas). *U.S. Reporting on Human Rights in El Salvador: Methodology at Odds with Knowledge*. New York, June 1982.

Americas Watch. *Human Rights in Honduras: Signs of "The Argentine Method."* New York, December 1982.

Americas Watch. *Almost Nine Years and Still No Verdict In the "Trial of Responsibilities."* New York, December 1992.

Americas Watch. *The Trial of Responsibilities: The García Meza Tejada Trial*. New York, September 10, 1993.

Andersen, Martin Edwin. *Dossier Secreto: Argentina's Desaparecidos and the Myth of the "Dirty War."* Boulder: Westview Press, 1993.

Anderson, Scott, and Jon Lee Anderson. *Inside the League*. New York: Dodd, Mead, 1986.

Arendt, Hannah. *Eichmann in Jerusalem: A Report on the Banality of Evil*. New York: Viking Press, 1963.

Armony, Ariel C. "Argentina and the Origins of Nicaragua's Contras." *Low Intensity Conflict and Law Enforcement* 2, no. 3 (winter 1993).

Armony, Ariel C. "The Former Contras," in Thomas W. Walker, ed. *Nicaragua Without Illusions: Regime Transition and Other Changes in the 1990s.* Wilmington: SR Books, 1997.

Armony, Ariel C., and Robert Chisholm. "Is Social Revolution Possible in a Liberal Era? Revolution and Compromise in Nicaragua 1979–1990." Paper delivered at the Annual Meeting of the American Political Science Association, New York, September 1994.

Amstrong, Scott, et al. *The Chronology: The Documented Day-by-Day Account of the Secret Military Assistance to Iran and the Contras.* New York: Warner Books, 1987.

Arnson, Cynthia. "Background Information on the Security Forces in El Salvador and U.S. Military Assistance." Institute for Policy Studies, Washington, D.C., March 1980.

Arnson, Cynthia J. *Crossroads: Congress, the President, and Central America 1976–1993*, 2nd. ed. University Park: Pennsylvania State University Press, 1993.

Arriagada Herrera, Genaro. "Ideology and Politics in the South American Military (Argentina, Brazil, Chile and Uruguay)." Paper presented at the Woodrow Wilson International Center for Scholars, Washington, D.C., March 21, 1979.

Arriagada Herrera, Genaro. *El pensamiento político de los militares (estudios sobre Chile, Argentina, Brasil y Uruguay).* Santiago, Chile: Editorial Aconcagua, 1981.

Bahbah, Bishara. *Israel and Latin America: The Military Connection.* New York: St. Martin's Press, 1986.

Bardini, Roberto. *Conexión en Tegucigalpa (El somocismo en Honduras).* Puebla: Universidad Autónoma de Puebla, 1982.

Bardini, Roberto. *Monjes, mercenarios y mercaderes: la red secreta de apoyo a los Contras.* México, D.F.: Alpa Corral, 1988.

Barry, Tom, and Kent Norsworthy. *Honduras: A Country Guide.* Albuquerque: Inter-Hemispheric Education Resource Center, 1990.

Beaufre, André. "La violencia." *Estrategia* 5 (January-February 1970).

Beaufre, André. "Perspectivas estratégicas en la década del 70." *Estrategia* 9 (January-February 1971).

Bendaña, Alejandro, ed. *Una tragedia campesina: testimonios de la resistencia.* Managua: Edit-Arte/CEI, 1991.

Bittencourt Emílio, L. A. "The 'Abertura' in Brazil: The Day-After of the Brazilian Intelligence 'Monster.'" Working paper, Instituto de Pesquisa Econômica Aplicada (IPEA), November 1992.

Bobbio, Norberto. *The Future of Democracy: A Defence of the Rules of the Game.* Minneapolis: University of Minnesota Press, 1987.

Booth, John A. *The End and the Beginning: The Nicaraguan Revolution,* 2nd. ed. Boulder: Westview Press, 1985.

Booth, John A., and Thomas W. Walker. *Understanding Central America,* 2nd. ed. Boulder: Westview Press, 1989.

Brinkley, Joel, and Stephen Engelberg, eds. *Report of the Congressional Committees Investigating the Iran-Contra Affair.* New York: Random House, 1988.

Brownstein, Ronald, and Nina Easton. *Reagan's Ruling Class: Portraits of the President's Top One Hundred Officials.* New York: Pantheon Books, 1983.

Brysk, Alison. "The Politics of Measurement: The Contested Count of the Disappeared in Argentina." *Human Rights Quarterly* 16, no. 4 (November 1994).

Brysk, Alison. *The Politics of Human Rights in Argentina: Protest, Change, and Democratization.* Stanford: Stanford University Press, 1994.

Butler, Judy. "A Nation Divided: A Chronicle of Nicaragua's Atlantic Coast." Unpublished manuscript, in author's files.

Bye, Vegard. *La paz prohibida: el laberinto centroamericano en la década de los ochenta.* San José, Costa Rica: Departamento Ecuménico de Investigaciones, 1991.

Calvo, Robert. "The Church and the Doctrine of National Security." *Journal of Interamerican Studies and World Affairs* 21, no. 1 (February 1979).

Cardoso, Oscar Raúl. "El último secreto del Proceso: apéndice sobre la experiencia argentina," in Christopher Dickey. *Con los Contras.* Buenos Aires: Sudamericana-Planeta, 1987.

Cardoso, Oscar R. Ricardo Kirschbaum, and Eduardo van der Kooy. *Malvinas, la trama secreta.* Buenos Aires: Sudamericana-Planeta, 1983.

Carothers, Thomas. *In the Name of Democracy: U.S. Policy Toward Latin America in the Reagan Years.* Berkeley: University of California Press, 1991.

Castañeda, Jorge G. *Utopia Unarmed: The Latin American Left After the Cold War*. New York: Alfred A. Knopf, 1993.

Centro de Estudios Legales y Sociales (CELS), "The Doctrine of Global Parallelism." MS, Buenos Aires, 1981, in author's files.

Centro de Estudios Legales y Sociales. *Uruguay/Argentina: coordinación represiva*. Buenos Aires: CELS, 1982.

Centro de Estudios Legales y Sociales. *Culpables para la sociedad, impunes por la ley*. Buenos Aires: CELS, 1988.

Centro de Investigación y Estudios de la Reforma Agraria (CIERA). *La reforma agraria en Nicaragua, 1979–1989*, vols. 4 and 6. Managua: CIERA, 1989.

Chamorro, Edgar. *Packaging the Contras: A Case of CIA Disinformation*. New York: Institute for Media Analysis, 1987.

Child, Jack. *Geopolitics and Conflict in South America*. New York: Praeger Publishers, 1985.

Chisholm, Robert. "From National Defence to National Security: 'Geopolitical Darwinism' and Military Thought in South America." Master's Thesis, Queen's University, Kingston, Ontario, Canada, 1989.

Christian, Shirley. *Nicaragua, Revolution in the Family*. New York: Vintage Books, 1986.

Cockburn, Andrew, and Leslie Cockburn. *Dangerous Liaison: The Inside Story of the U.S.-Israeli Covert Relationship*. New York: HarperCollins, 1991.

Cohn, Betsy, and Patricia Hynds. "The Manipulation of the Religion Issue," in Thomas W. Walker, ed. *Reagan versus the Sandinistas: The Undeclared War on Nicaragua*. Boulder: Westview Press, 1987.

Colburn, Forrest D. *Post-Revolutionary Nicaragua: State, Class, and the Dilemmas of Agrarian Policy*. Berkeley: University of California Press, 1986.

Colburn, Forrest D. "Foot Dragging and Other Peasant Responses to the Nicaraguan Revolution," in Forrest Colburn, ed. *Everyday Forms of Peasant Resistance*. Armonk: M. E. Sharpe, 1989.

Colburn, Forrest D. *Managing the Commanding Heights: Nicaragua's State Enterprises*. Berkeley: University of California Press, 1990.

Comblin, José. *The Church and the National Security State*. Maryknoll: Orbis Books, 1979.

Comisión Nacional sobre la Desaparición de Personas (CONADEP). *Nunca Más*. Buenos Aires: EUDEBA, 1984. Reprinted in English as *Nunca Más: The Report of the Argentine National Commission on the Disappeared*. New York: Farrar, Straus and Giroux, 1986.

Committee of Santa Fe. *A New Inter-American Policy for the Eighties*. Washington, D.C.: Council for Inter-American Security, 1980.

Corradi, Juan E. "The Mode of Destruction: Terror in Argentina." *Telos* 54 (1982–83).

Corradi, Juan E. "Toward Societies without Fear," in Juan E. Corradi, Patricia Weiss Fagen, and Manuel A. Garretón, eds. *Fear at the Edge: State Terror and Resistance in Latin America*. Berkeley: University of California Press, 1992.

Crahan, Margaret E. "National Security Ideology and Human Rights," in Margaret Crahan, ed. *Human Rights and Basic Needs in the Americas*. Washington, D.C.: Georgetown University Press, 1982.

Crahan, Margaret E. "Religion, Revolution, and Counterrevolution: The Role of the Religious Right in Central America," in Douglas A. Chalmers, Maria do Carmo Campello de Souza, and Atilio A. Boron, e *The Right and Democracy in Latin America*. New York: Praeger, 1

Dabat, Alejandro, and Luis Lorenzano. *Argentina: The Malvinas ar End of Military Rule*. London: Verso, 1984.

Danner, Mark. *The Massacre at El Mozote: A Parable of the Cc* New York: Vintage, 1994.

Deutsch, Sandra McGee, and Ronald H. Dolkart, eds. *The Right: Its History and Intellectual Origins, 1910 to the P* mington: SR Books, 1993.

Díaz Bessone, Ramón Genaro. *Guerra Revolucionaria en (1959–1978)*. Buenos Aires: Fraterna, 1986.

Dickey, Christopher. *With the Contras: A Reporter i Nicaragua*. New York: Simon and Schuster, 1987.

Dillon, Sam. *Comandos: The CIA and Nicaragua's C* York: Henry Holt, 1991.

Duhalde, Eduardo Luis. *El Estado terrorista argenti* Vergara, 1983.

Eich, Dieter, and Carlos Rincón. *The Contras: In dinistas*. San Francisco: Synthesis Publicatic

Enríquez, Laura. *Harvesting Change: Labor and Agrarian Reform in Nicaragua, 1979–1990.* Chapel Hill: University of North Carolina Press, 1991.

Escudé, Carlos. *La Argentina: ¿paria internacional?* Buenos Aires: Editorial de Belgrano, 1984.

Escudé, Carlos. *La Argentina vs. las grandes potencias (el precio del desafío).* Buenos Aires: Editorial de Belgrano, 1986.

Falcoff, Mark. *A Tale of Two Policies: U.S. Relations with the Argentine Junta, 1976–1983.* Philadelphia: Foreign Policy Research Institute, 1989.

Falla, Ricardo. *Massacres in the Jungle: Ixcán, Guatemala, 1975–1982.* Boulder: Westview Press, 1994.

Feldman, David Lewis. "The United States Role in the Malvinas Crisis, 1982: Misguidance and Misperception in Argentina's Decision to Go to War." *Journal of Interamerican Studies and World Affairs* 27, no. 2 (summer 1985).

Figueroa Ibarra, Carlos. *El recurso del miedo: ensayo sobre el Estado y el terror en Guatemala.* San José, Costa Rica: Editorial Universitaria Centroamericana, 1991.

Fitzgerald, E. V. K. "Estado y economía en Nicaragua," in Raúl Rubén and Jan de Gorot, eds. *El debate sobre la reforma agraria en Nicaragua.* Managua: Editorial Ciencias Sociales, 1988.

Fontana, Andrés. "Fuerzas armadas, partidos políticos y transición a la democracia en Argentina." Centro de Estudios de Estado y Sociedad (CEDES), Buenos Aires, 1984.

Fontana, Andrés. "De la crisis de Malvinas a la subordinación condicionada: conflictos intramilitares y transición política en Argentina." Working paper, Kellogg Institute, August 1986.

Foucault, Michel. *Discipline and Punish: The Birth of the Prison.* New York: Vintage, 1979.

Franco, Jean. "Gender, Death, and Resistance: Facing the Ethical Vacuum," in Juan E. Corradi, Patricia Weiss Fagen, and Manuel A. Garretón, eds. *Fear at the Edge: State Terror and Resistance in Latin America.* Berkeley: University of California Press, 1992.

Freedman, Lawrence, and Virginia Gamba-Stonehouse. *Signals of War: The Falklands Conflict of 1982.* Princeton: Princeton University Press, 1991.

Frontalini, Daniel, and María Cristina Caiati. *El mito de la guerra sucia.* Buenos Aires: Centro de Estudios Legales y Sociales (CELS), 1984.

García Lupo, Rogelio. *Paraguay de Stroessner.* Buenos Aires: Grupo Editorial Zeta, 1989.

Garretón, Manuel Antonio. *La posibilidad democrática en Chile.* Santiago: FLACSO, 1988.

Garretón, Manuel Antonio. "Fear in Military Regimes: An Overview," in Juan E. Corradi, Patricia Weiss Fagen, and Manuel A. Garretón, eds. *Fear at the Edge: State Terror and Resistance in Latin America.* Berkeley: University of California Press, 1992.

Gasparini, Juan. *La pista suiza.* Buenos Aires: Legasa, 1986.

Gasparini, Juan. *Montoneros: final de cuentas.* Buenos Aires: Puntosur, 1988.

Gasparini, Juan. *El crimen de Graiver.* Buenos Aires: Grupo Editorial Zeta, 1990.

Gianotten, Vera, Ton de Wit, and Rodrigo Montoya. *Nicaragua: cuestión agraria y participación campesina.* Lima: DESCO, 1987.

Gibson, Bill. "Overview of the Nicaraguan Economy," in Rose J. Spalding, ed. *The Political Economy of Revolutionary Nicaragua.* Boston: Allen and Unwin, 1987.

Gilbert, Dennis. *Sandinistas.* Oxford: Basil Blackwell, 1988.

Gillespie, Richard. *Soldiers of Perón: Argentina's Montoneros.* New York: Oxford University Press, 1982.

Goldstone, Jack A. "Revolution," in Mary Hawkesworth and Maurice Kogan, eds. *Encyclopedia of Government and Politics.* London: Routledge, 1992.

González Janzen, Ignacio. *La Triple-A.* Buenos Aires: Contrapunto, 1986.

Gould, Jeffrey L. *To Lead as Equals: Rural Protest and Political Consciousness in Chinandega, Nicaragua, 1912–1990.* Chapel Hill: University of North Carolina Press, 1990.

Goyret, José T. "El pensamiento estratégico del general Beaufre," part 1. *Estrategia* 7 (May-June, 1970).

Goyret, José T. "El pensamiento estratégico del general Beaufre," part 2. *Estrategia* 8 (July-August 1970).

Grabendorff, Wolf. "¿De país aislado a aliado preferido? Las relaciones entre la Argentina y los Estados Unidos: 1976–1981," in Peter Waldmann and Ernesto Garzón Valdez, eds. *El poder militar en la Argentina, 1976–1981*. Buenos Aires: Galerna, 1983.

Graziano, Frank. *Divine Violence: Spectacle, Psychosexuality, and Radical Christianity in the Argentine "Dirty War."* Boulder: Westview Press, 1992.

Guest, Iain. *Behind the Disappearances: Argentina's Dirty War Against Human Rights and the United Nations*. Philadelphia: University of Pennsylvania Press, 1990.

Guglialmelli, Juan E. "Las FF.AA. en América Latina (FF.AA. y Revolución Nacional)." *Estrategia* 17 (July-August 1972).

Guglialmelli, Juan E. "Fuerzas Armadas para la Liberación Nacional." *Estrategia* 23 (July-August 1973).

Guglialmelli, Juan E. "Geopolítica en la Argentina." *Estrategia* 46–47 (May-August 1977).

Guglialmelli, Juan E. "Economía, Poder Militar y Seguridad Nacional." *Estrategia* 51 (March-April 1978): 7–29.

Gutman, Roy. *Banana Diplomacy: The Making of American Policy in Nicaragua 1981–1987*. New York: Simon and Schuster, 1988.

Haig, Alexander M., Jr. *Caveat: Realism, Reagan, and Foreign Policy*. New York: Macmillan, 1984.

Halperin Donghi, Tulio. "Argentina's Unmastered Past," *Latin American Research Review* 23, no. 2 (1988).

Handy, Jim. *Gift of the Devil: A History of Guatemala*. Boston: South End Press, 1984.

Hodges, Donald C. *Argentina's "Dirty War": An Intellectual Biography*. Austin: University of Texas Press, 1991.

Hoffman, Bruce. *The PLO and Israel in Central America: The Geopolitical Dimension*. Santa Monica: RAND, 1988.

Honey, Martha. *Hostile Acts: U.S. Policy in Costa Rica in the 1980s*. Gainesville: University Press of Florida, 1994.

Human Rights Watch/Americas. *Honduras: The Facts Speak for Themselves*. New York, 1994.

Human Rights Watch/Americas. *The New Year's Rebellion: Violations of Human Rights and Humanitarian Law During the Armed Revolt in Chiapas, Mexico*. New York, March 1, 1994.

Jonas, Susanne. *The Battle for Guatemala: Rebels, Death Squads, and U.S. Power*. Boulder: Westview Press, 1991.

Kalmanowiecki, Laura. "Military Power and Policing During the Justo Administration, 1932–1938." Paper presented at the Eighteenth International Congress of the Latin American Studies Association, Atlanta, March 1994.

Kirkpatrick, Jeane. "Dictatorships and Double Standards." *Commentary* 68 (November 1979).

Kirkpatrick, Jeane. "U.S. Security and Latin America," in Howard J. Wiarda, ed. *Rift and Revolution: The Central American Imbroglio.* Washington, D.C.: American Enterprise Institute for Public Policy Research, 1984.

Klare, Michael T. "The Interventionist Impulse: U.S. Military Doctrine for Low-Intensity Warfare," in Michael Klare and Peter Kornbluh, eds. *Low-Intensity Warfare: Counterinsurgency, Proinsurgency, and Antiterrorism in the Eighties.* New York: Pantheon, 1988.

Klare, Michael T., and Peter Kornbluh. "The New Interventionism: Low-Intensity Warfare in the 1980s and Beyond," in Michael Klare and Peter Kornbluh, eds. *Low-Intensity Warfare: Counterinsurgency, Proinsurgency, and Antiterrorism in the Eighties.* New York: Pantheon, 1988.

Kornbluh, Peter. *Nicaragua: The Price of Intervention.* Washington, D.C.: Institute for Policy Studies, 1987.

Lapper, Richard, and James Painter. *Honduras: State for Sale.* London: Latin American Bureau, 1985.

Lernoux, Penny. *In Banks We Trust.* Garden City: Anchor Press, 1984.

Levine, Michael. *The Big White Lie: The CIA and the Cocaine/Crack Epidemic.* New York: Thunder's Mouth Press, 1993.

Loveman, Brian, and Thomas M. Davies, eds. *The Politics of Antipolitics: The Military in Latin America,* 2nd. ed. Lincoln: University of Nebraska Press, 1989.

Maas, Peter. *Manhunt.* New York: Random House, 1986.

Majul, Luis. *Los dueños de la Argentina.* Buenos Aires: Sudamericana, 1992.

Malamud-Goti, Jaime E. *Game Without End: State Terror and the Politics of Justice.* Norman: University of Oklahoma Press, 1996.

Malloy, James M. *Bolivia: The Uncompleted Revolution.* Pittsburgh: University of Pittsburgh Press, 1970.

Manwaring, Max G., and Court E. Prisk, eds. *El Salvador at War: An Oral History.* Washington, D.C.: National Defense University, 1988.

Martin, Lisa L., and Kathryn Sikkink. "U.S. Policy and Human Rights in Argentina and Guatemala, 1973–1980," in Peter B. Evans, Harold K. Jacobson, and Robert D. Putnam, eds. *Double-Edged Diplomacy: International Bargaining and Domestic Politics.* Berkeley: University of California Press, 1993.

Martínez Cuenca, Alejandro. *Sandinista Economics in Practice.* Boston: South End Press, 1992.

McCann, Frank. "Origins of the 'New Professionalism' of the Brazilian Military." *Journal of Interamerican Studies and World Affairs* 21, no. 4 (November 1979).

McClintock, Michael. *The American Connection: State Terror and Popular Resistance in El Salvador.* London: Zed Books, 1985.

McClintock, Michael. *The American Connection: State Terror and Popular Resistance in Guatemala.* London: Zed Books, 1985.

McSherry, Joan Patrice. "Democratization and the Politics of National Security in Argentina." Ph.D. dissertation, City University of New York, 1994.

Migdal, Joel S. *Peasants, Politics and Revolution: Pressures Toward Political and Social Change in the Third World.* Princeton: Princeton University Press, 1974.

Mignone, Emilio F. *Derechos humanos y sociedad: el caso argentino.* Buenos Aires: CELS/Ediciones del Pensamiento Nacional, 1991.

Millett, Richard. *Guardians of the Dynasty: A History of the U.S. Created Guardia Nacional de Nicaragua and the Somoza Family.* Maryknoll: Orbis Books, 1977.

Mittelbach, Federico. *Informe sobre desaparecedores.* Buenos Aires: La Urraca, 1986.

Molineu, Harold. *U.S. Policy Toward Latin America: From Regionalism to Globalism.* Boulder: Westview Press, 1990.

Monkman, Guillermo Alberto. "The Institutionalization of the Doctrine of National Security in Argentina: The Military and Foreign Policy." Ph.D. dissertation, University of South Carolina, 1992.

Moore, Barrington, Jr. *Social Origins of Dictatorship and Democracy: Lord and Peasant in the Making of the Modern World.* Boston: Beacon Press, 1966.

Morales Carazo, Jaime. *La Contra*. México, D.F.: Planeta, 1989.

Morley, Morris, and James Petras. *The Reagan Administration and Nicaragua: How Washington Constructs Its Case for Counterrevolution in Central America*. New York: Institute for Media Analysis, 1987.

Morrison, Andrew R., and Rachel A. May. "Escape from Terror: Violence and Migration in Post-Revolutionary Guatemala." *Latin American Research Review* 29, no. 2 (1994).

Naylor, R. T. *Hot Money and the Politics of Debt*. New York: Linden/Simon and Schuster, 1987.

Norden, Deborah. "Democratic Consolidation and Military Professionalism: Argentina in the 1980s." *Journal of Interamerican Studies and World Affairs* 32, no. 3 (fall 1990).

Núñez, Orlando, ed. *La guerra en Nicaragua*. Managua: Centro para la Investigación, la Promoción y el Desarrollo Rural y Social (CIPRES), 1991.

Paoletti, Alipio. *Como los Nazis, como en Vietnam*. Buenos Aires: Contrapunto, 1987.

Pastor, Robert A. *Condemned to Repetition: The United States and Nicaragua*. Princeton: Princeton University Press, 1987.

Pastor, Robert A. "The Carter Administration and Latin America: A Test of Principle," in John D. Martz, ed. *United States Policy in Latin America: A Quarter Century of Crisis and Challenge, 1961–1986*. Lincoln: University of Nebraska Press, 1988.

Perelli, Carina. "From Counterrevolutionary Warfare To Political Awakening: The Uruguayan and Argentine Armed Forces in the 1970s." *Armed Forces and Society* 20, no. 1 (fall 1993).

Persico, Joseph E. *Casey: From the OSS to the CIA*. New York: Viking, 1990.

Pinochet Ugarte, Augusto. *Geopolítica*, 2nd. ed. Santiago, Chile: Andrés Bello, 1974.

Pion-Berlin, David. "The National Security Doctrine, Military Threat Perception and the 'Dirty War' in Argentina." *Comparative Political Studies* 21 (1988).

Pion-Berlin, David. "Between Confrontation and Accommodation: Military and Government Policy in Democratic Argentina." *Journal of Latin American Studies* 23 (October 1991).

Pion-Berlin, David, and George A. Lopez. "Of Victims and Executioners: Argentine State Terror, 1975–1979." *International Studies Quarterly* 35 (1991).

Poder Ejecutivo Nacional. *Terrorism in Argentina*. Buenos Aires, January 7, 1980.

Potash, Robert A. *El ejército y la política en Argentina, 1928–1945*. Buenos Aires: Sudamericana, 1981.

Ranelagh, John. *The Agency: The Rise and Decline of the CIA*. New York: Simon and Schuster, 1986.

Reagan, Ronald. *A Time for Choosing: The Speeches of Ronald Reagan, 1961–1982*. Chicago: Regnery Gateway in cooperation with Americans for the Reagan Agenda, 1983.

Reimann, Elisabeth. *Confesiones de un Contra, historia de "Moisés" en Nicaragua*. Buenos Aires: Legasa, 1986.

Rock, David. *Authoritarian Argentina: The Nationalist Movement, Its History and Its Impact*. Berkeley: University of California Press, 1993.

Rodriguez, Felix I., and John Weisman. *Shadow Warrior: The CIA Hero of a Hundred Unknown Battles*. New York: Simon and Schuster, 1989.

Rouquié, Alain. *The Military and the State in Latin America*. Berkeley: University of California Press, 1987.

Russell, Roberto. "Las relaciones Argentina-Estados Unidos: del alineamiento heterodoxo a la recomposición madura," in Mónica Hirst, ed. *Continuidad y cambio en las relaciones América Latina-Estados Unidos*. Buenos Aires: Grupo Editor Latinoamericano, 1987.

Russell, Roberto, and Juan Tokatlian. *Argentina y la crisis Centroamericana, 1976–1985*. Research Report no. 36, Facultad Latinoamericana de Ciencias Sociales (FLACSO), 1986. Reprinted in Boris Yopo, Roberto Russell, and Juan Tokatlian. *La Unión Soviética y Argentina frente a la crisis Centroamericana*. San José, Costa Rica: Facultad Latinoamericana de Ciencias Sociales (FLACSO), 1987.

Saldomando, Angel, and Elvira Cuadra. "Los problemas de la pacificación en Nicaragua: recomposición de grupos armados y conflictos sociales." Coordinadora Regional de Investigaciones Económicas y Sociales (CRIES), February 1994.

Salimovich, Sofia, Elizabeth Lira, and Eugenia Weinstein. "Victims of Fear: The Social Psychology of Repression," in Juan E. Corradi, Patricia Weiss Fagen, and Manuel A. Garretón, eds. *Fear at the Edge:*

State Terror and Resistance in Latin America. Berkeley: University of California Press, 1992.

Salinas, Juan, and Julio Villalonga. *Gorriarán, la Tablada y las "guerras de inteligencia" en América Latina*. Buenos Aires: Mangin, 1993.

Salomón, Leticia. "The National Security Doctrine in Honduras: Analysis of the Fall of General Gustavo Alvarez Martínez," in Nancy Peckenham and Annie Street, eds. *Honduras: Portrait of a Captive Nation*. New York: Praeger, 1985.

Salomón, Leticia. *Política y militares en Honduras*. Tegucigalpa: Centro de Documentación de Honduras, 1992.

Schoultz, Lars. *Human Rights and United States Policy Toward Latin America*. Princeton: Princeton University Press, 1981.

Schoultz, Lars. *National Security and United States Policy Toward Latin America*. Princeton: Princeton University Press, 1987.

Schulz, Donald E., and Deborah Sundloff Schulz. *The United States, Honduras, and the Crisis in Central America*. Boulder: Westview Press, 1994.

Schwarz, Benjamin C. *American Counterinsurgency Doctrine and El Salvador: The Frustrations of Reform and the Illusions of Nation Building*. Santa Monica: RAND, 1991.

Scott, Peter Dale, and Jonathan Marshall. *Cocaine Politics: Drugs, Armies, and the CIA in Central America*. Berkeley: University of California Press, 1991.

Seligson, Mitchell A. "Trust, Efficacy and Modes of Political Participation: A Study of Costa Rican Peasants." *British Journal of Political Science* 10 (January 1980).

Selser, Gregorio. *Bolivia: El cuartelazo de los cocadólares*. México, D.F.: Mex-Sur, 1982.

Selser, Gregorio. *Honduras, república alquilada*. México, D.F.: Mex-Sur, 1983.

Sikkink, Kathryn. "The Effectiveness of U.S. Human Rights Policy: The Case of Argentina and Guatemala." Paper presented at the Sixteenth International Congress of the Latin American Studies Association, Washington, D.C., April 1991.

Sklar, Holly. *Washington's War on Nicaragua*. Boston: South End Press, 1988.

Skocpol, Theda. "What Makes Peasants Revolutionary?" *Comparative Politics* 14, no. 3 (April 1982).

Stepan, Alfred. "The New Professionalism of Internal Warfare and Military Role Expansion," in Alfred Stepan, ed. *Authoritarian Brazil: Origins, Policies and Future.* New Haven: Yale University Press, 1973.

Stepan, Alfred. *The State and Society: Peru in Comparative Perspective.* Princeton: Princeton University Press, 1978.

Stepan, Alfred. *Rethinking Military Politics: Brazil and the Southern Cone.* Princeton: Princeton University Press, 1988.

Stockholm International Peace Research Institute (SIPRI). *World Armaments and Disarmament Yearbook 1979.* London: Taylor and Francis, 1979.

Stockholm International Peace Research Institute. *Yearbook 1982.* London: Taylor and Francis, 1982.

Timerman, Jacobo. *Preso sin nombre, celda sin número.* Buenos Aires: El Cid Editor, 1982.

Tulchin, Joseph. *Argentina and the United States.* Boston: Twayne Publishers, 1990.

Uriarte, Claudio. *Almirante Cero: biografía no autorizada de Emilio Eduardo Massera.* Buenos Aires: Planeta, 1991.

Vacs, Aldo C. "The 1980 Grain Embargo Negotiations: The United States, Argentina, and the Soviet Union," rev. ed. Pew Case Studies in International Affairs, Washington, D.C., 1992.

Vacs, Aldo C. "A Delicate Balance: Confrontation and Cooperation Between Argentina and the United States in the 1980s." *Journal of Interamerican Studies and World Affairs* 31, no. 4 (winter 1989).

Vaky, Viron P. "Hemispheric Relations: 'Everything is Part of Everything Else.'" *Foreign Affairs* 60 (1980).

Verbitsky, Horacio. *La última batalla de la tercera guerra mundial.* Buenos Aires: Legasa, 1984.

Verbitsky, Horacio. *La posguerra sucia: un análisis de la transición.* Buenos Aires: Legasa, 1985.

Verbitsky, Horacio. *El vuelo.* Buenos Aires: Planeta, 1995.

Vergara, Raúl, Deborah Barry, and Rodolfo Castro. *Nicaragua: país sitiado.* Managua: CRIES, 1986.

Vilas, Acdel Edgardo. *Tucumán: el hecho histórico* ("El plan táctico que posibilitó la victoria contra el Ejército Revolucionario del Pueblo (ERP) en 1975"). Undated pamphlet.

Vilas, Carlos M. *Del colonialismo a la autonomía: modernización capital-*

ista y revolución social en la Costa Atlántica. Managua: Nueva Nicaragua, 1990.

Villegas, Osiris G. *Guerra Revolucionaria Comunista.* Buenos Aires: Pleamar, 1963.

Villegas, Osiris G. *Tiempo Geopolítico Argentino.* Buenos Aires: Pleamar, 1975.

Villegas, Osiris G. *Testimonio de un alegato.* Buenos Aires: Compañía Impresora Argentina, 1990.

Walker, Thomas W. *Nicaragua: The Land of Sandino,* 3d ed. Boulder: Westview Press, 1991.

Walter, Knut. *The Regime of Anastasio Somoza, 1936–1956.* Chapel Hill: University of North Carolina Press, 1993.

Washington Office on Latin America. *Contra Human Rights Abuses Against Honduran Civilians.* Washington, D.C., March 1986.

Weber, Henri. *The Sandinist Revolution.* London: Verso, 1981.

Weber, Henri. "The Struggle for Power," in Peter Rosset and John Vandermeer, eds. *Nicaragua: Unfinished Revolution.* New York: Grove Press, 1986.

Wesson, Robert, ed. *The Latin American Military Institution.* New York: Praeger, 1986.

Wheaton, Philip E. *Inside Honduras: Regional Counterinsurgency Base.* Washington, D.C.: EPICA, 1982.

Wickham-Crowley, Timothy P. *Guerrillas and Revolution in Latin America: A Comparative Study of Insurgents and Regimes Since 1956.* Princeton: Princeton University Press, 1992.

Willetts, Peter, ed. *Pressure Groups in the Global System.* New York: St. Martin's Press, 1982.

Williams, Philip J. "Dual Transitions from Authoritarian Rule: Popular and Electoral Democracy in Nicaragua." *Comparative Politics* 26 (January 1994).

Wolf, Eric. *Peasant Wars of the Twentieth Century.* New York: Harper and Row, 1969.

Wolfe, Alan. *The Limits of Legitimacy: Political Contradictions of Contemporary Capitalism.* New York: The Free Press, 1977.

Woodward, Bob. *Veil: The Secret Wars of the CIA, 1981–1987.* New York: Simon and Schuster, 1987.

Yankelovich, Daniel, and Larry Kaagan. "Assertive America." *Foreign Affairs* 60 (1980).

Yeves, Enrique. *La Contra: una guerra sucia.* Buenos Aires: Ediciones B, 1990.

Selected Documents

Arms Control and Foreign Policy Caucus. "Who are the Contras? An Analysis of the Makeup of the Military Leadership of the Rebel Forces, and of the Nature of the Private American Groups Providing Them Financial and Material Support." Research Report. Washington, D.C., April 18, 1985.

Comando General del Ejército, EMGE, Jefatura II Inteligencia. Annex 1 (Intelligence) to the secret directive of the Army General Commander no. 404/75, "War Against Subversion," signed by Gen. Roberto Eduardo Viola. Buenos Aires, October 28, 1975.

Comando General del Ejército, EMGE, Jefatura II Inteligencia. Annex 1 (Intelligence) to the secret directive of the Army General Commander no. 404/75, "Summary of the Origins, Evolution, and Doctrine of the PRT-ERP and JCR," signed by Col. Carlos Alberto Martínez, Army Intelligence vice chief. Buenos Aires, October 28, 1975.

Comando General del Ejército, EMGE, Jefatura II Inteligencia. Annex 1 (Intelligence) to the secret directive of the Army General Commander no. 504/77, "Continuation of the Offensive Against Subversion During the Period 1977/1978," signed by Gen. Roberto Eduardo Viola. Buenos Aires, April 20, 1977.

Comando General del Ejército, EMGE, Jefatura II Inteligencia. Annex 1 (Intelligence) to the secret directive of the Army General Commander no. 604/79, "Continuation of the Offensive Against Subversion," signed by Gen. Alberto Alfredo Valín, Army Intelligence chief. Buenos Aires, December 24, 1981.

Comisión Argentina de Derechos Humanos (CADHU). Affidavit of Rodolfo Peregrino Fernández. Madrid, April 26, 1983.

Comisión de Análisis y Evaluación de las Responsabilidades Políticas y Estratégico-Militares en el Conflicto del Atlántico Sur (CAERCAS). *Informe Rattenbach*. Buenos Aires: Ediciones Espartaco, 1988.

Francés, Héctor. Transcript of videotaped testimony before Sandinista authorities. December 6, 1982.

General Directorate of Military Industries (Dirección General de Fabricaciones Militares, DGFM). "Financiación de venta de material bélico a la República de Honduras," secret memo from Gen. Horacio Varela Ortiz to the president of the Central Bank, December 29, 1981.

General Directorate of Military Industries. Secret letter to the president, Central Bank, from Varela Ortiz, December 29, 1981.

General Directorate of Military Industries. "Financiación de venta de material bélico a la República de El Salvador," secret memo to army commander in chief, Gen. Leopoldo F. Galtieri, from Gen. Augusto J. B. Alemanzor, January 18, 1982.

General Directorate of Military Industries. Memo no. 624/33, re. E.02940/82, February 1, 1982.

General Directorate of Military Industries. Secret letter to the president, Central Bank, from Varela Ortiz, July 26, 1982.

General Directorate of Military Industries. Secret contract, signed by Varela Ortiz, DGFM director, and Gen. Oscar Mejía Víctores, Guatemala's defense minister, May 19, 1983.

International Court of Justice (ICJ). Case Concerning Military and Paramilitary Activities In and Against Nicaragua. Affidavit of Edgar Chamorro. Washington, D.C., September 5, 1985.

International Court of Justice. Case Concerning Military and Paramilitary Activities In and Against Nicaragua (*Nicaragua v. United States of America*). Merits, Judgment, ICJ Reports, 1986.

Juzgado Nacional en lo Criminal y Correccional Federal no. 5 (Dr. Norberto M. Oyarbide). Case no. 10,000, "Sivak, Osvaldo Fabio víctima de secuestro extorsivo." Deposition of Rafael López Fader. Buenos Aires, August 20, 1996.

National Security Archive, ed. *El Salvador: The Making of U.S. Policy, 1977–1984*. Microfiche collection. Alexandria: Chadwyck-Healey, 1989.

National Security Archive, ed. *The Iran-Contra Affair: The Making of a Scandal, 1983–1988.* Microfiche collection. Alexandria: Chadwyck-Healey, 1990.

National Security Archive, ed. *Nicaragua: The Making of U.S. Policy, 1978–1990.* Microfiche collection. Alexandria: Chadwyck-Healey, 1991.

Nicaragua, Ministry of the Interior, General Directorate for State Security. Secret memo in re participation of the Argentine armed forces and their intelligence services in the aggression against Nicaragua, circa 1984.

Research Publications. *Declassified Documents Reference System.* Microfiche collection. Woodbridge: Research Publications, various years.

U.S. Congress, House, Committee on Appropriations, Subcommittee on Foreign Operations and Related Agencies. *Foreign Assistance and Related Programs Appropriations for Fiscal Year 1981,* pt. 1. 96th Cong., 2d Sess., 1980.

U.S. Congress, House, Committee on Foreign Affairs, Subcommittee on Inter-American Affairs. *Review of the Presidential Certification of Nicaragua's Connection to Terrorism.* 96th Cong., 2d Sess., September 30, 1980.

U.S. Congress, House, Committee on Appropriations, Subcommittee on Foreign Operations and Related Programs. *Foreign Assistance and Related Programs Appropriations for 1982.* 97th Cong., 1st Sess., 1981.

U.S. Congress, House, Committee on Foreign Affairs, Subcommittee on Inter-American Affairs. *Foreign Assistance Legislation for Fiscal Year 1982.* 97th Cong., 1st Sess., 1981.

U.S. Congress, House, Committee on Foreign Affairs, Subcommittees on Human Rights and International Organizations and on Inter-American Affairs. *Review of United States Policy on Military Assistance to Argentina.* 97th Cong., 1st Sess., April 1, 1981.

U.S. Congress, Senate, Committee on Foreign Relations, Subcommittee on Terrorism, Narcotics, and International Operations. *Drugs, Law Enforcement, and Foreign Policy: Money Laundering.* Testimony of Leandro Sánchez Reisse, July 23, 1987.

U.S. Congress, Senate, Select Committee on Secret Military Assistance to Iran and the Nicaraguan Opposition, and House, Select Committee to Investigate Covert Arms Transactions with Iran. *Report of the Congressional Committees Investigating the Iran-Contra Affair.* Appendix A, Source Documents. Washington, D.C.: Government Printing Office, 1988.

U.S. Congress, Senate, Committee on Foreign Relations, Subcommittee on Terrorism, Narcotics, and International Operations. *Drugs, Law Enforcement and Foreign Policy: A Report.* Washington, D.C.: Government Printing Office, 1989.

U.S. Department of State. *American Foreign Policy Current Documents 1977–80.* Washington, D.C.: State Department, 1984.

U.S. Department of State. *American Foreign Policy Current Documents 1981.* Washington, D.C.: State Department, 1984.

U.S. Department of State. *Documents on the Nicaraguan Resistance: Leaders, Military Personnel, and Program.* Special Report no. 142. Washington, D.C.: Bureau of Public Affairs, 1986.

U.S. Department of State. *Nicaraguan Biographies: A Resource Book.* Special Report no. 174. Washington, D.C.: Bureau of Public Affairs, 1988.

U.S. President. *Public Papers of the Presidents of the United States. Ronald Reagan, 1981.* Washington, D.C.: Government Printing Office, 1982.

Periodicals

Acción Cívica (Managua)
Albuquerque Journal
Ambito Financiero (Buenos Aires)
Barricada (Managua)
Brecha (Montevideo)
Buenos Aires Herald
Caras y Caretas (Buenos Aires)
Clarín (Buenos Aires)
Convicción (Buenos Aires)

Covert Action
El Día (Mexico)
El Heraldo (Tegucigalpa)
El Legionario: Revista oficial de la Legión 15 de Septiembre
El Periodista de Buenos Aires
El Porteño (Buenos Aires)
Excelsior (Mexico)
Guardian (London)
Guatemala Newsletter (Guatemala City)
Humor (Buenos Aires)
La Nación (Buenos Aires)
La Prensa (Buenos Aires)
La Prensa (New York)
La Razón (Buenos Aires)
La Semana (Buenos Aires)
La Tribuna (Tegucigalpa)
La Voz (Buenos Aires)
Latin America Weekly Report
Le Monde Diplomatique
Los Angeles Times
Nation
New Republic
New York Times
Newsweek
Página 12 (Buenos Aires)
Patria Libre (Managua)
Pensamiento Propio (Managua)
Pregón (Buenos Aires)
Progressive
Resistencia (Costa Rica)
Siete Días (Buenos Aires)
Soberanía (Managua)
Somos (Buenos Aires)
Tiempo (San Pedro Sula, Honduras)
Uno Más Uno (Mexico)
Wall Street Journal
Washington Post

Selected Interviews
(conducted by the author)

Ampié Quiróz, Rodolfo. Managua, July 2 and 5, 1993.
Arana, César. Miami, July 9, 1993.
Ballester, Horacio P., Colonel (ret.). Buenos Aires, August 5, 1991, and July 28, 1993.
Borge, Tomás. Managua, July 8, 1993.
Bruschtein, Luis. Buenos Aires, July 30, 1993.
Cesio, Juan Jaime, Colonel (ret.). Buenos Aires, August 5, 1993.
Céspedes, Abel. Managua, July 7, 1993.
Chávez, Lizzeth. Managua, July 6, 1993.
D'Andrea Mohr, José Luis, former captain. Buenos Aires, August 14, 1991.
Dalton, Eugenio Alfredo, General (ret.). Buenos Aires, August 6, 1993.
Dormoz, Camilo. Bluefields, Nicaragua, June 29, 1993.
García, José Luis, Colonel (ret.). Buenos Aires, August 10, 1993.
García Lupo, Rogelio. Buenos Aires, July 30, 1993.
Goyret, José Teófilo, General (ret.). Buenos Aires, August 5, 1993.
Li Puma, Miguel Angel, Colonel (ret.). Buenos Aires, August 18, 1993.
López Meyer, Ernesto Víctor, General (ret.). Buenos Aires, August 4, 1993.
Mallea Gil, Miguel Angel, General (ret.). Buenos Aires, August 18, 1993.
Martínez Zelaya, Francisco. Managua, July 1, 1993.
Morales, Mariano. Managua, July 7, 1993.
Raimondi, Carlos H., Captain (ret.). Buenos Aires, August 4, 1993.
Rivera, Juan Angel. Managua, July 7, 1993.
Salinas, Juan José. Buenos Aires, July 31, 1993.
Seineldín, Mohamed Alí, former colonel. Military prison, Magdalena, Buenos Aires Province, August 21, 1993.
Sobalvarro García, Oscar. Managua, July 7, 1993.
Sosa, Miguel Angel. Managua, July 5, 1993.
Varela, Alberto R., Admiral (ret.). Buenos Aires, August 17, 1993.

Index

AAA. *See* Argentine Anti-Communist Alliance

ADREN. *See* Nicaraguan Democratic Revolutionary Alliance

Afghanistan, 58
Soviet invasion of, 38, 45, 196 n.65

Africa, 37, 126

Agencia Nacional de Servicios Especiales de El Salvador. *See* National Security Agency of El Salvador

Agency for International Development (AID), 124

Aguirre, Francisco, 48, 129, 209 n.47, 215 n.109

AIFLD. *See* American Institute for Free Labor Development

Aja Espil, Jorge, 65

Alfieri González, Roberto, 225 n.61, 232–33 n.115

Alfonsín administration, 19, 143, 194 n.48

Alfonsín, Raúl, 18, 99, 188 n.1, 209 n.45

Algeria, 3, 9, 193 n.43, 198 n.80

Alianza Anticomunista Argentina. *See* Argentine Anti-Communist Alliance

Alianza Democrática Revolucionaria Nicaragüense. *See* Nicaraguan Democratic Revolutionary Alliance

Alianza Republicana Nacionalista. *See* Nationalist Republican Alliance

Alianza Revolucionaria Democrática. *See* Democratic Revolutionary Alliance

Allen, Richard, 49

Allende, Salvador, 26, 27, 98

Alpha 66, 28, 146, 157–59, 162, 256 nn.68, 69

Altmann, Klaus (alias Klaus Barbie), 30

Alvarez Martínez, Gustavo, 95, 101, 135, 235 n.128, 246 n.100, 247 n.114, 250 n.5
background of, 230 n.103, 231 nn.105, 107
and Moon church, 259 n.98
national security doctrine under, 95–99, 232 n.113
ousting of, 231 n.108

American Institute for Free Labor Development (AIFLD), 134

American Security Council, 258 n.91

Americas Watch. *See* Human Rights Watch/Americas

Amnesty International, 84, 207 n.31

Ampié Quiróz, Rodolfo (alias Invisible), 129, 134, 219 nn.9, 10

Anaya, Jorge Isaac, 217 n.127

Andean Brigade, 31, 32, 150, 161

Andersen, Martin, 82

ANSESAL. *See* National Security Agency of El Salvador

anti-Semitism, 155

Arana, Frank, 120

Arana, Raúl, 135

Arancibia Clavel, Enrique L., 27, 202 n.108

Arce Gómez, Luis, 30, 31, 155, 204 n.123

ARDE. *See* Democratic Revolutionary Alliance

INDEX

Urbina Pinto, Bernardo, 164
Uruguay, 26–28, 67, 68, 76, 85, 87,
88, 162, 166, 201 n.102, 202
n.106
U.S. embassy (Buenos Aires), 8, 9, 19

Vaca Narvaja, Fernando, 81
Valdivia, Encarnación (alias Tigrillo),
116, 127
Valdivieso, Ricardo, 163
Valín, Alberto A., 23, 82, 129, 130
Valladares, Leo, 229 n.93
Vaquero, Antonio, 89
Vargas, Max, 120
Vega, Gualberto, 31
Vega, Pablo A., 123
Venezuela, 22, 29, 76, 226 n.67
Videla, Jorge Rafael, 4, 5, 14, 29,
43–45, 83
Vietnam, 11, 37, 39, 59, 68, 138, 139,
198 n.80, 255–56 n.61
Vilas, Acdel Edgardo, 137
Villagra, Hugo (alias Visage), 94, 120,
230 n.95
Villegas, Santiago. See Hoya, Santi-
ago
Viola, Roberto, 14, 44, 65, 77, 88, 199
n.91, 215 n.109

WACL. See World Anti-Communist
League
Walters, Vernon, 64, 88, 89, 134, 227
n.79
and Aguirre, 48, 215 n.109
and Mallea Gill, 215–16 n.112
Watergate scandal, 37
Weinberger, Caspar, 54
West Point, 13, 216 n.112
Wheelock, Jaime, 81
White House:
and CIA, 46, 58
and Haig, 54
hard-liners in, 57
World Anti-Communist League
(WACL), 146, 153, 160, 162–64,
256 n.69, 257 n.87
World War II, 36, 126

Yacimientos Petrolíferos Fiscales
(YPF), 161, 162, 167

Zapatista National Liberation Army
(Ejército Zapatista de Lib-
eración Nacional, [EZLN]), 169
Zarattini, Alfredo, 87, 94, 222 n.40
Zelaya, José Santos, 110

301

Monographs in International Studies

Titles Available from Ohio University Press, 1996

Southeast Asia Series

No. 56   **Duiker, William J.** Vietnam Since the Fall of Saigon. 1989. Updated ed. 401 pp. Paper 0-89680-162-4 $20.00.

No. 64   **Dardjowidjojo, Soenjono.** Vocabulary Building in Indonesian: An Advanced Reader. 1984. 664 pp. Paper 0-89680-118-7 $30.00.

No. 65   **Errington, J. Joseph.** Language and Social Change in Java: Linguistic Reflexes of Modernization in a Traditional Royal Polity. 1985. 210 pp. Paper 0-89680-120-9 $25.00.

No. 66   **Binh, Tran Tu.** The Red Earth: A Vietnamese Memoir of Life on a Colonial Rubber Plantation. Tr. by John Spragens. 1984. 102 pp. (SEAT*, V. 5) Paper 0-89680-119-5 $11.00.

No. 68   **Syukri, Ibrahim.** History of the Malay Kingdom of Patani. 1985. 135 pp. Paper 0-89680-123-3 $15.00.

No. 69   **Keeler, Ward.** Javanese: A Cultural Approach. 1984. 559 pp. Paper 0-89680-121-7 $25.00.

No. 70   **Wilson, Constance M. and Lucien M. Hanks.** Burma-Thailand Frontier Over Sixteen Decades: Three Descriptive Documents. 1985. 128 pp. Paper 0-89680-124-1 $11.00.

No. 71   **Thomas, Lynn L. and Franz von Benda-Beckmann,** eds. Change and Continuity in Minangkabau: Local, Regional, and Historical Perspectives on West Sumatra. 1985. 353 pp. Paper 0-89680-127-6 $16.00.

No. 72   **Reid, Anthony and Oki Akira,** eds. The Japanese Experience in Indonesia: Selected Memoirs of 1942–1945. 1986. 424 pp., 20 illus. (SEAT, V. 6) Paper 0-89680-132-2 $20.00.

No. 74   **McArthur M. S. H.** Report on Brunei in 1904. Introduced and Annotated by A. V. M. Horton. 1987. 297 pp. Paper 0-89680-135-7 $15.00.

* Southeast Asia Translation Project Group

No. 75   Lockard, Craig A. From Kampung to City: A Social History of Kuching, Malaysia, 1820–1970. 1987. 325 pp. Paper 0-89680-136-5 $20.00.

No. 76   McGinn, Richard, ed. Studies in Austronesian Linguistics. 1986. 516 pp. Paper 0-89680-137-3 $20.00.

No. 77   Muego, Benjamin N. Spectator Society: The Philippines Under Martial Rule. 1986. 232 pp. Paper 0-89680-138-1 $17.00.

No 79   Walton, Susan Pratt. Mode in Javanese Music. 1987. 278 pp. Paper 0-89680-144-6 $15.00.

No. 80   Nguyen Anh Tuan. South Vietnam: Trial and Experience. 1987. 477 pp., tables. Paper 0-89680-141-1 $18.00.

No. 82   Spores, John C. Running Amok: An Historical Inquiry. 1988. 190 pp. paper 0-89680-140-3 $13.00.

No. 83   Malaka, Tan. From Jail to Jail. Tr. by Helen Jarvis. 1911. 1209 pp., three volumes. (SEAT V. 8) Paper 0-89680-150-0 $55.00.

No. 84   Devas, Nick, with Brian Binder, Anne Booth, Kenneth Davey, and Roy Kelly. Financing Local Government in Indonesia. 1989. 360 pp. Paper 0-89680-153-5 $20.00.

No. 85   Suryadinata, Leo. Military Ascendancy and Political Culture: A Study of Indonesia's Golkar. 1989. 235 pp., illus., glossary, append., index, bibliog. Paper 0-89680-154-3 $18.00.

No. 86   Williams, Michael. Communism, Religion, and Revolt in Banten in the Early Twentieth Century. 1990. 390 pp. Paper 0-89680-155-1 $14.00.

No. 87   Hudak, Thomas. The Indigenization of Pali Meters in Thai Poetry. 1990. 247 pp. Paper 0-89680-159-4 $15.00.

No. 88   Lay, Ma Ma. Not Out of Hate: A Novel of Burma. Tr. by Margaret Aung-Thwin. Ed. by William Frederick. 1991. 260 pp. (SEAT V. 9) Paper 0-89680-167-5 $20.00.

No. 89   Anwar, Chairil. The Voice of the Night: Complete Poetry and Prose of Chairil Anwar. 1992. Revised Edition. Tr. by Burton Raffel. 196 pp. Paper 0-89680-170-5 $20.00.

No. 90   Hudak, Thomas John, tr., The Tale of Prince Samuttakote: A Buddhist Epic from Thailand. 1993. 230 pp. Paper 0-89680-174-8 $20.00.

No. 91   Roskies, D. M., ed. Text/Politics in Island Southeast Asia: Essays in Interpretation. 1993. 330 pp. Paper 0-89680-175-6 $25.00.

No. 92   Schenkhuizen, Marguérite, translated by Lizelot Stout van Balgooy. Memoirs of an Indo Woman: Twentieth-Century Life in the East Indies and Abroad. 1993. 312 pp. Paper 0-89680-178-0 $25.00.

No. 93   **Salleh, Muhammad Haji.** Beyond the Archipelago: Selected Poems. 1995. 247 pp. Paper 0-89680-181-0 $20.00.

No. 94   **Federspiel, Howard M.** A Dictionary of Indonesian Islam. 1995. 327 pp. Bibliog. Paper 0-89680-182-9 $25.00.

No. 95   **Leary, John.** Violence and the Dream People: The Orang Asli in the Malayan Emergency 1948–1960. 1995. 275 pp. Maps, illus., tables, appendices, bibliog., index. Paper 0-89680-186-1 $22.00.

No. 96   **Lewis, Dianne.** *Jan Compagnie* in the Straits of Malacca 1641–1795. 1995. 176 pp. Map, appendices, bibliog., index. Paper 0-89680-187-x. $18.00.

No. 97   **Schiller, Jim and Martin-Schiller, Barbara.** Imagining Indonesia: Cultural Politics and Political Culture. 1996. 384 pp., notes, glossary, bibliog. Paper 0-89680-190-x. $30.00.

No. 98   **Bonga, Dieuwke Wendelaar.** Eight Prison Camps: A Dutch Family in Japanese Java. 1996. 233 pp., illus., map, glossary. Paper 0-89680-191-8. $18.00.

No. 99   **Gunn, Geoffrey C.** Language, Ideology, and Power in Brunei Darussalam. 1996. 328 pp., glossary, notes, bibliog., index. Paper 0-89680-192-6. $24.00.

No. 100   **Martin, Peter W., Conrad Ozog, and Gloria R. Poedjosoedarmo, eds.** Language Use and Language Change in Brunei Darussalam. 1996. 390 pp., maps, notes, bibliog. Paper 0-89680-193-x. $26.00.

Africa Series

No. 43   **Harik, Elsa M. and Donald G. Schilling.** The Politics of Education in Colonial Algeria and Kenya. 1984. 102 pp. Paper 0-89680-117-9 $12.50.

No. 45   **Keto, C. Tsehloane.** American-South African Relations 1784–1980: Review and Select Bibliography. 1985. 169 pp. Paper 0-89680-128-4 $11.00.

No. 46   **Burness, Don, ed.** Wanasema: Conversations with African Writers. 1985. 103 pp. paper 0-89680-129-2 $11.00.

No. 47   **Switzer, Les.** Media and Dependency in South Africa: A Case Study of the Press and the Ciskei "Homeland." 1985. 97 pp. Paper 0-89680-130-6 $10.00.

No. 51   **Clayton, Anthony and David Killingray.** Khaki and Blue: Military and Police in British Colonial Africa. 1989. 347 pp. Paper 0-89680-147-0 $20.00.

Latin America Series

No. 13   Henderson, James D. Conservative Thought in Latin America: The Ideas of Laureano Gomez. 1988. 229 pp. Paper 0-89680-148-9 $16.00.

No. 17   Mijeski, Kenneth J., ed. The Nicaraguan Constitution of 1987: English Translation and Commentary. 1991. 355 pp. Paper 0-89680-165-9 $25.00.

No. 18   Finnegan, Pamela. The Tension of Paradox: José Donoso's *The Obscene Bird of Night* as Spiritual Exercises. 1992. 204 pp. Paper 0-89680-169-1 $15.00.

No. 19   Kim, Sung Ho and Thomas W. Walker, eds. Perspectives on War and Peace in Central America. 1992. 155 pp., notes, bibliog. Paper 0-89680-172-1 $17.00.

No. 20   Becker, Marc. Mariátegui and Latin American Marxist Theory. 1993. 239 pp. Paper 0-89680-177-2 $20.00.

No. 21   Boschetto-Sandoval, Sandra M. and Marcia Phillips McGowan, eds. Claribel Alegría and Central American Literature. 1994. 233 pp., illus. Paper 0-89680-179-9 $20.00.

No. 22   Zimmerman, Marc. Literature and Resistance in Guatemala: Textual Modes and Cultural Politics from El Señor Presidente to Rigoberta Menchú. 1995. 2 volume set 320 + 370 pp., notes, bibliog. Paper 0-89680-183-7 $50.00.

No. 23   Hey, Jeanne A. K. Theories of Dependent Foreign Policy: The Case of Ecuador in the 1980s. 1995. 280 pp., map, tables, notes, bibliog., index. paper 0-89680-184-5 $22.00.

No. 24   Wright, Bruce E. Theory in the Practice of the Nicaraguan Revolution. 1995. 320 pp., notes, illus., bibliog., index. Paper 0-89680-185-3. $23.00.

No. 25   Mann, Carlos Guevara. Panamanian Militarism: A Historical Interpretation. 1996. 243 pp., illus., map, notes, bibliog., index. Paper 0-89680-189-6. $23.00.

No. 26   Armony, Ariel. Argentina, the United States, and the Anti-Communist Crusade in Central America, 1977–1984. 1997. 312 pp., illus., maps, notes, bibliog., index. Paper 0-89680-196-9. $26.00.

Ordering Information

Individuals are encouraged to patronize local bookstores wherever possible. Orders for titles in the Monographs in International Studies may be placed directly through the Ohio University Press, Scott Quadrangle, Athens, Ohio 45701-2979. Individuals should remit payment by check, VISA, or Master-Card.* Those ordering from the United Kingdom, Continental Europe, the Middle East,. and Africa should order through Academic and University Publishers Group, 1 Gower Street, London WC1E, England. Orders from the Pacific Region, Asia, Australia, and New Zealand should be sent to East-West Export Books, c/o the University of Hawaii Press, 2840 Kolowalu Street, Honolulu, Hawaii 96822, USA.

Individuals ordering from outside of the U.S. should remit in U.S. funds to Ohio University Press either by International Money Order or by a check drawn on a U.S. bank.** Most out-of-print titles may be ordered from University Microfilms, Inc., 300 North Zeeb Road, Ann Arbor, Michigan 48106, USA.

Prices are subject to change.

* Please add $3.50 for the first book and $.75 for each additional book for shipping and handling.

** Outside the U.S. please add $4.50 for the first book and $.75 for each additional book.

Ohio University
Monographs in International Studies

The Ohio University Center for International Studies was established to help create within the university and local communities a greater awareness of the world beyond the United States. Comprising programs in African, Latin American, Southeast Asian, Development and Administrative studies, the Center supports scholarly research, sponsors lectures and colloquia, encourages course development within the university curriculum, and publishes the Monographs in International Studies series with the Ohio University Press. The Center and its programs also offer an interdisciplinary Master of Arts degree in which students may focus on one of the regional or topical concentrations, and may also combine academics with training in career fields such as journalism, business, and language teaching. For undergraduates, major and certificate programs are also available.

For more information, contact the Vice Provost for International Studies, Burson House, Ohio University, Athens, Ohio 45701.